GENDER
WORK STRESS AND
HEALTH

GENDER
WORK STRESS AND
HEALTH

**EDITED BY DEBRA L. NELSON
AND RONALD J. BURKE**

American Psychological Association

Washington, DC

Published by
American Psychological Association
750 First Street, NE
Washington, DC 20002
www.apa.org

To order
APA Order Department
P.O. Box 92984
Washington, DC 20090-2984

Tel: (800) 374-2721, Direct: (202) 336-5510
Fax: (202) 336-5502, TDD/TTY: (202) 336-6123
On-line: www.apa.org/books/
E-mail: order@apa.org

In the U.K., Europe, Africa, and the Middle East, copies may be ordered from
American Psychological Association
3 Henrietta Street
Covent Garden, London
WC2E 8LU England

Typeset in Goudy by NOVA Graphic Services, Inc., Ft. Washington, PA
Printer: Port City Press, Inc., Baltimore, MD
Cover Designer: NiDesign, Baltimore, MD
Project Manager: NOVA Graphic Services, Inc., Ft. Washington, PA

The opinions and statements published are the responsibility of the authors, and such opinions and statements do not necessarily represent the policies of the American Psychological Association.

Library of Congress Cataloging-in-Publication Data
Gender, work stress, and health / edited by Debra L. Nelson and Ronald J. Burke.
   p. cm.
   Includes bibliographical references and index.
   ISBN 1-55798-923-0
   1. Job stress—Health aspects.   2. Sex role—Health aspects.   3. Sex factors in disease.
   I. Nelson, Debra L., 1956-   II. Burke, Ronald J.

   RC963.48 .G46 2002
   158.7'2'082—dc21

2002022842

British Library Cataloguing-in-Publication Data
A CIP record is available from the British Library.

Printed in the United States of America
First Edition

CONTENTS

Contributors vii

Preface ix

Chapter 1.   A Framework for Examining Gender,
             Work Stress, and Health 3
             Debra L. Nelson and Ronald J. Burke

I. Stressors, Individual Differences, and Coping 15

Chapter 2.   Managerial Stress: Are Women More at Risk? 19
             Sandra L. Fielden and Cary L. Cooper

Chapter 3.   Men, Masculinity, and Health 35
             Ronald J. Burke

Chapter 4.   Women and Corporate Restructuring: Sources
             and Consequences of Stress 55
             Rekha Karambayya

Chapter 5.   Assessing the Role of Negative Affectivity
             in Occupational Stress Research:
             Does Gender Make a Difference? 71
             Steve M. Jex, Gary A. Adams, and Michele L. Ehler

Chapter 6.   Work Stress, Coping, and Social Support:
             Implications for Women's Occupational Well-Being 85
             Esther R. Greenglass

II. Stress and Family Dynamics 97

Chapter 7. Do Men and Women Benefit From Social
            Support Equally? Results From a Field Examination
            Within the Work and Family Context 101
            Pamela L. Perrewé and Dawn S. Carlson

Chapter 8. The Allocation of Time to Work and Family Roles 115
            Jeffrey H. Greenhaus and Saroj Parasuraman

Chapter 9. Gender Asymmetry in Crossover Research 129
            Mina Westman

III. Prevention and Interventions 151

Chapter 10. Reduced Work Arrangements for Managers
            and Professionals: A Potential Solution to
            Conflicting Demands 155
            Marcia Brumit Kropf

Chapter 11. Reduced-Load Work Arrangements: Response to
            Stress or Quest for Integrity of Functioning? 169
            *Mary Dean Lee, Shelley M. MacDermid,
            and Michelle L. Buck*

Chapter 12. An Affirmative Defense: The Preventive
            Management of Sexual Harassment 191
            *Myrtle P. Bell, Cyndy S. Cycyota,
            and James Campbell Quick*

Chapter 13. Do Family-Friendly Policies Fulfill Their Promise?
            An Investigation of Their Impact on Work–Family
            Conflict and Work and Personal Outcomes 211
            Hazel M. Rosin and Karen Korabik

IV. Conclusion 227

Chapter 14. New Directions for Studying Gender,
            Work Stress, and Health 229
            Debra L. Nelson, Ronald J. Burke, and Susan Michie

Author Index 243

Subject Index 253

About the Editors 259

CONTRIBUTORS

Gary A. Adams, Department of Psychology, University of Wisconsin–Oshkosh

Myrtle P. Bell, Department of Management, University of Texas at Arlington

Michelle L. Buck, Faculty of Management, McGill University, Montreal, Quebec, Canada

Ronald J. Burke, Schulich School of Business, York University, Toronto, Ontario, Canada

Dawn S. Carlson, Department of Management, Baylor University, Waco, TX

Cary L. Cooper, Manchester School of Management, University of Manchester Institute of Science and Technology, Manchester, England

Cyndy S. Cycyota, Department of Management, University of Texas at Arlington

Michele L. Ehler, Dow Chemical Corporation, Midland, MI

Sandra L. Fielden, Manchester School of Management, University of Manchester Institute of Science and Technology, Manchester, England

Esther R. Greenglass, Department of Psychology, York University, Toronto, Ontario, Canada

Jeffrey H. Greenhaus, Department of Management, Drexel University, Philadelphia, PA

Steve M. Jex, Department of Psychology, University of Wisconsin–Oshkosh

Rekha Karambayya, Schulich School of Business, York University, Toronto, Ontario, Canada

Karen Korabik, Department of Psychology, University of Guelph, Guelph, Ontario, Canada

Marcia Brumit Kropf, Catalyst, New York

Mary Dean Lee, Faculty of Management, McGill University, Montreal, Quebec, Canada

Shelley M. MacDermid, Department of Child Development & Family Studies, Purdue University, West Lafayette, IN

Susan Michie, Department of Management, Oklahoma State University, Stillwater

Debra L. Nelson, Department of Management, Oklahoma State University, Stillwater

Saroj Parasuraman, Department of Management, Drexel University, Philadelphia, PA

Pamela L. Perrewé, Department of Management, Florida State University, Tallahassee

James Campbell Quick, Department of Management, University of Texas at Arlington

Hazel M. Rosin, Schulich School of Business, York University, Toronto, Ontario, Canada

Mina Westman, Faculty of Management, Tel Aviv University, Tel Aviv, Israel

PREFACE

Our duty, as men and women, is to proceed as if limits to our ability did
not exist. We are collaborators in creation.

Pierre Teilhard de Chardin (1881–1955),
French philosopher, paleontologist

Our own experiences in studying gender and work have revealed to us
several insights. One on which we both agree is this: We need to know more.
It is in that spirit that we embarked on the collaboration to publish this collection. Our aim was simple: to present a collection of leading-edge research
on gender, work stress, and health. It is of necessity an interdisciplinary ven-
ture, combining knowledge from management, psychology, sociology, epidemiology, and medicine, among other fields. Gender permeates every
aspect of life, but it is especially salient to the work environment. While
considerable progress has been made in studying gender in a broad fashion,
far less progress has been made in terms of gender as it specifically affects
work stress and health. We must enhance our knowledge of this specific gender area in order to develop more effective interventions in organizations.

The research on gender, work stress, and health is eclectic in terms of
subject matter and study methods. As a body of knowledge, it is limited by a
lack of attention to underrepresented constituencies, a focus on disease
rather than health, and a lack of understanding of the relationship between
biobehavioral responses and social roles. We will discuss these limitations
more fully in the final chapter of this book. Yet, as the chapters in this volume demonstrate, while some questions remain, significant findings are
emerging. One of the more consistent findings in the stress literature underscores the importance of social support, as explored in chapters 6 and 7 of this
volume. Another important finding is the complex interplay between work
and home dynamics in relationship to health, as presented in chapters 8 and
9 of this volume. We can conclude that research on gender, work stress, and
health remains a fertile field, but significant progress has been made.

The features of this collection are many and varied. Our contributors are an international set of prolific writers and researchers who were kind enough to share some of their best work with us. Although many gender-based studies end up being about women, this collection integrates the masculine viewpoint as well. The book's organization reflects a comprehensive stress management framework.

We believe that many groups will be served by this collection. Undergraduate and graduate students and researchers in management, business, occupational psychology, sociology, and women's studies who are working to understand the complex interplay of gender, work stress, and health will find interest here. Another audience comprises professionals in human resource management, consulting, training and development, occupational health, and women's networks.

In chapter 1, we present an overall framework that details the organization of the book. We believe much can be gained by examining the gender literature in terms of a three-part framework: stressors, individual characteristics, and coping; stress and family dynamics; and prevention and interventions. These are the contemporary issues that are on the minds of practicing managers and researchers alike. Using these three themes, our opening chapter critically reviews the existing research literature.

Part I, Stressors, Individual Differences, and Coping, contains five chapters that focus on the dynamic connection between stressors and health, including the individual characteristics and coping methods that intervene in this linkage. In chapter 2, Sandra L. Fielden and Cary L. Cooper explore the stressors encountered by managers and the factors influencing how female and male managers respond to these stressors in terms of personal characteristics and coping styles. They also evaluate the particular health risks facing female managers. Fielden and Cooper conclude that much of the burden of helping female managers remain healthy is on organizations. In chapter 3, Ronald J. Burke explores gender role strain, masculinity, and the health risks men face. He asserts that men's roles are undergoing massive changes and that there is considerable confusion about the expectations men face and their associated health risks. In chapter 4, Rekha Karambayya focuses on a particularly stressful situation, that of corporate restructuring. She asserts that organizational restructuring is a gendered process that contains structural, political, and cultural biases and that women are especially at risk during the process. A better understanding of the health consequences of restructuring will benefit women and men alike and may keep organizations from experiencing what Karambayya calls a "quiet exodus" of the organization's best employees. In chapter 5, Steve M. Jex, Gary A. Adams, and Michelle L. Ehler take a critical look at research on negative affectivity, an underresearched variable in gender and work stress studies. They conclude from this review that negative affect is a more salient strain for women than for men; therefore, the role of negative affect in the stress–strain relationship may differ by gender. Esther R. Greenglass, in chapter 6, examines a paradox. While research suggests that multiple roles benefit women's well-being, other studies demonstrate that multiple roles mean more role conflict. Greenglass suggests that social support and coping skills must be engaged to effectively manage role conflict and that gender must be incorporated into future research on role conflict and stress.

Part II, Stress and Family Dynamics, examines the work and family roles of men and women, with particular attention to gender differences in the experience and enactment of these roles. In chapter 7, Pamela L. Perrewé and Dawn S. Carlson discuss a study that posed the question, "Do men and women benefit from social support equally?" The answer, according to their study, is that social support may be more beneficial for women than for men, particularly social support from family sources. In chapter 8, Jeffrey H. Greenhaus and Saroj Parasuraman report on their study of time allocation to work and family roles. They found that conflict between work and family roles was a significant source of stress for both men and women. They also found that work and family roles were consistent determinants of decisions on how to allocate time. Mina Westman, in chapter 9, explores the role of gender in crossover, in which work stress is transmitted from job incumbents to their spouses or partners, thus affecting their psychological and physical health. Westman proposes that, although gender is largely ignored in crossover studies, it has potential effects on many mechanisms of the crossover process.

Part III, Prevention and Interventions, highlights the theme of prevention and interventions, or what organizations can do to manage issues surrounding work stress and health. In chapter 10, Marcia Brumit Kropf summarizes the studies conducted by Catalyst on reduced-work arrangements. She presents the importance of such arrangements, the potential difficulties for organizations, and strategies for successful reduced-work arrangements. In chapter 11, Mary Dean Lee, Shelley M. MacDermid, and Michelle L. Buck report their study of reduced-load work arrangements among a group of managers and professionals. They propose that such arrangements may be less a response to stress and more a strategy for individuals to achieve integrity of functioning—more freedom, balance, and opportunities to pursue personal fulfillment. Myrtle P. Bell, Cyndy S. Cycyota, and James Campbell Quick present a unique perspective on sexual harassment in chapter 12. They cast sexual harassment as a chronic social problem and apply a preventive management, data-based approach. They also suggest ways of applying the approach to prevent harassment and to reduce its adverse effects. In chapter 13, Hazel Rosin and Karen Korabik pose the question, "Do family-friendly policies fulfill their promise?" They examine these policies in terms of whether they serve to reduce work–family conflict.

Our final chapter in Part IV explores six questions that we believe should guide future research on gender, work stress, and health. First, in what ways have the new economy and a new psychological contract affected men and women's work stress and health, and how has the contemporary work environment influenced gender role expectations? Second, are there particular occupational and demographic or family structure groups that need greater research attention? Third, are the differences we think of as gender-based really biological in nature? Fourth, is a more positive approach possible, focusing on health rather than distress? Fifth, is a focus on gender, stress, and health at odds with higher education programs and the demands of corporate life? Finally, how can employers be encouraged to take an active role in supporting women and men's health? These themes can occupy managers and researchers for years to come.

ACKNOWLEDGMENTS

We would like to thank our colleagues in the Management Department at Oklahoma State University for their encouragement, support, and friendship. We would also like to acknowledge the support provided by the School of Business, York University, for this undertaking. Debra Nelson is grateful for Ron Burke's generosity and friendship—he makes projects like this one enjoyable. Ron Burke thanks his friend and colleague, Debra Nelson, for a fruitful and rewarding collaboration. Our contributors are to be commended for their scholarship, and we thank them for collaborating with us on this collection. We are also grateful to our international contributors for joining with us in furthering our understanding of gender, work stress, and health.

GENDER
WORK STRESS AND
HEALTH

1

A FRAMEWORK FOR EXAMINING GENDER, WORK STRESS, AND HEALTH

DEBRA L. NELSON AND RONALD J. BURKE

Since the dawn of time, gender differences have fascinated us. In recent years, gender differences have been a focus of much of the writings and research on work stress and health. The concept of gender consists of the ways men and women are defined through cultural processes. The lines between sex and gender are blurry ones; the concepts often overlap. Masculinity and femininity are socially constructed states. In Western cultures, the gender perspective has traditionally meant that men and women are seen as having natural, distinctive psychological and behavioral differences based on their sex. These differences are supported by clear definitions of "men's work" versus "women's work" and by divisions of labor (Burke & Nelson, 1998).

These socially constructed roles place many demands on men and women that affect both their work lives and their family lives. Organizations, as socially constructed entities, reinforce the gender role distinctions. Men have traditionally been seen as breadwinners, providers for and protectors of the family, while women were the caretakers of the home and nurturers of children. Western cultures associate specific behaviors and attitudes with each gender. In these cultures, masculinity means technical competence, competitiveness, aggressiveness, and rationality. Femininity, meanwhile, involves emotionality, nurturance, passivity, and relationships. As more women enter the workforce, these traditional social roles are becoming less distinct.

Gender roles are acquired through socialization. Girls and boys are taught appropriate role behaviors at early ages, and are reinforced when they display gender-appropriate behavior. Girls tend to play in small groups or with a close friend. Preferred activities include playing house or other relationship-building pretend games in which intimacy is the norm. Boys play in large, hierarchically structured groups (like most organizations). Boys tend to take part in contests in which there are clear winners and losers;

integration, rather than intimacy, is the norm. These gender roles continue throughout adult life.

In this chapter, we will set forth a framework for examining contemporary literature on gender differences with regard to work stress and health. Our aim is to facilitate a careful look at the significance, meaning, and consequences of what society defines as masculine versus feminine, and how these culturally shaped definitions affect individuals' experiences of stress and health at work. Questions arising from taking this perspective include:

- Do men and women experience different sources of stress at work?
- Does one gender experience more stress than the other?
- Are stressors more strongly linked with ill health for one gender?
- Do men and women experience different symptoms related to distress?
- How do men and women cope with work stress?
- What are organizations doing to help men and women cope with stress at work?

Examining the contemporary themes of research conducted by leading scholars was the impetus for our framework. There are four broad thematic areas that call for attention: (a) the link between contemporary work stressors and health, (b) the role of individual characteristics in the stress process, (c) family dynamics, and (d) the role of prevention and intervention, involving individual and organizational efforts to manage the stress process.

STRESSORS AND HEALTH

Researchers have studied gender differences in stressors and in health outcomes related to stress. There is little evidence that men and women experience acute stressors at different rates; however, there is evidence of differences in chronic stressors. Men and women share some common chronic work-related stressors. Both genders experience role ambiguity, job insecurity, downsizing, and time pressures. There are, however, some notable differences in the experience of other stressors. Women report higher total workload, which includes both vocational and domestic, paid and unpaid work. Women carry an average total workload of 78 hours per week, while men's total workload averages 68 hours per week (Frankenhaeuser, 1991). Evidence from a 20-year study (1977–1997) showed that the number of hours men spend with their children and doing household chores has increased slightly; however, the gap in total workload remains (Bond, Galinsky & Swanberg, 1998).

This increased workload makes it difficult for women to wind down and threatens their physical and mental health. Studies show that levels of stress hormones such as epinephrine, norephinephrine, and cortisol remain high after work hours for women, which can lead to feelings of fatigue and eventually to ill health (Lundberg & Frankenhaeuser, 1999). Women also are particularly prone to role overload, which is the experience of multiple, conflicting expectations from others. Those activities traditionally considered women's work, such as dependent care and housework, tend to be less flexible than those considered men's work and are less disposable; consequently, women have less discretionary time. In addition, tasks such as these are often "low-schedule-control," meaning they have to be done despite other interferences and cannot be postponed (Barnett & Shen, 1997).

Women also report more obstacles to achievement in the workplace, such as the "glass ceiling," an invisible barrier that keeps women from rising to top positions in organizations. Women are still relatively rare in the upper levels of organizations. Discrimination is a likely culprit, in terms of biased recruiting efforts and the selection and promotion processes. Women also may be less likely to receive developmental opportunities (such as mentoring relationships) that would prepare them for such positions (Nelson & Burke, 2000).

In addition, women report experiencing the "maternal wall," in which they receive less desirable assignments or limited career opportunities once they have had children (Williams, 1999). Employers sometimes assume that once a woman has a child, her commitment is to the child rather than the career—that mothers cannot be good employees. There are three conditions of employment that often drive mothers from the workforce. The first is the executive schedule, which typically spans 50 to 80 hours per week. The second is the marginalization of part-time work, with its restricted career opportunities, lack of benefits, and low pay. The third is the expectation that managers will relocate their families to further their careers. This is socially acceptable if it is the man's career, and much less common if it is the woman's career. Because of relocation expectations, women often turn down promotions they might otherwise accept.

Women may also experience tokenism when they are the first of their gender to enter management or executive positions. Tokens often feel isolated and excluded from informal networks, and experience stereotyping and discrimination from the majority group (Kanter, 1990). Women also report more sexual harassment and nonharassing social–sexual behavior than do men. Social–sexual behavior may include flirting and making sexual jokes. Women in nontraditional occupations, such as construction or police work, are especially prone to these stressors, which have been linked with symptoms such as nausea, headaches, and psychological illnesses (Goldenhar, Swanson, Hurrell, Ruder, & Deddens, 1998). Women also report more stress from organizational politics than do men (Nelson, Hitt, & Quick, 1989). They may have difficulty in obtaining information, may be barred from informal networks, and may lack legitimate power in organizations because they tend to be clustered in lower-level positions in the organizational hierarchy. As a consequence, women may also have little upward influence, and fewer resources.

Jobs that are held more often by men than women have burdens as well as benefits. Stressors include long working hours, considerable travel, little time for developing relationships with children, corporate politics and competition at work, and high risk of being fired for poor performance (Alvesson & Billing, 1997). Men, because of their socialization experiences, are likely to experience gender role strain, which is a long-term failure to fulfill male role expectations. Pleck (1995) identified three distinct types of gender role strain. *Discrepancy strain* occurs when a man cannot live up to his own internalized masculine ideal (typically that of traditional masculinity). This form of strain has been linked with anxiety and depression. *Dysfunctional strain* occurs when men, as a result of meeting the requirements of traditional masculinity, display negative side effects such as sexual harassment, absent fathering, and relationship dysfunctions. *Trauma strain* is a result of the male socialization experience, and may include the inability to express emotions or engage in relationships.

Another stressor that plagues men is the confusion surrounding men's contemporary roles (Burke & Nelson, 1998). Many men report not knowing exactly what is expected of them these days; others report feeling like a disenfranchised minority; still others feel that they are the victims of reverse discrimination. In current gender roles, men are not only expected to be breadwinners, but they are also expected to take on greater household responsibilities, be more disclosive of their feelings, and be more active in raising children. There is increased interest in exploring men's roles and men's development in the popular press.

Females tend to report more distress than do males, but their distress symptoms tend to be at the less lethal end of the spectrum (Matuszek, Nelson, & Quick, 1995). Women report higher levels of psychophysiological symptoms such as insomnia, nervousness, headaches, pounding heart, dizziness, nightmares, trembling, and lack of motivation. Women consistently report more symptoms of mental ill health; they have higher rates of acute illnesses and more chronic conditions, and make more health care visits. Women are higher users of medical services and prescriptions, and suffer more psychological distress and somatic disorders than do men (Jenkins, 1991). This may occur either because women are more willing to disclose their symptoms and to seek care, or because they are more likely to consider a broader spectrum of symptoms (i.e., both psychological and physical symptoms) in evaluating their health. In addition, it may be more socially acceptable for women to discuss health issues, or that medical professionals are more likely to attribute women's symptoms to somatic complaints or mental ill health. Finally, the results may reflect actual gender differences in symptom rates.

Men's distress, in contrast, tends to be of a more lethal nature. Men have higher rates of the chronic conditions that cause death (e.g., coronary heart disease), and more injuries. The gap in life expectancy between men and women is 8 years, favoring women, and many researchers (cf. Harrison, Chin, & Ficarrotto, 1989) attribute the early deaths to the masculine role. Men tend to internalize stress and are socialized to avoid asking for help with physical or psychological problems.

Behavioral symptoms of distress also differ by gender. Women are more likely to smoke, whereas men are more likely to drink. Anorexia and bulimia are more common among women than among men. Female managers are more likely to abuse tranquilizers, antidepressants, and sleeping pills than male managers (Quick, Quick, Nelson, & Hurrell, 1997).

The variance in the distress symptoms may be due to the different ways women and men cope with stress. Men tend to use problem-focused coping strategies, planned and rational actions, humor, and fantasy as ways of coping (Jenkins, 1991). Women, on the other hand, gravitate toward emotion-focused strategies. Some of these strategies, such as expression of emotions and seeking social support, are positive. Others, such as self-blame, denial, and avoidance, are less functional.

Women are more likely to use social support than men, and can especially benefit from support in the family or home arena. Support from spouses buffers working women from depression (Beatty, 1996). Women's health is related to the total number of supportive relationships they hold, and from support they receive from family and friends. Men have been shown to benefit more from support in the work arena (Baruch, Biener, & Barnett, 1987). Even when men and women receive the same amount of support from supervisors and coworkers, men reap more health benefits.

Women tend to maintain healthier diets than men, which increases their resilience against stress (Lindquist, Beilin, & Knuiman, 1997). They view diet as an important coping device. Men are more likely to turn to exercise as a coping technique, which helps them manage their fitness in response to stress (Nelson, Hitt, & Quick, 1989).

In summary, there are gender differences in stressors experienced by men and women, in the distress symptoms they report, and in the ways they choose to cope with stress. In addition, important individual differences affect each gender's experience of the stress process and its attendant health outcomes.

INDIVIDUAL CHARACTERISTICS

Gender, as an individual characteristic, has had an interesting history in work stress literature. Most of the early studies, particularly of the "fight-or-flight response," involved men. Yet, in more contemporary literature, the work on gender has concentrated on the stress experiences of working women. A more balanced perspective is in order. Our understanding of masculinity and femininity as socially constructed gender ideals and the way these ideals affect working life needs expansion. Williams (1999) noted that current gender roles restrict the potential of both men and women. Conventional femininity tends to marginalize and disempower women, whereas traditional masculinity constrains men's ability to engage fully in family life and traps them in a life of hard labor.

A new paradigm, based on gender research in animals and humans, has emerged to complement the fight-or-flight response. Taylor and her colleagues (Azar, 2000; Taylor et al., 2000) propose that females respond to stressful situations by protecting themselves and others through nurturing behaviors, and by forming relationships with others (referred to as "tend-and-befriend"). The tend-and-befriend response derives from the brain's attachment system. Differences in each gender's neuroendocrine patterns may be related to the differential responses. Oxytocin, often present in higher levels in females than in males, and which promotes caregiving behavior, also decreases the fight-or-flight response. Men probably also exhibit the tend-and-befriend response in certain situations. This response also may be a factor in studies that have shown that women seek out and benefit from social support.

Other individual differences, in addition to gender, affect the stress process. *Negative affect* is the propensity for viewing life pessimistically and negatively (Watson & Clark, 1984). Individuals high in negative affect report greater distress, and perceptions of decreased control (Ball, Trevino, & Sims, 1994). Overall, women report more negative affect than men (Jick & Mitz, 1985). Women who are employed in low-control positions are particularly vulnerable to negative affect.

Type A behavior is linked with higher blood pressure, higher cardiac output, and other increased risk factors for coronary heart disease in both sexes (Borysenko, 1987). Originally thought to be a male phenomenon, Type A behavior and associated health risks are found increasingly among women in managerial roles (Matuszek et al., 1995).

Workaholism is another individual difference variable with implications for work stress. Workaholism has three facets: work involvement, feeling driven to work, and work enjoyment (Spence & Robbins, 1992). One study of MBA graduates indicated some salient gender differences among the facets of workaholism (Burke, 1999). Women reported lower work involvement, but were similar to men in levels of work enjoyment and work drive. Women also reported greater levels of self-imposed perfectionism and overall job stress than did men. The experience of workaholism may thus differ for men and women.

Individual difference variables should be the focus of increased attention in future studies of work stress and health. Some of the above-mentioned personality variables may, in fact, account for what were previously thought to be simple gender differences.

WORK–HOME CONFLICT AND FAMILY DYNAMICS

There are many gender role expectations affecting the work–family interface. Chief among these is that men should be breadwinners, a norm that has persisted despite women's increased participation in the labor force. Masculinity is often defined by the size of a man's paycheck; whereas femininity is equated with caregiving; mothers should have "all the time in the world to give." Women are still expected to take primary responsibility for the home and family. Both men and women are subject to the ideal worker norm; that is, the ideal of an employee who works full time and overtime, and does not take time off for childbearing or child rearing (Williams, 1999). Thus, caregiving is in direct conflict with the ideal worker norm; hence the prevalence of conflict between the demands of work and family.

Work and family affect each other in a complex interplay. Much of the literature on the work–family interface has concentrated on work–home conflict. The total workload shouldered by both partners in a relationship is related to this conflict. Total workload varies by gender, age, occupational level, and number of children. Women have heavier total workloads than men, and the overall workload increases with the number of children in the home (Lundberg, Mardberg, & Frankenhaeuser, 1994).

Work–home conflict has been linked with anxiety, depression, and hostility among working women, and its deleterious effects are stronger for women who have children (Beatty, 1996). Other researchers have examined the conflict in two forms: work's interference with family, and family's interference with work. Both forms of conflict have been associated with depression, poor physical health, and alcohol use among both sexes (Frone, Russell, & Barnes, 1996). Another study of members of dual-earner families found no gender differences in work–family conflict per se; however, mothers in the study reported less task sharing from their partners (Schwartzberg & Dytell, 1996).

Culture doubtless plays a role in work–family conflicts. In Finland, one study indicated that work–family conflict was reported more often than family–work conflict among both sexes, but no gender differences were found in either form of conflict. It is more common in Finland for caregiving roles to be shared, and the norm is combining multiple roles for both sexes (Kinnunen & Mauno, 1998).

Crossover is a form of stress contagion whereby one spouse's work stress creates stress for the other. Burnout, in particular, may be contagious. One study of Israeli military officers and their wives (all professionals) showed that husbands' burnout was related to wives' burnout, and vice versa (Westman & Etzion, 1995). In addition, when one spouse had a sense of control, it also benefited the partner.

Children are also affected by parents' stress. Galambos, Sears, Almeida, and Kolaric (1995) noted that parent–child conflict was highest when both parents were stressed. In a similar vein, Barling, Dupre, and Hepburn (1998) found that children who witnessed their parents' job insecurity and layoffs had more negative work attitudes themselves.

It should be noted that there is little knowledge concerning the positive side of the work–family interface; that is, work and family roles might have enriching, rather than conflicting, effects on each other. Two mechanisms would promote the enhancement hypothesis (Greenhaus & Parasuraman, 1999). One is status enhancement, in which resources from one role promote well-being in another. Such resources include salary, relationships and networking, and status. Another mechanism whereby work and family roles might enrich each other is personality enhancement, which is the transfer of skills or perspectives learned in one role to solve problems in another. Organizing skills learned at work may transfer well into managing a home, and vice versa.

Work–home conflict is an important stressor for both women and men, and plays an important role in frameworks for understanding gender and stress at work. Examining gender role expectations, crossover processes, and the broader family dynamics will enhance our knowledge of the ways in which work and family roles affect health.

PREVENTION AND INTERVENTIONS

A final theme in gender and work stress is the prevention of distress and ill health in the workplace, and organizational intervention programs that are aimed at either enhancing health or preventing ill health. One theory through which interventions can be evaluated is *preventive stress management*, with its basis in public health methods of disease prevention (Quick et al., 1997). The basic tenet of preventive stress management is that prevention efforts should begin at the primary level. *Primary interventions* focus on changing the cause of stress, or changing one's perception of stressors. Examples of primary prevention are sexual harassment programs, which focus on alleviating harassment in the workplace, and cognitive restructuring, which teaches individuals to reframe stressful situations as challenges rather than threats. Primary level interventions are to be supplemented with *secondary interventions*, which focus on changing the individual's response to stress so that he or she is better equipped psychologically and physically to deal with it. Examples of secondary interventions include exercise and fitness programs, and meditation training. A final avenue for prevention is tertiary prevention, or healing the wounds of distress. *Tertiary prevention* usually involves referrals to qualified medical professionals and counselors and is focused on symptoms of distress.

Another basic tenet of preventive stress management is that individuals and organizations share the burden of responsibility for health and well-being. Unfortunately, too often the responsibility for stress management is left with the individual. Many organizations place the burden of adjustment on the employee, conveying the message that the individual must change in order to be healthy. Yet primary prevention, in which the sources of stress are altered, most often requires that changes be made in the job or in the organization.

Few organizations engage in gender-specific programs. Most interventions can help both men and women manage health risks and enhance well-being. Alternative work arrangements such as flextime, part-time work, and job sharing can help individuals manage work–home conflicts and time pressures. Childcare and eldercare, offered mainly by large organizations, also help both genders deal with dependent care issues. Women may be the main beneficiaries of such arrangements, however, because the responsibility for dependent care usually rests with them.

If organizations want to design gender-specific interventions, they should focus on eliminating the stressors to which each gender is especially vulnerable. For women, the stressors include total workload, the glass ceiling, the maternal wall, tokenism, and political–networking issues. Barriers to achievement can be eliminated through reward and development systems that promote equitable treatment among all individuals. Pay equity programs are one example. Audits should be conducted to ensure that women are not disadvantaged when it comes to training and development opportunities. Because social support is important, programs such as mentoring may be helpful for women. In addition, programs (secondary level prevention) that encourage and enable women to exercise should be made available. This may mean providing on-site facilities, and assistance with child care. Increased smoking among women warrants greater implementation of smoking cessation programs.

For men, primary interventions should target gender role strain and role confusion. Programs that assist men in exploring their own emotional development are warranted. "Corporate masculinity" is the term used by Maier (1991) to describe men's behavior in the workplace. Such behavior is characterized as objective, competitive, adversarial, logical, and task-oriented, and is rewarded by organizations. While this may be functional in some respects, there is ample evidence that more flexible, relationship-oriented, nurturing styles of behavior, especially for managers, are necessary. Thus, corporate masculinity limits men's effectiveness and potential as managers. It places men in the position of considering work as life's most important role, and encourages workaholism. This male model of work overvalues traditional masculine characteristics and breeds excessive attachment to achievement, at considerable health risk. Interventions that help men discover the limitations of corporate masculinity and develop a more balanced approach to life will improve their health. Because alcohol abuse is common among men, substance abuse programs are warranted.

It should be noted that interventions targeted for a particular gender can still benefit both sexes, and therefore should be offered to both. Many stressors are related to gender roles, and there are no quick fixes for culturally proscribed behaviors that are strongly ingrained. Educating employees about the health risks of such roles and behaviors is a start, but this must be combined with changes in organizational cultures, particularly those that reinforce corporate masculinity. In addition, managers should focus on corporate practices such as long work hours and excessive overtime that impact both men and women, because these practices negatively affect both health and productivity.

CONCLUSION

We believe much can be gained by examining the gender literature in terms of differences in stressors and health, individual characteristics, work–home dynamics, and interventions. These are the contemporary issues that are on the minds of practicing managers and researchers alike. The following chapters will expand our knowledge of these critical issues, and serve as the impetus for enhanced understandings that will make work life more satisfying, productive, and healthy for both men and women.

REFERENCES

Alvesson, M., & Billing, A. D. (1997). *Understanding gender and organizations.* London: Sage.

Azar, B. (2000). A new stress paradigm for women. *American Psychologist, 55,* 42–43.

Ball, G. A., Trevino, L. K., & Sims, H. P., Jr. (1994). Just and unjust punishment: Influences on subordinate performance and citizenship. *Academy of Management Journal, 37,* 299–322.

Barling, J., Dupre, K. E., & Hepburn, C. G. (1998). Effects of parents' job insecurity in children's work beliefs and attitudes. *Journal of Applied Psychology, 83,* 112–118.

Barnett, R. C., & Shen, Y. C. (1997). Gender, high- and low-schedule-control housework tasks, and psychological distress: A study of dual-earner couples. *Journal of Family Issues, 18,* 403–428.

Baruch, G. K., Beiner, L., & Barnett, R. C. (1987). Women and gender research on work and family stress. *American Psychologist, 42,* 130–136.

Beatty, C. A. (1996). The stress of managerial and professional women: Is the price too high? *Journal of Organizational Behavior, 17,* 233–252.

Bond, J. T., Galinsky, E., & Swanberg, J. E. (1998). *The 1997 national study of the changing workforce.* New York: Families and Work Institute.

Borysenko, J. (1987). *Minding the body, mending the mind.* New York: Bantam.

Burke, R. J. (1999). Workaholism in organizations: Gender differences. *Sex Roles, 41,* 333–345.

Burke, R. J., & Nelson, D. L. (1998). Organizational men: Masculinity and its discontents. In C. L. Cooper, & I. T. Robertson, *International Review of Industrial and Organizational Psychology, 13,* 225–271.

Frankenhaueser, M. (1991). The psychophysiology of workload, stress, and health: Comparisons between the sexes. *Annals of Behavioral Medicine, 13,* 197–204.

Frone, M. R., Russell, M., & Barnes, G. M. (1996). Work–family conflict, gender, and health-related outcomes: A study of employed parents in two community samples. *Journal of Occupational Health Psychology, 1,* 57–69.

Galambos, N. L., Sears, H. A., Almeida, D. M., & Kolaric, G. C. (1995). Parents' work overload and problem behavior in young adolescents. *Journal of Research on Adolescence, 5,* 201–223.

Goldenhar, L. M., Swanson, N. G., Hurrell, J. J., Ruder, A., & Deddens, J. (1998). Stressors and adverse outcomes for female construction workers. *Journal of Occupational Health Psychology, 3,* 19–32.

Greenhaus, J. H., & Parasuraman, S. (1999). Research on work, family, and gender: Current status and future directions. In G. Powell (Ed.), *Handbook of gender and work* (pp. 391–412). Thousand Oaks, CA: Sage.

Harrison, J., Chin, J., & Ficarrotto, T. (1989). Warning: Masculinity may be dangerous to your health. In M. S. Kimmel, & M. A. Messner (Eds.), *Men's lives* (pp. 296–309). New York: Macmillan.

Jenkins, R. (1991). Demographic aspects of stress. In C. L. Cooper, & R. Payne (Eds.), *Personality and stress: Individual differences in the stress process* (pp. 107–132). Chichester: Wiley.

Jick, T., & Mitz, L. (1985). Sex differences in work stress. *Academy of Management Review, 10,* 408–420.

Kanter, R. M. (1990). Token women in the corporation. In J. Heeren, & M. Mason (Eds.), *Sociology: Windows on society* (pp. 186–294). Los Angeles: Roxbury.

Kinnunen, U., & Mauno, S. (1998). Antecedents and outcomes of work–family conflict among employed women and men in Finland. *Human Relations, 51,* 157–177.

Lindquist, T. L., Beilin, L. J., & Knuiman, M. W. (1997). Influence of lifestyle, coping, and job stress on blood pressure in men and women. *Hypertension, 29,* 1–7.

Lundberg, U., & Frankenhaeuser, M. (1999). Stress and workload of men and women in high-ranking positions. *Journal of Occupational Health Psychology, 4,* 142–151.

Lundberg, U., Mardberg, B., & Frankenhaeuser, M. (1994). The total workload of male and female white collar workers as related to age, occupational level, and number of children. *Scandinavian Journal of Psychology, 35,* 315–327.

Maier, M. (1991). The dysfunctions of "corporate masculinity": Gender and diversity issues in organizational development. *Journal of Management in Practice, 8,* 49–63.

Matuszek, P. A. C., Nelson, D. L., & Quick, J. C. (1995). Gender differences in distress: Are we asking all the right questions? *Journal of Social Behavior and Personality, 10*, 99–120.

Nelson, D. L., & Burke, R. J. (2000). Women executives: Health, stress and success. *Academy of Management Executive, 14*, 107–121.

Nelson, D. L., Hitt, M. A., & Quick, J. C. (1989). Men and women of the personnel profession: Some similarities and differences in their stress. *Stress Medicine, 5*, 145–152.

Pleck, J. H. (1995). The gender role strain paradigm: An update. In R. F. Levant, & W. S. Pollack (Eds.), *A new psychology of men* (pp. 11–32). New York: Basic Books.

Quick, J. C., Quick, J. D., Nelson, D. L., & Hurrell, J. J., Jr., (1997). *Preventive stress management in organizations.* Washington, DC: American Psychological Association.

Schwartzberg, N. S., & Dytell, R. S. (1996). Dual-earner families: The importance of work stress and family stress for psychological well being. *Journal of Occupational Health Psychology, 1*, 211–23.

Spence, J. T., & Robbins, A. S. (1992). Workaholism: Definition, measurement and preliminary findings. *Journal of Personality Assessment, 58*, 160–178.

Taylor, S., Klein, L., Lewis, B., Gurung, R., Gruenewald, T., & Updegraff, J. (2000). Biobehavioral responses to stress in females: Tend and befriend, not fight or flight. *Psychological Review, 107*, 411–429.

Watson, D., & Clark, L. A. (1984). Negative affectivity: The disposition to experience aversive emotional states. *Psychological Bulletin, 96*, 465–490.

Westman, M., & Etzion, D. (1995). Cross-over of stress, strain and resources from one spouse to another. *Journal of Organizational Behavior, 16*, 169–181.

Williams, J. (1999). *Unbending gender: Why work and family conflict and what to do about it.* New York: Oxford University Press.

I

STRESSORS, INDIVIDUAL DIFFERENCES, AND COPING

INTRODUCTION: STRESSORS, INDIVIDUAL DIFFERENCES, AND COPING

Much of our understanding of gender differences in work stress comes from studies that have focused on causes of stress, the characteristics of individuals that intervene in the stressor–strain relationship, and ways of coping. *This part of the book represents where we are now in terms of our research.* In this section, we highlight leading-edge work in each area. Chapters 2 and 3 provide a backdrop for focusing on gender differences, with chapter 2 detailing comparisons between men and women, and chapter 3 focusing on the underrepresented research area of masculinity in organizations. Chapter 4 examines a very distressful contemporary phenomenon, that of restructuring, and the stress women encounter. Chapter 5 highlights a controversial individual difference variable, negative affectivity, and puts a unique twist on it by examining gender differences. Chapter 6 describes a study representing the growing body of research on social support.

2

MANAGERIAL STRESS: ARE WOMEN MORE AT RISK?

SANDRA L. FIELDEN AND CARY L. COOPER

One of the greatest social and economic changes over the past 2 decades has been the increase of women entering the labor market. This change has taken place throughout Western Europe, North America, and Australia (Davidson & Burke, 2000), and means that women are now in direct competition with men. For example, the United Kingdom has one of the highest growth rates of women entering the workforce, and, at 69%, has the third-highest employment rate of all European Union countries, just behind Denmark with 72% and Sweden with 71% (Labour Market Trends, 2001). This increase has not been across all occupations or occupational levels, however. Occupational segregation by sex persists as a primary characteristic of the United Kingdom labor market, and throughout Europe, women continue to be underrepresented at all senior management levels (Davidson & Burke, 2000).

Employment is important to both men and women as a source of income and a defining factor in self-conceptions. However, attitudes and social patterns mean that employment, and specifically managerial employment, still appears to be linked with masculinity. Although the proportion of women entering management in the United Kingdom has increased from 9.5% in 1994 to 18% in 1998, they earn less even at director level and on average are younger at each level of management than their male counterparts (Institute of Management and Remuneration Economics, 1998). These figures do represent increases at all management levels, yet it is clearly a slow progression toward true equality, with the greatest rate of growth occurring at the lowest management levels and the poorest rate of growth at director levels. The "think manager = think white male" mindset continues to prevent the progression of women in management (Schein, 2001). This means that women managers not only have to deal with the same sources of stress as their male counterparts but also have to contend with additional stressors as a direct result of being female.

This chapter considers the sources of stress encountered by managers, and the factors influencing how female and male managers respond to the demands placed on them. It also seeks to evaluate the risks facing female managers, compared to their male counterparts, as a result of their position within the workplace.

OCCUPATIONAL STRESS

The term *stress* has been conceptualized in several fundamentally different ways, and these conceptualizations can lead to confusion regarding the concept of stress. It is now generally accepted that occupational stress can be adequately explored only by taking a multidisciplinary approach (Cooper, 1996; Cooper, Cooper, & Eaker, 1988), one that investigates a combination of psychological, sociological, and physiological problems that tax individuals. Pressure in itself is not always a negative experience and can have substantial motivational benefits for those who have the resources to meet the demands placed on them. Stress is regarded as a response to a situation in which individuals are unable to meet the demands placed on them, resulting in a negative outcome (Cooper, Sloan, & Williams, 1988).

This definition of stress recognizes that the sources of stress, and its effects, are multiple and not just limited to a particular situation (e.g., work). It views stress as not just a function of being under pressure in an occupational sense but as a function of an individual's whole life situation. It includes factors intrinsic to the job (workload); relationships at work; organizational structure and climate; role ambiguity and conflict; opportunities for career development and progression; and the home–work interface (Cooper, 1996). In doing so it recognizes the environmental agents that disturb structure and function, while taking into account an individual's psychological, physiological, and behavioral attempts to adjust to both internal and external pressure.

A number of organizational and extraorganizational sources of stress have been isolated as being particularly pertinent to women managers (i.e., work stress and home–work conflicts). Organizational stressors include problems associated with being part of a minority group (e.g., discrimination and prejudice, including career blocks and sexual harassment) and being the "token" woman (including isolation, stereotyping, exclusion, and a lack of role models) (Davidson & Cooper, 1992). Extraorganizational stressors focus on the interface between work and home commitments, including issues such as poor domestic support and dilemmas about starting a family (Davidson & Fielden, 1999). These stressors are interactive and cumulative, forming an integrated whole that affects performance, behavior, job satisfaction, and well-being.

Stress exerts a high price throughout the Western world. It is estimated that 360 million working days are lost annually in the United Kingdom as a result of sickness absence, costing organizations a staggering £7–9 billion (O'Driscoll & Cooper, 1996). In the United States, of the 550 million days' productivity lost through sickness absence, it is estimated that 54% are stress related in some way (Elkin & Rosch, 1990). Although paid employment provides many positive benefits, the cost to individuals in terms of well-being is obviously high, a cost that appears to be significantly higher for women managers. Excessive pressure and scarcity of time can adversely affect women's ability to cope, often leading to reduced well-being and the increased use of maladaptive coping strategies (e.g., alcohol and drug abuse).

A recent study by Long (1998) suggests that the impact of such stressors on female managers is mitigated by other factors, however. Greater access to coping resources, such as an increased sense of personal control, leads to higher levels of job satisfaction and lower levels of job distress for managers than those in clerical positions. Therefore, female managers may be less at risk than their nonmanagerial counterparts, but in comparison to their male managerial counterparts they are still likely to be faced with additional sources of stress and poorer access to coping resources (e.g., Barnett & Brennan, 1997; Jamieson, 1998).

MANAGERIAL STRESSORS

Recent research clearly shows that while both male and female managers consider their jobs challenging and stimulating, men are still in a more favorable position than women (Lundberg & Frankenhaeuser, 1999). Women continue to be concentrated in the lower management levels, where they are paid less than their male counterparts yet are expected to perform at a higher standard (Davidson & Burke, 2000). Those in such positions frequently report high levels of mental and physical ill-health and job dissatisfaction, regardless of the type of industry or employing organization (Davidson, Cooper, & Baldini, 1995). In addition, many women report that promotion from such positions is substantially inhibited by the "glass ceiling," with organizations failing to afford them the same opportunities as their male counterparts, despite the existence of equal opportunity policies (Equal Opportunities Commission, 1996). Only organizations with a genuine commitment to the implementation of equal opportunities have made progress in successfully removing the barriers to women's progression into the higher management levels. However, that progress appears to be limited to a small number of organizations in traditionally female-dominated industries (Equal Opportunities Commission, 1996).

Chapter 1 discusses many of the stressors faced by women managers, such as workload, role overload, the glass ceiling, the maternal wall, tokenism, and sexual harassment. These will not be discussed again in this chapter but a number of additional stressors are explored below.

Gender Stereotypes

The assumption that women lack the commitment and motivation needed to succeed is often responsible for the indirect discrimination experienced by women during their managerial careers. Male managers are often seen as highly motivated and success-orientated individuals because they are constantly on the lookout for any means of progression and will exploit every reasonable opportunity to get ahead (White, Cox, & Cooper, 1992). In contrast, a common perception is that women will only move if they feel competent to do so. This approach has been interpreted as a demonstration that women are unwilling to be recruited into executive positions (Wahl, 1995). It has often been contended that women fail to demonstrate as much interest in managerial careers as men, or have the real business understanding that is required for senior management (Marshall, 1995; White et al., 1992). This presumed lack of interest has been used consistently to explain the underrepresentation of women in management, thereby placing the blame for their predicament firmly with women (Adler, 1993; Wahl, 1995).

Minority Employees

Few studies have explored the work stressors experienced by minority employees. However, the work that has been conducted has revealed that women from minority ethnic backgrounds are doubly disadvantaged in terms of career progression as a result of unique stressors (Greenhaus, Parasuraman, & Wormley, 1990; Hite, 1996). Research has shown that perceived prejudice and discrimination are a source of stress for minority workers, above and beyond normal sources of work stress (Frone, Russell, & Cooper, 1990; James, 1994). Other studies of Black women managers found that these women perceive themselves as living in a bicultural world, and experience a "push and pull" between the demands placed on them by those different worlds (Bell, 1990). These bicultural role stressors, combined with the effects of sexism and racism, enhance the high levels of stress already encountered by the majority of Black female managers (Bell, 1990; Davidson, 1997).

Marital Support

Women continue to report greater levels of stress as a consequence of their experiences in and out of the working environment (Barnett & Brennan, 1997). Many managerial occupations are so demanding they are considered to be a "two-person" career, which implies that the support of a spouse is essential. For men marriage provides a platform of support and security from which to manage their careers, but for women it is a competing demand and an obstacle representing a barrier to their career progression (Cooper & Davidson, 1994; Greenglass, 1993). In addition, Cooper and Lewis (1998) found that while many organizations acknowledged wives as an asset, husbands were viewed as a liability. Furthermore, women managers with children are potentially even more at risk from higher stress levels because of the greater levels of emotional and physical demand they encounter (Jamieson, 1998). The stress that arises from the conflicting nature of work and home pressures can also have a significant impact on career development and progression (Cooper and Lewis, 1998).

Organizational Culture

The cultures found in an organization generally reflect societal norms, being largely dominated by male values (Corcoran-Nates & Roberts, 1995). Even though the number of women managers is rising, management is still seen as a male-dominated profession in which women are marginalized by this masculine model of the successful manager (Schein, 2001). In order to achieve success, women typically have to adapt to the organizational culture by taking on male values and attitudes, becoming masculine in their gender role orientations (Sachs, Chrisler, & Devlin, 1992). However, while this may appear to benefit the individual, it frequently leads to the overall marginalization of women (Marshall, 1995). Successful female managers often hold very negative attitudes toward other women managers, and reject the notion that women's problems are external in origin (Apter & Garnsey, 1994). Thus, women managers are not only constrained by male power, but also by women's own attitudes toward the male model of management and their resistance toward other successful women (Apter & Garnsey, 1994; Nelson & Burke, 2000).

Business Networks

Men's desire to maintain the status quo in management is frequently achieved through the exclusion of women from management networks. Informal business networks can provide knowledge, information, support, advice, and sponsors (Burke, Rothstein, & Bristor, 1995). A lack of access to such networks not only denies an individual the benefits such associations afford, but also places individuals at a disadvantage. Women managers appear to be reluctant to engage in the politics that are an integral part of organizational life and business networks. Welsh (1980) believes that a lack of self-esteem is one of the factors that makes women so hesitant to use business networks, although Arroba and James (1989) suggest that there is a more important factor that explains the reluctance of women managers to engage in politics. They propose that women managers frequently choose not to become involved in business networks because they view political activity with distaste, believing that they would be compromising their own principles if they were to enter into such relationships. The reluctance of women managers to play the "network game" is compounded by the tradition upheld by many male managers of looking after their own, thereby successfully excluding women (Davidson & Cooper, 1992). When male managers need assistance, such as in a promotion situation, they turn to other men for assistance. As male networks tend to be more influential than those of females, women are often denied the same information and assistance as their male counterparts (Nelson, Hitt, & Quick, 1997).

INDIVIDUAL AND PERSONALITY CHARACTERISTICS

It is not only the pressures that individuals encounter that contribute to the levels of stress they experience. The way in which the individuals themselves react to those pressures also has a significant impact on the stress response. Work is a highly valued activity and members of occupational groups, such as managers, often develop occupational self-images that provide motivation and work satisfaction. Positive self-images can maintain or increase psychological resistance to work-based pressures, protecting individuals from the adverse effects of stress (Kaufman, 1982). As women tend to hold less prestigious management positions and experience lower levels of job control than their male counterparts, they are less likely to benefit from positive occupational self-images.

Self-Esteem

Women's lack of positive professional self-image is further exaggerated by differences in the ways in which men and women perceive levels of self-esteem. Although self-esteem is intrinsically linked to self-concept, its influence on an individual's psychological well-being is to some degree independent of self-concept, and therefore warrants separate consideration (Jex, Cvetanovski, & Allen, 1994). Self-esteem is generally defined as the degree to which we like and value ourselves. Individuals with low self-esteem tend to report greater levels of anxiety and depression than those with higher levels of self-esteem (Pierce, Gardner, Dunham, & Cummings, 1993). In addition, those with low self-esteem are prone to doubt the efficacy and accuracy of their beliefs and behaviors, demonstrating greater responsivity to social cues and an increased desire to please (Jex et al., 1994)

Overall, working women tend to hold more positive reflected appraisals (i.e., the opinions they believe others hold of them) than working men, suggesting that they have higher levels of self-esteem (Bala & Lakshmi, 1992). However, the disparity between the managerial levels held by men and women, coupled with the lack of recognition afforded most women managers (Schein, 2001), makes it likely that the personal evaluations of women managers will be less favorable than those of men. Evidence suggests that both global and domain-specific feelings of self-esteem moderate the relationship between stressors and stress outcomes (Jex, Cventanovski, & Allen, 19934). Because women managers are unlikely to have the same degree of access to this buffer, it is anticipated that they will be more at risk from the adverse effects of stress than their male counterparts.

Self-Efficacy

The effects of low self-esteem interact with an individual's self-efficacy to further reduce the individual's ability to deal effectively with workplace pressures. Self-efficacy has been defined as the belief in one's ability to perform a task, or more specifically to execute a specified behavior successfully (Bandura, 1982). According to this theory two types of expectancies exert powerful influences on behavior: *outcome expectancy*, the belief that certain behaviors will lead to certain outcomes, and *self-efficacy expectancy*, the belief that one can successfully perform the behaviors in question (Maddux, Sherer, & Rogers, 1982). These expectations influence individuals' choices of activities, the amount of effort they will expend, and how long they will persist in the face of obstacles or adverse experiences. Those with a poor sense of self-efficacy will doubt their own capabilities, and as these doubts grow, the individuals are likely to reduce their efforts or give up altogether. Those with a strong sense of self-efficacy will exert the greatest effort to master the challenges, maintaining high levels of performance (Bandura, 1982).

Wells-Parker, Miller, and Topping (1990) found that for women, outcome expectancies were the main predictors of active or passive coping orientations in relation to occupational roles. They suggest that the more experienced people are in management tasks, the greater their self-efficacy. Compared to men, women tend to have less experience with managerial tasks, their jobs are more task restricted, overall they receive less verbal support, and as a result experience greater psychological tension (Vianen & Keizer, 1996). As a consequence their self-efficacy is frequently lower than that of their male counterparts, a situation that has significant implications for the way in which women managers perceive pressure at work.

Personal Control

The way in which individuals perceive their situation and attribute causes of events is also dependent upon the degree of personal control they experience. According to Rotter (1966), people have generalized expectancies regarding whether or not their actions will be influenced by the degree to which they have control over a situation, i.e. whether or not control is internal or external. The generalized expectancy of internal control refers to the perception of events, whether positive or negative, as being a consequence of one's own actions and thereby potentially under personal control. In contrast, the generalized expectancy of external control refers to the perception of positive or negative events as being unrelated to one's own behavior and therefore beyond personal control (Lefcourt, 1982). Although people tend to be classified as "internals" or "externals," the concept is not dichotomous, but rather a continuum ranging from highly internal to highly external (Weiten, 1989).

Individuals with an internal locus of control tend to have a high need for achievement, exhibit a strong desire to assume personal responsibility for performing a task, take more initiatives in their efforts to attain their goals, seek high levels of information, and adopt behavior patterns that facilitate personal control (Cherrington, 1991; Kapalka & Lachenmeyer, 1988; Lefcourt, 1982). In general, people with an internal locus of control tend to develop fewer psychological disorders than those with an external locus of control (Weiten, 1989). Internals tend to perceive less stress, employ more task-centered coping behaviors and employ fewer emotion-centered behaviors than externals (Anderson, 1977). Previous research has shown that, in general, individuals employed in supervisory and management positions experience higher internal locus of control than those working in non-supervisory positions (Kapalka & Lachenmeyer, 1988; Mellinger & Erdwins, 1985; St.-Yves, Contant, Freeston, Huard, & Lemieux, 1989). However, women managers tend to report lower levels of internal control and are more likely to employ emotion-centered behaviors than male managers, thereby increasing their chances of experiencing psychological ill health as a result of work stress (Hochwarter, Perrewe, & Dawkins, 1995; Vingerhoets & Heck, 1990).

COPING STYLES

The process of coping with occupational stress is complex, highly dynamic, and is directed toward moderating the impact of stressful events on an individual's physical, social, and emotional functioning. The coping strategies adopted by an individual are determined by a number of personal and environmental factors, and their effectiveness depends on the approach the individual takes. It is common to distinguish between two major dimensions of coping: *problem-focused coping*, which addresses the stressful situation, and *emotion-focused coping*, which deals with the feelings and reactions to the stressful event (Latack, Kinicki, & Prussia, 1995). Problem-focused coping has been found to decrease emotional distress and is negatively related to depression, whereas emotion-focused coping increases emotional distress and is positively related to depression (Mitchell, Cronkite, & Moos, 1983; Vitaliano, Maiuro, Russo, & Becker, 1987). Vingerhoets and Van Heck (1990) found that men are more inclined to use active problem-focused coping strategies, planning and rationalizing their actions, and engaging in positive thinking, perseverance, self-adaptation and personal growth. In contrast, women prefer emotion-focused solutions, engaging in self-blame and wishful thinking. They also seek social support and a forum for the expression of their emotions which, while being recognized as a positive coping strategy, can have serious negative outcomes when the level of support is less than that sought or is not at a level of intimacy desired (Fielden & Davidson, 1998). This tendency to engage in emotion-focused strategies serves to exacerbate the negative effect of a lack of personal control, further increasing women managers' risk factors.

Women managers' tendency toward emotion-focused coping behaviors may not be the only reason they are faced with different sources of stress than their male counterparts. Research suggests that their ability to cope with stress may also be adversely affected by their tendency toward Type A behavior patterns (Greenglass, 1993). *Type A behavior* refers to the overall style of behavior that is observed in people who are excessively time-conscious, aggressive, competitive, ambitious, and hard-driving, and has been found to be a significant predictor of stress-related illness (Edwards, Baglioni, & Cooper, 1990; Greenglass, 1993). It has been reported that Type A behavior patterns are often elicited by environmental stressors or challenges, which are frequently encountered by women managers, especially in male-dominated organizations. Type A individuals are particularly challenged by situations in which their control is threatened; their primary response in such situations is an attempt to aggressively exert and maintain control over their environment (Caplan, 1983).

The effect of Type A behavior patterns on an individual's psychological and psychosomatic reactions to stress is strongly influenced by the type of coping strategy employed by that individual (Edwards et al., 1990). Problem-focused coping in conjunction with Type A behavior results in a decrease in stress-related symptoms, whereas emotion-focused coping in conjunction with Type A behavior results in an increase in symptoms. Although not all studies have found significant gender differences in Type A behavior, some studies have revealed that women managers tend to display higher levels of Type A behavior than their male counterparts (Davidson & Cooper, 1987; Rees & Cooper, 1990). This discrepancy may arise from differences in the prevailing organizational environment rather than in the behavior of women managers, however, with male-dominated environments leading to higher levels of Type A behavior patterns expressed in women managers.

Gender differences have been reported in relation to occupational stress, and previous research has indicated that female managers react differently than do male managers in terms of reported stress outcomes (Davidson et al., 1995). Stress-related illness tends to manifest itself in terms of physical ill health for male executives, whereas for female executives it is more likely to develop into mental ill health (Cooper & Melhuish, 1984). As poor mental health is not necessarily regarded as an illness and frequently only physical sickness is seen as "genuine," male managers may consider physical illness more compatible with their self-concept and more acceptable in others' appraisals of them than they would consider mental illness (Miles, 1988). In contrast, although findings suggest that women experience higher levels of psychological distress, they also indicate that women tend to normalize their mental health problems (Walters, 1993).

Because evidence relating to the effects of work stress on female managers is limited, it is important to consider the wider context of women in general in order to extrapolate relevant information (Nelson & Burke, 2000). One of the most consistent results in mental health surveys is that women report significantly more symptoms than men (Tuosignant, Brousseau, & Tremblay, 1987). The evidence suggests that this difference may arise for one or more the following reasons:

1. Women are more willing to disclose their symptoms to others, either because of greater social acceptance of sickness among women or greater concern for health among women.
2. The "vocabulary of illness" differs for men and women; women elaborate more about their symptoms, often discussing the psychological effects of their symptoms, not just the physical outcomes.
3. Women genuinely experience poorer mental health than men (Verbrugge, 1985; Vermeulen & Mustard, 2000).

Eckerman (2000) proposes that indicators of well-being need to be contextualized if the differences in the mental health of men and women are to be more than merely a reflection of the gender socialization process and the role it plays in influencing attitudes and behaviors. This has particular relevance to women managers, who find themselves not only compared to the male model of management (Schein, 1992), but also to a model of mental health that is based on the assumption that "normality = white, middle-class male" (Frosh, 1987).

Nelson, Hitt, & Quick (1997) maintain that women suffer from poorer mental health, not because they are inherently less stable than men, but because they experience greater sources of both psychological and physiological stress than men. Women are also more likely to experience psychosocial sources of stress than their male counterparts (Vermeulen & Mustard, 2000), and a significant relationship between psychosocial stressors and susceptibility to infectious disease has been found (Arnetz et al., 1987). In addition, recent research suggests that women's susceptibility to physiological impairment is increasing, and the links between stress and heart disease are of great concern for both male and female managers (Elliott, 1995).

Overall, the evidence clearly indicates that there are differences between the psychological, physiological, and behavioral reactions of men and women to stressors. Nelson et al. (1997) found that women reported higher levels of anxiety, depression, and sleep disturbances, with women now more likely to commit suicide than men. Women are more likely to smoke in stressful situations than men, and their rate of smoking is increasing faster than men's (Hammarstrom & Janlert, 1994). In contrast, men have been far more likely to experience health problems as a result of higher rates of alcohol consumption, although this situation appears to be changing rapidly (Lahelma, Kangas, & Manderbacka, 1995; Nelson & Burke, 2000).

CONCLUSION

Female managers are faced with a higher number of sources of stress than their male counterparts because of their minority status. Women must strive harder for less reward, both at work and in the home, with poorer access to effective coping strategies. There appears to be a failure by organizations to recognize the difficulties women must overcome to succeed in management. This has repercussions not only for organizations but for society as a whole.

The literature would strongly suggest that women managers are more at risk from managerial stressors than their male counterparts. If this position is not addressed, the future for women managers, in terms of health and well-being, does not look positive. The increase in the number of women entering managerial positions during the past decade has been minimal, yet there is an extremely strong argument to be made in favor of the employment of women at all managerial levels. However, if business are to take advantage of such benefits they need to provide women with an environment that aids, rather than hinders, their progression. Although initiatives such as equal opportunities and family-friendly policies are becoming more widespread, organizations need to be proactive in the implementation of such policies if they are to avoid the negative repercussions resulting from the high levels of stress experienced by women managers.

The policies implemented by organizations should also be appropriate in meeting the needs of both current and potential women managers. However, such initiatives do not have to benefit women managers alone. A move away from the long-hours culture present in many organizations has positive implications for the whole workforce, sending a clear message that work is not the only valued activity in an individual's life. Culture change programs can be effective in fostering an environment in which all employees experience an improved sense of self-worth and greater job satisfaction.

If real progress is to be made in increasing the number of women at all management levels, especially senior levels, organizations must be more proactive in protecting them from the deleterious effects that working in such positions currently exposes them to. Individuals can employ coping strategies, such as time management, seeking social support, exercise, and improved diet to help themselves handle stress. The success of such strategies is not only dependent on the individuals but also on the environment in which they live and work. Individuals only can take small steps; it is up to organizations to take the great strides necessary to effect real change.

REFERENCES

Adler, N. J. (1993). An international perspective on the barriers to the advancement of women managers. *Applied Psychology: An International Review, 42*, 289–300.

Anderson, C. R. (1977). Locus of control, coping behaviors, and performance in a stress setting: a longitudinal study. *Journal of Applied Psychology, 62*, 446–451.

Apter, T., & Garnsey, E. (1994). Enacting inequality: structure, agency and gender. *Women's Studies International Forum, 17*, 19–31.

Arnetz, B. B., Wasserman, J., Petrini, B., Brenner, S. O., Levi, L., Eneroth, P., et al. (1987). Immune function in unemployed women. *Psychosomatic Medicine, 49*, 3–12.

Arroba, T., & James, K. (1989). Are politics palatable to women managers? How women can make wise moves at work. *Women in Management Review, 3*, 123–130.

Bala, M., & Lakshmi, M.(1992). Perceived self in educated employed and educated unemployed women. *International Journal of Social Psychiatry, 38*, 257–261.

Bandura, A. (1982). Self-efficacy mechanism in human agency. *American Psychologist, 37*, 122–147.

Barnett, R. C., & Brennan, R. T. (1997). Changes in job conditions, changes in psychological distress and gender: A longitudinal study of dual-earner couples. *Journal of Organizational Behavior, 11*, 459–478.

Bell, E. L. (1990). The bicultural life experiences of career-oriented Black women. *Journal of Organizational Behavior, 11*, 459–478.

Burke, R. J., Rothstein, M. G., & Bristor, J. M. (1995). Interpersonal networks of managerial and professional women and men: Descriptive characteristics. *Women in Management Review, 10*, 21–27.

Caplan, R. D. (1983). Person-environment fit: Past, present and future. In C. L. Cooper, (Ed.), *Stress research*. Chichester: John Wiley & Son.

Cherrington, D. J. (1991). Needs theory of motivation. In R. M. Steers, & L. W. Porter, (Eds.), *Motivation and work behavior*. New York: McGraw-Hill.

Cooper, C. L. (1996). *Handbook of stress, medicine and health*. Boca Raton, FL: CRC Press.

Cooper, C. L., Cooper, C. R., & Eaker, L. H. (1988). *Living with stress*. London: Penguin.

Cooper, C. L., & Davidson, M. J. (1994). *Women in management*. London: Heinemann.

Cooper, C. L., & Lewis, S. (1998). *Balancing your career, work and family*. London: Kogan Page.

Cooper, C. L., & Melhuish, A. (1984). Executive stress and health: Differences between men and women. *Journal of Occupational Medicine, 26*, 99–103.

Cooper, C. L., Sloan, S. J., & Williams, S. (1988). *Occupational stress indicator: Management guide*. Windsor, Berks.: NFER-Nelson.

Corcoran-Nates, Y., & Roberts, K. (1995). 'We've got one of those': The peripheral status of women in male dominated industries. *Gender, Work and Organisation, 2*, 21–33.

Davidson, M. J. (1997). *The Black and ethnic minority woman manager*. London: Paul Chapman Publishing.

Davidson, M. J., & Burke, R. J. (2000). *Women in management: Current research issues, Volume II*. London: Sage.

Davidson, M. J., & Cooper, C. L. (1987). Female managers in Britain—A comparative review. *Human Resource Management, 26*, 217–242.

Davidson, M. J., & Cooper, C. L. (1992). *Shattering the glass ceiling: The woman manager*. London: Paul Chapman Publishing Ltd.

Davidson, M. J., Cooper, C. L., & Baldini, V. (1995). Occupational stress in female and male graduate managers. *Stress Medicine, 11*, 157–175.

Davidson, M. J., & Fielden, S. L. (1999). Stress and the working woman. In G. Powell (Ed.), *Handbook of gender & work*. Thousand Oaks, CA: Sage.

Eckerman, L. (2000). Gendering indicators of health and well-being: Is quality of life gender neutral? *Social Indicators Research, 52*, 29–54.

Edwards, J. R., Baglioni, A. J., & Cooper, C. L. (1990). Stress, Type-A, coping, and psychological and physical symptoms: A multi-sample test of alternative models. *Human Relations, 43*, 919–956.

Elkin, A., & Rosch, P. (1990). Promoting mental health at the workplace: The prevention side of stress management. *Occupational Medicine: State of the Art Review, 5*, 739–754.

Elliott, S. J. (1995). Psychological stress, women and heart health: A critical review. *Social Science Medicine, 40*, 105–115.

Equal Opportunities Commission (1996). *Equal Opportunities Review, 65*, 5–6.

Fielden, S. L., & Davidson, M. J. (1998). Social support during unemployment: Are women managers getting a fair deal? *Women in Management Review, 13*, 264–273.

Frone, M. R., Russell, M., & Cooper, M. L. (1990). *Occupational stressors, psychological resources and psychological distress: A comparison of Black and White workers*. Paper presented at annual meeting of the Academy of Management, San Francisco, CA.

Frosh, S. (1987). *The politics of psychoanalysis: An introduction to Freudian and post-Freudian theory.* London: MacMillan Educational.

Greenglass, E. R. (1993). Structural and social–psychological factors associated with job functioning by women managers. *Psychological Reports, 73,* 979–986.

Greenhaus, J. H., Parasuraman, S., & Wormley, W. M. (1990). Effects of race on organizational experiences, job performance, evaluation and career outcomes. *Academy of Management Review, 33,* 66–86.

Hammarstrom, A., & Janlert, U. (1994). Unemployment and change of tobacco habits. *Addiction, 89,* 1691–1696.

Hite, L. M. (1996). Black women managers and administrators: Experiences and implications. *Women in Management Review, 11,* 11–17.

HMSO (2001). Labour Market Trends. *Employment Service, 109,* 107–118.

Hochwarter, W. A., Perrewé, P. L., & Dawkins, M. C. (1995). Gender differences in perceptions of stress-related variables: Do the people make the place or does the place make the people? *Journal of Managerial Issues, 7,* 62–74.

Institute of Management and Remuneration Economics (1998). *UK national management survey.* London: Institute of Management.

James, K. (1994). Social identity, work stress and minority workers' health. In G. P. Keita, & J. J. Hurrell (Eds.), *Job stress in a changing workforce.* Washington, DC: American Psychological Society.

Jamieson, L. (1998). *Intimacy: Personal relationships in modern society.* Malden, MA: Polity.

Jex, S. M., Cvetanovski, J., & Allen, S. J. (1994). Self-esteem as a moderator of the impact of unemployment. *Journal of Social Behavior and Personality, 9,* 69–80.

Kapalka, G. M., & Lachenmeyer, J. R. (1988). Sex-role flexibility, locus of control, and occupational status. *Sex Roles, 19,* 417–427.

Kaufman, H. G. (1982). *Professionals in search of work: Coping with the stress of job loss and unemployment.* New York: Wiley Int.

Lahelma, E., Kangas, R., & Manderbacka, K. (1995). Drinking and unemployment: Contrasting patterns among men and women. *Drug and Alcohol Dependency, 37,* 71–82.

Latack, J. C., Kinicki, A. J., & Prussia, G. E. (1995). An integrative process model of coping with job loss. *Academy of Management Review, 20,* 311–342.

Lefcourt, H. M. (1982). *Locus of control: Current trends in theory and research.* Hillsdale, NJ: LEA.

Long, B. (1998). Coping with workplace stress: A multiple-group comparison of female managers and clerical workers. *Journal of Counselling Psychology, 45,* 65–78.

Lundberg, U., & Frankenhaeuser, M. (1999). Stress and workload of men and women in high-ranking positions. *Journal of Occupational Health Psychology, 4,* 142–151.

Maddux, J., Sherer, M., & Rogers, R. (1982). Self-efficacy expectancy and outcome expectancy. *Cognitive Therapy and Research, 6,* 207–211.

Marshall, J. (1995) Working at senior management and board levels: Some of the issues for women. *Women in Management Review, 10,* 21–25.

Mellinger, S., & Erdwins, P. (1985). Personality correlates of age and life roles in adult women. *Psychology of Women Quarterly, 9,* 503–514.

Miles, A. (1988). *Women and mental illness.* Brighton: Wheatsheaf.

Mitchell, R. E., Cronkite, R. C., & Moos, R. H. (1983). Stress, coping, and depression among married couples. *Journal of Abnormal Psychology, 92,* 433–448.

Nelson, D. L., & Burke, R. J. (2000). Women executives: Health, stress and success. *Academy of Management Executive, 14,* 107–121.

Nelson, D. L., Hitt, M. A, & Quick, J. C. (1997). Men and women of the personnel profession: Some similarities and differences in their stress. *Stress Medicine, 5,* 145–152.

O'Driscoll, M. P., & Cooper, C. L. (1996). Sources and management of executive job stress and burnout. In P. Warr (Ed.), *Psychology at work* (pp. 188–223) London: Penguin.

Pierce, J. L., Gardner, D. G., Dunham, R. B., & Cummings, L. L. (1993). Moderation by organisation-based self-esteem of role condition–employee response relationship. *Academy of Management Journal, 36,* 271–288.

Rees, D., & Cooper, C. L. (1990). Occupational stress in health service workers in the UK. *Stress Medicine, 8,* 79–80.

Rotter, J. B. (1966). Generalized expectancies for internal versus external control of reinforcement. *Psychological Monographs, 80* (Whole No. 609).

Sachs, R., Chrisler, J. C., & Devlin, A. S. (1992). Biographic and personal characteristics of women in management. *Journal of Vocational Behavior, 41,* 89–100.

Schein, V. E. (1993). The work–family interface. *Women in Management Review, 8,* 22–27.

Schein, V. E. (2001). *Think manager, think male: A global perspective.* Unpublished conference paper. European Group of Organizational Studies. Lyon: France.

St.-Yves, A., Contant, F., Freeston, M. H., Huard, J., & Lemieux, B. (1989). Locus of control in women occupying middle-management and non-management positions. *Psychological Reports, 65,* 483–486.

Tuosignant, M., Brousseau, R., & Tremblay, L. (1987). Sex biases in mental health scales: Do women tend to report less serious symptoms and confide more than men? *Psychological Medicine, 17,* 203–215.

Verbrugge, L. M. (1985). Gender and health: An update on hypothesis and evidence. *Journal of Health and Social Behavior, 26,* 156–182.

Vermeulen, M., & Mustard, C. (2000). Gender differences in job strain, social support at work, and psychological distress. *Journal of Occupational Health Psychology, 5,* 428–440.

Vianen, A. E. M., & Keizer, W. A. J. (1996). Gender differences in managerial intention. *Gender, Work and Organisation, 3,* 103–114.

Vingerhoets, A. J. M., & Van Heck, G. L. (1990). Gender, coping and psychosomatic symptoms. *Psychological Medicine, 20,* 125–135.

Vitaliano, P. P., Maiuro, R. D., Russo, J., & Becker, J. (1987). Raw versus relative scores in the assessment of coping strategies. *Journal of Behavioral Medicine, 10,* 1–18.

Wahl, A. (Ed.) (1995). *Men's perceptions of women and management*. Stockholm: Norstedts Tryckeri.

Walters, V. (1993). Stress, anxiety and depression: Women's accounts of their health problems. *Social Science and Medicine, 36,* 393–402.

Weiten, W. (1989). *Psychology themes and variations*. Pacific Grove, CA: Brooke/Cole.

Wells-Parker, E., Miller, D. I., & Topping, J. S. (1990). Development of control-of-outcome sclaes and self-efficacy scales for women in four life roles. *Journal of Personality Assessment, 54,* 564–575.

Welsh, M. S. (1980). *Networking, the great new way for women to get ahead?* London: Sage.

White, B., Cox, C., & Cooper, C. L. (1992). *Women's career development: A study of high flyers*. Oxford: Blackwell.

3

MEN, MASCULINITY, AND HEALTH

RONALD J. BURKE

Why do we need a chapter on men, masculinity, and health? Don't we know enough about them? It is true that although most research on work and health has involved men, the experiences of men as men have been virtually ignored (Hearn, 1994). In the 1970s and 1980s, attention was focused on women, spearheaded by scholars who called attention to the fact that increasing numbers of women were entering the workforce and women's roles were changing (Powell, 1999). In the mid 1990s, the focus shifted to men and men's roles, which are still undergoing sweeping changes (Levant, 1996).

The popular press has suggested that considerable confusion currently exists about men's roles (Kimmel & Messner, 1989). Questions such as "What are men supposed to do?" and "What do women want from men?" convey the general tenor of this uncertainty (Kimmel, 1993). Part of the confusion may be the result of pressures on men to exhibit behavior that conflicts with traditional notions of masculinity. Such pressures include those to commit to relationships, communicate one's deepest feelings, share in household responsibilities, nurture children, and to limit aggression and violence (Levant, 1996).

In addition, many men find it increasingly difficult to fulfill the expectations of the provider role. Historically, men have defined themselves by their work, a profession, and a paycheck (Kimmel, 1993, 1996). Now, men are having to redefine themselves as a result of women's influx into the workplace and the greater difficulties men face in working (acting as provider) as a result of corporate downsizing and restructuring. These forces require men to reevaluate what it means to be a success at work and in the home, because the worker–provider role is no longer what it once was (Cohen, 1993; Faludi, 1999).

Preparation of this manuscript was supported in part by the School of Business, York University, Toronto, Canada. Shelley Peterson assisted in collecting material for the chapter, Debra Nelson provided helpful feedback, and Sandra Osti prepared the manuscript.

My intent in this chapter is to explore the topic of men, masculinity, and health. I am concerned that the chapter not come across as "male bashing," because that is not my intent. Instead, I advocate a careful examination of the research evidence and consider the issue part of men's life planning in the broadest sense. My objectives are to review and integrate a diverse body of research and writing; to identify what we know and don't know about men, masculinity, and health; and to suggest a research agenda for this under-studied area.

WHAT IS MASCULINITY?

The central construct in research that examines men and men's roles is *masculinity ideology*, which views masculinity as a socially constructed gender ideal for men (Thompson & Pleck, 1995). The roots of the masculine gender ideal are instilled through the socialization process.

West and Zimmerman (1991) describe gender as an achieved status, or an accomplishment constructed through psychological, cultural, and social means. While the terms "male" and "masculine" are used interchangeably, there is a critical distinction between *maleness*, as a biologically determined state, and *masculinity*, a socially constructed state. In Western societies, the shared cultural perspective of gender views women and men as naturally and clearly defined categories having distinctive psychological and behavioral characteristics based on their sex. Differences between women and men are seen as fundamental and enduring, supported by sexual division of labor, and clear definitions of women's and men's work. This division follows as a natural consequence of biological differences that form the basis for the observed differences in psychological, behavioral, and social outcomes (Korabik, 1999).

These processes place unique pressures and expectations on men that influence men's work, private life, and health. For example, men historically have been judged on their ability to fill the breadwinner role (Ehrenreich, 1983, 1989), and by the size of their paychecks (Gould, 1974).

In general, contemporary adult men were socialized as boys to learn risk-taking, teamwork, assertiveness, and calmness in the face of danger, all of which are action skills. In contrast, contemporary adult women were socialized to learn emotional skills such as empathy, the ability to access and feel intense emotions, and the ability to express those emotions through both verbal and nonverbal means (Levant, 1995). Thus, traditional masculine and feminine ideology prevailed in the socialization process, and became reflected in adult behavior.

Because masculinity is a social construct, men's views of what constitutes masculinity vary widely. Despite this range of views, it is possible to identify what some refer to as traditional masculinity ideology (Pleck, 1995). Brannon (1976) identified four themes in traditional masculine ideology:

1. *No sissy stuff*—Avoid anything feminine.
2. *Be a big wheel*—Be powerful, strong and competitive since men must be admired to be real.
3. *Be a sturdy oak*—Show no emotion.
4. *Give 'em hell*—Take risks, go for it, face danger and demonstrate bravado.

Building on Brannon's four themes of the male role, Thompson and Pleck (1987) developed and validated a 57-item self-report questionnaire of the male sex role. Data were obtained from male college students. Factor analysis of their data yielded three prevailing attitudes: *status*—achieve status and others' respect; *toughness*—be mentally, physically and emotionally tough and self-reliant; and *anti-femininity*—avoid stereotypically feminine attitudes and occupations. They concluded that men in their sample did not fully endorse traditional male norms.

More recently, Levant et al. (1992) described traditional masculine ideology as having seven dimensions: avoid anything feminine; restrict one's emotional life; display toughness and aggression; be self-reliant; work to achieve status above all else; adopt nonrelational, objectifying attitudes toward sexuality; and fear and hate homosexuals.

IMPLICATIONS FOR MEN

In this section, we review the consequences of masculinity ideology, both positive and negative. Kaufman (1993) observes that the ways in which societies have defined male power for thousands of years have granted men access to great power and privilege but also caused them pain and insecurity. This pain remained hidden until the emergence of feminism. As women began to identify and challenge men's power and privilege, men felt under attack, vulnerable, confused, empty, and introspective.

There are many virtues to be found in men's masculinity: physical and emotional strength, sexual desire, the ability to operate under pressure, courage, creativity, intellect, self-sacrifice, and dedication to the task at hand (Kaufman, 1993). Although these qualities exist in all humans, many of them become distorted in men. Some men work too hard, drink too much, are isolated and alienated from other men, distant from their children, and present a facade that all is well. Men's power is a source of both privilege and painful isolation.

Kaufman further contends that society's definition of masculinity creates a shell that protects men from the fear of *not* being manly. Ironically, it is almost impossible to live up to our society's image of masculinity and manhood. It should come as no surprise that many men have concerns about their ability to "measure up" to this image. The development of a sense of what constitutes masculinity starts early in life for most men as they learn to discipline their bodies and unruly emotions. Men eventually come to accept relationships built on power and hierarchy (Butts & Whitty, 1993). Men generally learn to become leery of emotions, and to deny feelings and needs that are not considered masculine. Men come to suppress a range of emotions, needs and possibilities, including nurturing, receptivity, empathy, and compassion, which are seen as inconsistent with the power of manhood. These are suppressed because they are associated with femininity. With the passage of time, men lose their ability to identify and express emotions. Sadly, men often are unaware they are behaving in this way (Jourard, 1964).

Brod (1987) also weighs the costs and benefits (economic, legal, social, and political) men obtain from patriarchy. The male role is associated with heart attacks, hypertension, ulcers, suicide, early death, and greater general life dissatisfaction (Harrison, 1978). Brod, like Kaufman, sees the possession of power (and privilege) as double-edged. Yet there are vested interests of the powerful and privileged in keeping the roots of their power and privilege secretive, since this is one way to remain powerful or privileged. Leaving men's lives unexamined is one way to keep men's power and privilege unexamined.

Kaufman (1993) cautions that there is a danger in placing undue emphasis on the costs, rather than the benefits, of masculinity. These benefits include the freedom to fully commit to the workplace, the luxury of a back-up resource on the home front (in many cases), the positive perception of a strong father figure, and the ability to achieve comfort and stability in their lives (Weiss, 1990), the exclusion of women, and the wider availability of privilege. Focusing on the downside of masculinity diverts attention away from the ways in which masculinity excludes and burdens women.

It is curious that although men seem to have all the power, many men feel powerless. There are two basic reasons for this apparent contradiction. First, only a small proportion of men meet the definition of masculinity. Second, there is discrimination among men on the basis of race, age, ethnicity, class, and sexual preference. Kaufman (1993) asserts that men's power comes with a high price in terms of pain, isolation, and alienation from both women and men. Yet an appreciation of this pain is important to understand men and masculinity. In addition, it sheds light on the ways men are socialized in society and on the process of gender acquisition.

The masculine role has been implicated in men's health (Courtenay, 2001). For example, the gap in life expectancy between males and females increased from 2 years in 1900 to 8 years in 1988. Men also suffer heart attacks and ulcers at a consistently higher rate than do women. Harrison, Chin, and Ficarrotto (1989) estimate that three quarters of men's early deaths are related to the male sex role. Men rarely ask for help with physical or emotional problems. Men internalize stress; men cope with stress through use of alcohol, tobacco, and drugs; men take more unnecessary risks, and therefore have higher rates of accidental injury; and men are more successful at committing suicide (Jourard, 1964).

Males comprise the majority of many problem groups. Such groups include perpetrators of violence, sex offenders, substance abusers, victims of homicide, suicide, participants in fatal auto accidents, parents estranged from their children, and victims of stress-related illnesses (Levant, 1996). These problems affect not only men, but society as a whole. Many of these problems may be related in part to gender role strain.

Gender Role Strain

Pleck (1995) provided an update on research relating to his *gender role strain* model of masculinity (Pleck, 1981). Three broad ideas underlie the model's ten different propositions:

1. A considerable number of males experience long-term failure to fulfill male role expectations. This is known as *gender role discrepancy or incongruity.*
2. Even if male role expectations are fulfilled, the process and/or the fulfilment itself is traumatic.
3. The successful fulfilment of work role expectations leads to undesirable side effects for men or for others (e.g., low family involvement). Three types of strain result: discrepancy, trauma, and dysfunction strain.

I will elaborate on gender role strain as a cost of masculinity when I consider implications later in the chapter.

Brannon and Juni (1984) reported that college males endorsing violence and adventure as important for men also reported being in fist fights. Among male college students, Thompson, Grisanti, and Pleck (1985) found that greater endorsement of traditional masculinity was associated with having more power and engaging in less self-disclosure in heterosexual dating relationships. Perceptions of masculinity were also found to be related to college males' use of psychological violence in dating relationships (Thompson, 1990) and having myths about rape (Bunting & Reeves, 1983).

In a sample of teenaged males, Pleck, Sonenstein, and Ku (1993a, 1993b) noted that traditional attitudes toward male roles were associated with such adolescent problem behaviors as alcohol consumption, drug use, being picked up by the police, careless or negative attitudes towards condoms, and coercive sex.

Health Problems

Men traditionally have difficulty maintaining positive health care in terms of nutrition, exercise, relaxation, and stress management. Men have been socialized to ignore the physical symptoms that lead to acute illness or chronic health problems. The male gender role depicts men as tireless, achieving workers without limits. Some men have limited awareness of changes in their physiological processes, often because they are socialized to ignore them in order to get the job done. If a man cannot sense the signals from his body that all is not well, he is likely to become sick, exhausted, suffer heart attacks or premature death.

Since asking for help is associated with femininity, many men deny their physical problems. Goldberg (1977) believes that the basic bodily processes, attitudes, and behaviors that sustain life and maintain health are feminine, whereas the body-destroying attitudes and behaviors are masculine. Feminine characteristics men avoid include expressing emotions and pain, asking for help, attention to diet and alcohol consumption, self care, dependence, and being touched. Masculine attitudes and behaviors include limited need for sleep, enduring pain, excessive alcohol consumption, poor eating habits, emotional independence, denial, and repression.

Masculine gender role stress has predicted negative psychosocial and somatic consequences in men (Eisler, Skidmore, & Ward, 1988; Lash, Eisler, & Schulman, 1990) including anger and anxiety (Eisler & Skidmore 1987). Men's traditional gender role attitudes have been associated with attitudes supporting the use of physical force and marital violence (Finn, 1986). The masculine orientation was found to be correlated with self-reported drug use, aggressive behavior, dangerous driving following alcohol consumption, and delinquent behavior during high school (Mosher & Sirkin, 1984). Gender role conflict has been found to be negatively correlated with psychological well-being (Davis & Walsh, 1988), self-esteem, and intimacy (Sharpe & Heppner, 1991). Gender role conflict has also been positively correlated with depression and anxiety (Good & Mintz, 1990; Sharpe & Heppner, 1991) and directly related to decreased likelihood of seeking help (Good, Dell, & Mintz, 1989).

In a sample of male college students, Sharpe and Heppner (1991) studied gender role conflict, sex role orientation, self-esteem, anxiety, depression, relationship intimacy, and relationship satisfaction. They found that gender role conflict was negatively correlated with self-esteem, relationship intimacy, and relationship satisfaction (partial support), but positively correlated with anxiety and depression. Surprisingly, gender role conflict was not correlated with masculinity.

Pollack (1998) provides a review of the "costs" of masculinity. Men appear to be at risk from the moment of birth. Infant males are more likely to experience complications during labor and delivery and to have more birth defects than are females. Boys often exhibit behavioral difficulties and learning difficulties in primary schools, and in middle school are less likely to have professional or career aspirations. Boys are nine times more likely to suffer from hyperactivity than are girls and more than twice as likely to be suspended from school. Men are less likely to attend a university or graduate school than are women. Compared to young women, young men are four times more likely to be victims of homicide and are five times more likely to kill themselves (Pollack, 1998).

Men suffer under a code of masculinity requiring them to be aggressive, dominant, achievement oriented, competitive, rigidly self-sufficient, adventure-seeking, willing to take risks, emotionally restrictive, and avoidant of all things feminine (Levant & Pollack, 1995; Maier, 1999; Mooney, 1995). This code is bound to influence men's health and longevity. The average life expectancy for males in North America is 8 years shorter than that for women. Both Harrison (1978) and Waldron (1976) estimate that the difference in life expectancy between women and men is accounted for more strongly by sex role-related behaviors than biological or genetic factors. The traditional male role not only prevents men from seeking medical help in the early stage of illness and disease but also from paying attention to early warning signs of illness (Waldron & Johnson, 1976).

While women have shown higher rates of affective, anxiety, and somatic disorders, men have demonstrated higher rates of substance abuse and antisocial personality disorders (Landers, 1989). Such men are overly invested in work, emotionally unavailable to their families, and oblivious to the effects their lifestyle may have on their partners, their children, and their emotional and physical health (Brooks, 1992; Pleck, 1995). Men are rewarded for being competitive at work, where control of one's emotions, aggression, and assertiveness are considered "effective" while expressing feelings of weakness and vulnerability are not (Kofodimos, 1993; Maier, 1999). Young boys suppress those skills that would better equip them to participate in adult intimate relationships and care for their emotional and physical needs.

Socially negative components of masculinity (aggressive or exploitative) have been found to be correlated with tendencies toward fighting (Spence, Helmrich, & Holahan, 1979) and alcohol and drug use (Snell, Belk, & Hawkins, 1987). Mosher and Sirkin (1984) found that areas on their Hypermasculinity Inventory were correlated with self-reported drug use, aggressiveness, driving after drinking, and delinquent behavior. Helgeson (1990) noted that, among males with coronary heart disease, a masculinity scale predicted Type A behavior, poor health practices, impaired social networks, and an overall predictive indicator of heart attack severity.

Costs of Corporate Masculinity

By the time boys reach the age of five, they are socialized into masculine role behavior (Paley, 1984). Boys are taught to believe they should be controlled, aggressive, competitive, loud, loyal, and self-directed. As boys move into their teens, they learn that to fill the masculine role they must also be providers and protectors of their families. These values are consistent with a social commitment to work and the tenets of corporate masculinity (Maier, 1991).

As a consequence, men come to put work first and family second (Bardwick, 1984; Stroh & Reilly, 1999). They experience tension and stress from work overload, work–family conflict, and the discrepancy between what they say is important (family) and what they put energy toward (work). Few men have taken advantage of the Family and Medical Leave Act in the United States (Hawthorne, 1993); women still do the vast majority of second shift work (Hochschild, 1989, 1997). Men are sometimes unaware of their internal states and personal needs, given their tendency to fit with external demands, called a market orientation (Fromm, 1974, 1976). A majority of corporate men seem to be satisfied with their lives and life experiences but a minority feel trapped, alienated, and victimized. There is widespread pressure to achieve and to accumulate materialistic possessions in a capitalistic society. Corporate men's feelings of self-worth become linked to successfully overcoming challenges along the path of upward career mobility. These men must feel valued by others before they can value themselves (Korman & Korman, 1980).

The answer lies in freeing men from the requirements to be "success objects" while filling the provider role. This involves breaking the masculine mold. This is challenging for a variety of reasons. Some men are unaware of how strongly they have been socialized. For them, giving up masculinity is a sign of weakness. New behavior will be uncomfortable for these men. Benefits of freedom from the masculine role include becoming a more effective manager, obtaining career and family balance, and becoming less work addicted.

Corporate masculinity thus has costs not only for individual men but for organizations as well. Another consequence of masculinity in organizations is Type A behavior.

The Type A Experience

The Type A behavior syndrome has captured considerable attention in medical and psychological research circles during the past 2 decades. An important series of studies has strongly implicated the Type A pattern in the pathogenesis of coronary heart disease (CHD) independent of standard risk factors such as age, hypertension, diet, and heredity generally associated with the condition (Friedman & Rosenman, 1974). Research evidence finds that Type A individuals' risk of developing CHD and of having fatal heart attacks is approximately twice that of Type Bs in the population.

Certain identifying elements of the Type A pattern include exaggerated expressions of achievement striving, a strong sense of time urgency and competitiveness, and an aggressive demeanor. The Type A individual is described as an unrelenting worker, dominated by the success ethic, eager to outperform others and to constantly better his or her productivity. A psychological vigilance, hurried and restless movements, polyphasic behavior, and overtones of free-floating hostility are other Type A features (Friedman & Rosenman, 1974). Type Bs are characterized as individuals displaying opposing behavioral characteristics, and having a more relaxed, calmer approach to life in general.

Type A behavior poses a threat to careers, personality, and life itself. Type A behavior threatens careers through impatience, anger, and burnout. Type A tendencies threaten personality by increasing interpersonal conflict, narrowing the possibilities for joy (limiting oneself to things that can be counted—becoming boring and dull). Finally, Type A threatens life by fostering the development of arterial disease and its association with cigarette smoking.

As opposed to their Type B counterparts, Type As work more hours per week, travel more days per year, take less vacation and sick time off work, and are more job involved and organizationally committed (Howard, Cunningham, & Rechnitzer, 1977). Type As are more likely to experience high self-esteem at work (Burke & Weir, 1980). This encourages Type As to be more invested and committed to their work than their Type B counterparts. Type As are not necessarily more satisfied in their jobs, however. Type A behavior has typically been found to bear no relationship to job satisfaction (Burke & Weir, 1980; Howard, Cunningham, & Rechnitzer, 1977). Two questions still remain unanswered: (a) Are Type As more productive or effective in their jobs than Type Bs?; (b) Are Type As more likely to be promoted (or found) at the top of organizations? The limited data that is available suggests that Type As were in fact more likely to receive greater organizational rewards than were Type Bs (Mettlin, 1976). In addition, Type As were more likely to be promoted and to have higher performance ratings than were Type Bs (Chesney & Rosenman, 1980). In spite of this, Type As were not more satisfied in their jobs. Burke and Deszca (1982) reported that Type As were more likely to report mid-career experiences of personal and social alienation and pessimism, which Korman and Korman (1980) refer to as "career success and personal failure," than Type Bs. Thus, although Type As invest more of themselves in their work role and report greater occupational self-esteem, they are not necessarily more satisfied in their jobs and run the risk of increased feelings of personal failure later in their careers.

Type As report less marital satisfaction, and a more adverse effect of their job demands on personal, home, and family lives (Burke & Weir, 1980). Spouses of Type A job incumbents agree with their husbands. They also report less marital satisfaction, and a more adverse effect of their partner's job demands on personal, home, and family lives (Burke, Weir, & Duwors, 1979). Thus, there probably is a link between Type A behavior and marital distress, and ultimately marital dissolution. It is also likely that Type A individuals are less involved with their children. Friedman and Rosenman (1974) provide anecdotal information that is consistent with the research conclusions that Type A individuals and their partners report a less satisfying home and family life.

It is interesting to note that the facets of Type A behavior are almost synonymous with traditional masculine ideology. Aggressiveness, competitiveness, and achievement striving are part of traditional masculinity. Anger and hostility, perhaps the most noxious components of Type A, are the common pathways for strong feelings among men (Pollack, 1998). Male gender role stress has been associated with anger and anxiety, which is consistent with higher Type A risk (Eisler, 1995; Price, 1982). Type A might well turn out to be "Type M" for men because of its association with masculinity (Pollack, 1998).

Workaholism

Schaef and Fassel (1988) conclude that addictive (greedy) organizations promote workaholism. Many men (and women) are structurally rewarded for colluding with addictive work systems. In these addictive organizations, destroying one's life and loved ones is acceptable if it produces something useful in the society. Schaef and Fassel argue that denial about workaholism is pervasive because of an attachment to an economically based system, capitalism, and a social structure that supports this system (Fassel, 1990).

Shortened work weeks coupled with increased leisure time have not been realized; in fact, the opposite is true. With increases in single-parent households and dual-income families, more people are caught in a time squeeze (Schor, 1991). The consequences of busy, time-pressured lives, while often ignored, are significant (see Robinson, 1998, for review).

Porter (1996) defines workaholism as "excessive involvement with work evidenced by neglect in other areas of life and based on internal motives of behavior maintenance rather than requirements of the job or organization" (p. 71). She takes the position that an addictive pattern of excessive work impairs both immediate and long-term work performance. Consistent with other addictions such as alcoholism, Porter's review includes material on identity issues, rigid thinking, withdrawal, progressive involvement, and denial. Her definition has two elements: excessive involvement with work, and neglect of other areas of life. Workaholism makes it difficult to even think about anything other than work; family, friends, and self are neglected.

Burke (1999b) compared self-reported work and psychological well-being outcomes of three types of workaholics: work enthusiasts, work addicts, and enthusiastic addicts. The three types of workaholics worked similar hours per week (approximately 55 hours on average). The work addicts, however, indicated significantly less satisfying work outcomes and poorer psychological well-being than did the two other workaholic types. What distinguished the work addicts from the other two groups were higher scores on feeling driven to work (the addictive–compulsive factor) and lower scores on work enjoyment.

Kofodimos (1993) suggests that the imbalance in the lives of American managers results from their basic character (masculinity). She notes the similarity of the character structure of male managers and the values and beliefs of organizations, which are consistent with a male model of success. Both external and internal forces operate so that individuals who capably manage large organizations lose control of their own lives. External forces include organizational pressures, values, and rewards. These forces are seductive, resulting in more time and energy being devoted to work with the accompanying neglect of family life. Internal forces include needs, wants, and drives.

Kofodimos implicates two broad polarities to explain men's escalating commitment of time and energy to work to the neglect of personal and family life. The first, *striving for mastery*, shows up for men in both work and family life. It embodies an emphasis on task accomplishment, rationality in decision making, and viewing other people as resources for getting the job done. The second polarity, *avoidance of intimacy*, includes a lack of empathy and compassion, an unawareness of one's own and other's feelings, an unwillingness to be spontaneous and playful and an inability to admit weakness.

The imbalance resulting from mastery striving and intimacy avoidance has long-term costs. These include both difficulties in one's personal life (family crises, distant relationships) as well as failures in management (anger, intimidation overcontrol, not asking for help, avoiding feedback), ultimately increasing stress levels and health care costs. Imbalances such as workaholism may affect entire families, with particular consequences for children (Burke, 2000).

Career Success and Personal Failure

Korman and Korman (1980) highlighted and elaborated on the career success and personal failure phenomenon. *Career success and personal failure* is a syndrome that afflicts some managerial and professional men in midlife and midcareer. Career success and personal failure refers to experiences reported among men who have attained an unquestionable level of success according to society's criteria (high occupational status, prestige, power and responsibility, substantial income, relative material worth, status in the community). However, concurrent with this experience of oneself as a career success is a growing disaffection with one's life as a whole. The individual feels victim to feelings of frustration, grief, loneliness, alienation and despair, and to pressing questions about the meaning and direction of his life. The discrepancy between the individual's career identity with its external trappings and rewards, and the individual's more personal sense of self, creates varying degrees of psychological distress which demand resolution.

Why should an individual who is so obviously successful in his career develop feelings of personal failure? One set of antecedents proposed by Korman and Korman results from new appreciations of life realities developed from particular work experiences. These include the realization that life demands are contradictory (one cannot necessarily have it all); the realization that one's view of cause–effect relationships was wrong; the realization that many of one's choices or decisions were made to please others; and the realization that one has few close friends and is basically alone. A second set of antecedents results from the male midlife stage itself. These include an awareness of physical decline, advancing age, and goals that will never be achieved; changes in family and personal relationships among self and others; and increased feelings of obsolescence. The combination of these antecedents results in career-successful men feeling personally and socially alienated. With these feelings come a loss of work interest and dissatisfaction with one's job, career, or life in general. In turn, this leads to psychological distress and a desire to rearticulate a sense of purpose and meaning in one's life.

Kofodimos defines balance as "a satisfying, healthy and productive life that includes work, play, and love; that integrates a range of life activities with attention to self and to personal and spiritual development; and that expresses a person's unique wishes, interests, and values" (1993, p. xiii). Several factors have made the striving for balance a higher priority among some managers. These include the presence of more women in the workforce, increasing pressures for harder work and longer hours, the movement of baby-boomers into midlife and management, and the realization by some that the simple-minded pursuit of career success has fallen short in providing happiness.

CHANGING MEN AND ORGANIZATIONS

There is increasing evidence that educational and counseling initiatives can prove useful in reducing the most lethal aspects of the male role. Friedman and his colleagues (Friedman & Rosenman, 1974; Friedman & Ulmer, 1984) indicate clearly that Type A behavior can be modified, resulting in a corresponding reduction in incidence of CHD. Their program (Friedman & Ulmer, 1984) provides detailed information on ways to alleviate time urgency, free-floating hostility, and self-destructive tendencies. The program involves cognitive restructuring, behavior modification, self monitoring, social support, and reinforcement. These authors provide evidence of the effectiveness of this program in preventing heart disease-related deaths.

Williams and Williams (1993) describe a program for controlling hostility, one of the key components of coronary-prone behavior (Williams, 1989). The major strategies involve learning how to deflect anger, improve relationships, and adopt positive attitudes.

There are also a number of workshops available allowing both men and women to confront the discontents of masculinity. Silverstein and Rashbaum (1994) offer one such workshop, titled, "The courage to raise good men." The workshop questions traditional motives of manhood and encourages both mothers and fathers to refuse to sanction the emotional shutdown traditionally demanded of boys. Silverstein and Rashbaum also encourage a new way of valuing traditional "feminine" behaviors such as empathy, nurturing, and compassion. As Kaufman (1993) writes, it is time to start "cracking the armor."

Achieving balance requires changes in both individuals and organizations. Kofodimos (1993) advocates, at the broadest level, that individuals change their approach to living, and that organizations review and change their norms, values, and practices. Individuals need to identify the allocation of time and energy that fits their values and needs. Organizations that support balance need to examine and redefine effective performance at work (to be more than hours worked per week) as well as redefine the notions of a career and career success.

Korman and Korman (1980) offer some suggestions for societal and organizational interventions that can be considered to reduce career success and personal failure experiences. First, with greater recognition of the existence of the problem, professionals in our society can develop programs explicitly designed to help individuals anticipate or resolve the problem of career success and personal failure. This may involve developing personal growth and life planning workshops, assessment centers, career and personal counseling facilities, and self-help materials, all specifically designed to aid individuals in coping with or preventing the severity of this experience.

Another intervention at the societal level might involve the educational system. Students in high schools and universities could be exposed to the different meanings of the word "success"; to viable lifestyle options; to stages of adult development and their relevant tasks, issues and problems; to the interactive effects of work and family life; and to goal setting and career and life-planning activities. There is an obvious need to portray the reality of success more accurately. The societal model pushed so enthusiastically by schools offering business and corporate management development programs (i.e., hard work will bring success, success automatically creates the good life, the healthy life) grossly distorts the reality. As individuals begin their careers, unrealistic expectations can result in eventual disillusionment in midlife, followed by psychosomatic symptoms, physical illness, alcoholism, and heart attacks. The costs of success must be presented if a balanced view is to be had.

Interventions at the organizational level are crucially important yet at the present time are virtually nonexistent. Organizations are in a position to provide assessment and career planning programs for their employees and many do. Fortunately, there is a growing recognition that these kinds of programs make little sense without giving consideration to personal life needs and goals. In addition, it is impossible to ignore the fact that individuals' work life and personal life influence each other to a significant degree. It is not unreasonable to expect organizations to consider the impact they are having on the families of their employees; to understand the extent of that impact by surveys of both employees and their spouses; to providing adequate counseling facilities for employees and their families; and to take a more active role in involving and preparing families for the job and career changes that might affect them.

At an early stage in an individual's career, organizations can identify those who are prone to career success and personal failure. Every top management group knows who their workaholics and Type As are and can begin developing a program to educate these individuals on the possible effects such behavior could have on themselves and their families. Another interesting possibility for organizations is to make provisions for individuals to take sabbaticals, or to be assigned to special assignments that significantly change their day-to-day work and life patterns and free them to re-examine their life situation and gain new perspective.

CONCLUSION

Reconstructing or redefining masculinity requires social change. It must occur in early childhood, in schools, in the media (especially television), in universities, in organizations, and through government policies and initiatives. The current trend toward corporate and government restructuring has resulted in massive downsizing and job losses. Might these serve as stimuli for change? Some men may be forced out of the traditional breadwinner role, and some may adopt new definitions of masculinity as a result. Others, however, may respond with fear and a rigid adherance to traditional masculine ideology.

Brod and Kaufman (1994) suggest that contemporary men need to be open to women's presence and suppressed knowledge; consider men's lives and experiences as those of men and not humans in general; appreciate how men assume the privileges of a patriarchical society; become aware of how the masculine role oppresses women; and understand why it is so difficult for men to change. Theoretical understanding of men's experiences necessarily becomes personal understanding since it is men's lives that are being examined. It is men's responsibility to challenge an oppressive status quo through changes in men's personal lives as well as in ideas, structures, processes and organizations.

Men who develop the capacity to provide a gender-sensitive empathic form of fathering may benefit in reducing levels of masculinity ideology. First, they can see the positive effects of their emotional commitment to their children's well-being, raising their children's self-esteem. Second, they can learn from their female partners how to better nurture. Robinson (1998) and Friedman and Ulmer (1984) provide useful insights on reducing the harmful habits of workaholism and Type A behavior respectively. Interestingly, Burke (1999a, 1999b) has found that the need to prove oneself is an individual difference characteristic associated with both levels of Type A behavior and work addiction.

How can men change? Men do not need to discard parts of themselves as much as they need to change them. Autonomy and aggressiveness are not negative unless they become extreme. These traits need to be tempered and balanced.

Orton (1993) defines social change as a process of *unlearning* gender- and power-based behaviors that have proved harmful and then *relearning* respectful empowering behaviors that have no reference to gender. This process will take considerable time and practice to realize benefits from it. Orton believes that it is the job of men to point out to other men the dysfunctional aspects of traditional masculinity and support and model new behaviors.

Kimmel (1987) raises the question of how we can change those components of masculinity that limit "men's development as healthy and fully responsive people." He identifies three approaches: personal change by men, the creation of political organizations that communicate and lobby for change, and the emergence of broadly based social movements. He further suggests that men are changing, but points out that few do so in response to the downside and limitations of masculinity, but rather from pressures of external forces (e.g., the women's movement).

Brannon's four basic rules of manhood highlight the dilemma for men. These rules have limited men and channeled them away from whatever their real potential might have been. How can men free themselves from their prison? Suggestions include getting out of the corporate rat race; rejecting competition and aggression; and regaining emotional spontaneity. What was missing in all this was a new model of manhood.

Kimmel (1996) offers "democratic manhood" as the model of masculinity of the future. Democratic manhood involves inclusion, fighting injustice based on difference, and private and public commitments. Men need to change themselves, foster relationships, and nurture their families. In addition, men need to challenge and remake social systems so that they and women will prosper.

REFERENCES

Bardwick, J. (1984). When ambition is no asset. *New Management, 1*, 22–28.

Brannon, R. (1976). The male sex role: Our culture's blueprint for manhood and what it's done for us lately. In D. David, & R. Brannon (Eds.), *The forty-nine percent majority: The male sex role* (pp. 1–48). Reading, MA: Addison-Wesley.

Brannon, R., & Juni, S. (1984). A scale for measuring attitudes about masculinity. *Psychological Documents, 14*, 6–7.

Brod, H. (1987). *The making of the masculinities: The new men's studies.* Boston: Unwin Hyman.

Brod, H., & Kaufman, M. (1994). *Theorizing masculinities.* Thousand Oaks, CA: Sage.

Brooks, G. R. (1992). Gender-sensitive family therapy in a violent culture. *Topics in Family Psychology and Counseling, 1*, 24–36.

Bunting, A. B., & Reeves, J. B. (1983). Perceived male sex orientation and beliefs about rape. *Deviant Behavior, 4*, 281–295.

Burke, R. J. (1999a). Workaholism in organizations: The role of beliefs and fears. *Anxiety, Stress, and Coping, 12*, 1–12.

Burke, R. J. (1999b). It's not how hard you work but how you work hard: Evaluating workaholism components. *International Journal of Stress Management, 6*, 225–239.

Burke, R. J. (2000). Workaholism in organizations: Concepts, results and future research directions. *International Journal of Management Reviews, 2*, 1–16.

Burke, R. J., & Deszca, E. (1982). Type A behaviour and career success and personal failure. *Journal of Occupational Behaviour, 3*, 161–170.

Burke, R. J., & Weir, T. (1980). The Type A experience: Occupational and life demands, satisfaction and well-being. *Journal of Human Stress, 6*, 28–38.

Burke, R. J., Weir, T., & Duwors, R. E. (1979). Type A behavior of administrators and wives' reports of marital satisfaction and well-being. *Journal of Applied Psychology, 64*, 57–65.

Butts, D., & Whitty, M. (1993). Why men work? Money, power, success and deeper values. *Masculinities, 1*, 35–33.

Chesney, M., & Rosenman, R. H. (1980). Type A behavior in the work setting. In C. L. Cooper, & R. Payne (Eds.), *Current concerns in occupational stress* (pp. 187–212). New York: John Wiley.

Cohen, T. F. (1993). What do fathers provide? Reconsidering the economic and nurturant dimensions of men as parents. In J. Hood (Ed.), *Men, work and family* (pp. 1–22). Newbury Park, CA: Sage.

Courtenay, W. H. (2001). Constructions of masculinity and their influence on men's well-being: A theory offender and health. *Social Science and Medicine, 51*, 203–217.

Davis, F., & Walsh, W. B. (1988). *Antecedents and consequences of gender role conflict: An empirical test of sex role strain analysis.* Paper presented at the 96th Annual Convention of the American Psychological Association, Atlanta, GA.

Ehrenreich, B. (1983). *The hearts of men: American dreams and the flight from commitment*. New York: Anchor Press.

Ehrenreich, B. (1989). A feminist's view of the new man. In M. Kimmel, & M. A. Messner (Eds.), *Men's lives* (pp. 34–43). New York: MacMillan.

Eisler, R. M. (1995). The relationship between masculine gender role stress and men's health risk: The validation of a construct. In R. F. Levant, & W. S. Pollack (Eds.), *A new psychology of men* (pp. 207–225). New York: Basic Books.

Eisler, R. M., & Skidmore, J. R. (1987). Masculine gender role stress: Scale development and components factors in appraisal of stressful situations. *Behavior Modification, 11*, 123–136.

Eisler, R. M., Skidmore, J. R., & Ward, C. H. (1988). Masculine gender-role stress: Predictor of anger, anxiety and health-risk behaviors. *Journal of Personality Assessment, 52*, 133–141.

Faludi, S. (1999). *Stiffed: The betrayal of the American male*. New York: William Morrow & Co.

Fassel, D. (1990). *Working ourselves to death*. San Francisco: Harper.

Finn, J. (1986). The relationship between sex role attitudes and attitudes supporting marital violence. *Sex Roles, 14*, 235–244.

Friedman, M., & Rosenman, R. (1974). *Type A behaviour and your heart*. New York: Knopf.

Friedman, M., & Ulmer, D. (1984). *Treating Type A behavior and your heart*. New York: Alfred Knopf.

Fromm, E. (1974). *Man for himself*. New York: Rinehart.

Fromm, E. (1976). *To have or to be?* New York: Harper & Row.

Goldberg, H. (1977). *The hazards of being male*. New York: New American Library.

Good, G. E., Dell, D. M., & Mintz, L. B. (1989). Male role and gender role conflict: Relations in help seeking in men. *Journal of Counseling Psychology, 36*, 295–300.

Good, G. E., & Mintz, L. B. (1990). Gender role conflict and depression in college men: Evidence for compounded risk. *Journal of Counseling and Development, 69*, 17–21.

Gould, R. E. (1974). Measuring masculinity by the size of a paycheque. In J. Pleck, & J. Sawyer (Eds.), *Men and masculinity* (pp. 96–100). Englewood Cliffs, NJ: Prentice-Hall.

Harrison, J. C. (1978). Warning: The male role may be hazardous to your health. *Journal of Social Issues, 34*, 65-86.

Harrison, J. C., Chin, J., & Ficarrotto, T. (1989). Warning: Masculinity may be dangerous to your health. In M. S. Kimmel, & M. A. Messner (Eds.), *Men's lives* (pp. 296–309). New York: MacMillan.

Hawthorne, F. (1993). Why family leave shouldn't scare employers. *Institutions Investor, 27*, 31–34.

Hearn, J. (1994). Changing men and changing managements: Social change, social research and social action. In M. Davidson, & R. J. Burke (Eds.), *Women in management: Current research issues* (pp. 192–209). London: Paul Chapman.

Helgeson, V. S. (1990). The role of masculinity as a prognostic predictor of heart attack severity. *Sex Roles, 22,* 755–776.

Hochschild, A. R. (1989). *The timebind: When work becomes home and home becomes work.* New York: Metropolitan.

Hochschild, A. R. (1997). *The timebind.* New York: Metropolitan.

Howard, J. M., Cunningham, D. A., & Rechnitzer, P. A. (1977). Work patterns associated with Type A behavior: A managerial population. *Human Relations, 36,* 825–836.

Jourard, S. M. (1964). Some lethal aspects of the male role. In S. M. Jourard, *The transparent self* (pp. 46–55). Princeton, NJ: Van Nostrand.

Kaufman, M. (1993). *Cracking the armor.* Toronto: Viking.

Kimmel, M. S. (1987). *Changing men: New directions in research on men and masculinity.* Newbury Park, CA: Sage.

Kimmel, M. S. (1993). What do men want? *Harvard Business Review, 71,* 50–63.

Kimmel, M. S. (1996). *Manhood in America.* New York: The Free Press.

Kimmel, M. S., & Messner, M. A. (1989). *Men's lives.* New York: Macmillan Publishing Company.

Kofodimos, J. (1993). *Balancing act.* San Francisco, CA: Jossey-Bass.

Korabik, K. (1999). Sex and gender in the new millennium. In G. N. Powell (Ed.), *Handbook of gender and work* (pp. 3–16). Thousand Oaks, CA: Sage.

Korman, A., & Korman, R. (1980). *Career success and personal failure.* New York: Prentice-Hall.

Landers, S. (1989) In U.S., marital disorders affect 15 percent of adults. *APA Monitor, 20,* 16.

Lash, S. J., Eisler, R. M., & Schulman, R. S. (1990). Cardiovascular reactivity to stress in men: Effects of masculine gender role stress appraisal and masculine performance challenge. *Behavior Modification, 14,* 3–20.

Levant, R. F. (1995). Toward the reconstruction of masculinity. In R. F. Levant, & W. S. Pollack (Eds.), *A new psychology of men* (pp. 229–251). New York: Basic Books.

Levant, R. F. (1996). The new psychology of men. *Professional Psychology: Research and Practice, 27,* 259–265.

Levant, R. F., Hirsch, L., Celentano, E., Cozza, T., Hill, S., MacEachern, M., et al. (1992). The male role: An investigation of norms and stereotypes. *Journal of Mental Health Counseling, 14,* 325–337.

Levant, R. F., & Pollack, W. S. (1995). *A new psychology of men.* New York: Basic Books.

Maier, M. (1991). The dysfunctions of "corporate masculinity": Gender and diversity issues in organization development. *Journal of Management in Practice, 8,* 49–63.

Maier, M. (1999). On the gendered substructure of organization: Dimensions and dilemmas of Corporate Masculinity. In G. N. Powell (Ed.), *Handbook of gender and work* (pp. 69–93). Thousand Oaks, CA: Sage.

Mettlin, C. (1976). Occupational careers and the prevention of coronary-prone behavior. *Social Science and Medicine, 10,* 367–372.

Mooney, T. F. (1995). Cognitive behavior therapy for men. In R. F. Levant, & W. S. Pollack (Eds.), *A new psychology of men* (pp. 57–82). New York: Basic Books.

Mosher, D. L., & Sirkin, M. (1984). Measuring a macho personality constellation. *Journal of Research Personality, 18,* 150–163.

Orton, R. S. (1993). Outside in: A man in the movement. In E. Buckwald, P. R. Fletcher, & M. Rother (Eds.), *Transforming a rape culture* (pp. 237–246). Minneapolis, MN: Milkweed Editions.

Paley, V. G. (1984). *Boys and girls: Superheroes in the ball corner.* Chicago: University of Chicago Press.

Pleck, J. H. (1981). *The myth of masculinity.* Cambridge, MA: MIT Press.

Pleck, J. H. (1995). The gender role strain paradigm: An update. In R. F. Levant, & W. S. Pollack (Eds.), *A new psychology of men* (pp. 11–32). New York: Basic Books.

Pleck, J. H., Sonenstein, F. L., & Ku, L. C. (1993a). Masculinity ideology: Its impact on adolescent males' heterosexual relationships. *Journal of Social Issues, 49,* 11–29.

Pleck, J. H., Sonenstein, F. L., & Ku, L. C. (1993b). Attitudes toward male roles among adolescent males: A discriminant validity analysis. *Sex Roles, 30,* 481–501.

Pollack, W. S. (1998). *Real boys.* New York: Henry Holt.

Porter, G. (1996). Organizational impact of workaholism: Suggestions for research-ing the negative outcomes of excessive work. *Journal of Occupational Health Psychology, 1,* 70–84.

Powell, G. N. (1999). *Handbook of gender and work.* Thousand Oaks, CA: Sage.

Price, V. A. (1982). *Type A behavior pattern: A model for research and practice.* New York: Academic Press.

Robinson, B. E. (1998). *Chained to the desk: A guidebook for workaholics, their part-ners and children and the clinicians who treat them.* New York: NYU Press.

Schaef, A. W., & Fassel, D. (1988). *The addictive organization.* San Francisco: Harper.

Schor, J. (1991). *The overworked American: The unexpected decline of leisure.* New York: Basic Books.

Sharpe, M. J., & Heppner, P. P. (1991). Gender role, gender role conflict, and psy-chological well-being in men. *Journal of Counseling Psychology, 38,* 323–330.

Silverstein, O., & Rashbaum, B. (1994). *The courage to raise good men.* New York: Viking.

Snell, W. E., Belk, S. S., & Hawkins, R. C. (1987). Alcohol and drug use in stress-ful times: The influence of the masculine role and sex-related personality attributes. *Sex Roles, 16,* 359–373.

Spence, J. T., Helmreich, R. L., & Holahan, C. K. (1979). Negative and positive components of psychological masculinity and femininity and their relationship to self-reports of neurotic and acting-out behaviors. *Journal of Personality and Social Psychology, 37,* 1673–1682.

Stroh, L. H., & Reilly, A. H. (1999). Gender and careers: Present experiences and emerging trends. In G. N. Powell (Ed.), *Handbook of gender and work* (pp. 307–324). Thousand Oaks, CA: Sage.

Thompson, E. H. (1990). Courtship violence and the male role. *Men's Studies Review, 7*, 4–13.

Thompson, E. H., Grisanti, C., & Pleck, J. H. (1985). Attitudes toward the male role and their correlates. *Sex Roles, 13*, 413–427.

Thompson, E. H., & Pleck, J. H., (1987). Reformulating the male role. In M. S. Kimmel (Ed.), *Changing men* (pp. 25–36). Newbury Park, CA: Sage.

Thompson, E. H., & Pleck, J. H. (1995). Masculine ideology: A review of research instrumentation on men and masculinities. In R. F. Levant, & W. S. Pollack (Eds.), *A new psychology of men* (pp. 129–163). New York: Basic Books.

Thompson, E. H., Pleck, J. H., & Ferrera, D. C. (1992). Men and masculinities: Scales for masculinity ideology and masculinity-related constructs. *Sex Roles, 27*, 573–607.

Waldron, I. (1976). Why do women live longer than men? *Journal of Human Stress, 2*, 1–13.

Waldron, I., & Johnson, S. (1976). Why do women live longer than men? *Journal of Social Stress, 2*, 19–29.

Weiss, R. S. (1990). *Staying the course.* New York: The Free Press.

West, C., & Zimmerman, D. H. (1991). Doing gender. In J. Lorber, & S. A. Farrell (Eds.), *The social construction of gender* (pp. 13-37). Newbury Park, CA: Sage.

Williams, R. (1989). *The trusting heart: Great news about Type A behavior.* New York: Random House.

Williams, R., & Williams, V. (1993). *Anger kills.* New York: Random House.

4

WOMEN AND CORPORATE RESTRUCTURING: SOURCES AND CONSEQUENCES OF STRESS

REKHA KARAMBAYYA

Organizational restructuring refers to radical change in organizational structures and processes, often in response to or in anticipation of organizational decline. While in theory organizational restructuring can include any significant change in structures or processes, it is often a euphemism for downsizing, and in practice almost always involves downsizing to some degree. For purposes of discussion here restructuring is used as a general term involving significant organizational change in response to environmental pressures. Downsizing is one form that restructuring may take. Freeman and Cameron (1993) define downsizing as an intentional strategy of workforce reduction with the intent of improving organizational performance.

Since the early 1980s, restructuring in general, and downsizing in particular, have been touted as a route to competitiveness during an era of mergers and acquisitions. McKinley, Sanchez, and Schick (1995) point out that more than 85% of Fortune 1000 companies downsized their white collar workforces between 1987 and 1991. There has been much debate on the subject of whether organizational restructuring in general, and downsizing in particular, have actually achieved their intended results (Cascio, 1993; Noer, 1993). Gordon (1996) argues that most organizations in their attempts to become "lean and mean" have only managed to go halfway to "fat and mean." Most of the research on the effects of restructuring suggests that organizations engaged in restructuring processes often experience a decline in innovation and creativity (Amabile & Conti, 1999; Mone, McKinley, & Barker, 1998), accompanied by a decline in communication and trust, often at a time when it is most needed (Cascio, 1993; Noer, 1993). These processes appear to follow the predictions of the threat–rigidity model (Staw, Sandelands, & Dutton, 1981) in which an external threat is met with an internal paralysis and reliance on well-learned, obsolete responses.

Bedian and Armenakis (1998) suggest that organizations in decline suffer from a "cesspool syndrome," in which the departure of qualified and valuable employees results in incompetent managers rising to the top of the organization. The end result is a vicious cycle in which failing organizations become less capable of reversing their decline because they have fewer resources to devote to the task.

Recently, considerable attention has been paid to the effects of downsizing on individuals, particularly managers, who survive the process. Most of this work recognizes the need to address the loss and stress caused by layoffs, also known as "survivors syndrome" (Brockner, 1988; Cascio, 1993; Noer, 1993). In addition, there appears to be a tendency among managers to respond to the unpleasantness of layoffs by either distancing themselves from the consequences of their decisions (Folger & Skarlicki, 1998), or by becoming "toxic handlers," absorbing some of the toxicity that emerges during organizational restructuring at considerable personal expense (Frost & Robinson, 1999).

Clearly, restructuring is a stressful event for managers as well as employees. It involves uncertainty, the reality or the prospect of job loss, loss of support networks, and additional pressure to work long hours and achieve short-term results. For managers it involves making or communicating unpopular decisions, and taking responsibility for decisions and outcomes that are often outside their sphere of control (Cascio, 1993; Noer, 1993).

This chapter presents the argument that restructuring may present unique stresses for women in organizations, partly because of their organizational and personal circumstances, and partly because of their means of coping with such stress. This is an exploratory analysis that integrates research on gender, stress, and organizational restructuring to come up with conceptual arguments to map the effects of organizational restructuring on women. While there is some research in each of these areas, it rarely has been integrated to explore the impact of restructuring on women in organizations.

GENDER AND STRESS

There is considerable dispute on the issue of whether women experience unique forms of occupational stress. Some research suggests that, in general, women tend to occupy organizational positions with less control, power, and authority, and that they typically have more career interruptions than men (Barnett, Beiner, & Baruch, 1987). In addition, women are more likely to be embedded in family and community networks, are expected to be nurturing, and tend to suffer from "other people's problems" (Belle, 1987; Wethington & McLeod, 1987). Others suggest that the research evidence is not quite so clear cut. While women may experience unique stressors and respond to them differently than do men, gender interacts with stressors in such complex ways that trying to isolate the role of gender in stress may be almost impossible (Nelson & Burke, 2000).

In general, women in organizations occupy positions of less status and power than do men, are often paid less than men in comparable positions, face a "glass ceiling," have less career and organizational support, and are often subject to sexual harassment and inhospitable workplace cultures (Dunahoo, Geller, & Hobfoll, 1996; see also chapter 6). For a detailed discussion of work stressors faced by women including workload, role overload, the glass ceiling, tokenism, and sexual harassment, see chapter 1.

Among nonwork stressors, family life and roles have dominated the research agenda. What is evident is that the movement of women into the workplace has not had much impact on the definition and adoption of family roles. Women are burdened with most of the "second shift," including caring for children and the elderly, family maintenance, shopping, cooking and cleaning (Hochschild, 1989; see also chapter 1).

Models of stress categorize coping behaviors as either *problem focused* (directed at the source of the stress), or *emotion focused* (directed at the reactions to stress) (Barnett, Beiner, & Baruch, 1987). While some research suggests that women tend to engage in emotion-focused coping, while men are more problem oriented in their coping behavior (Barnett, Beiner, & Baruch, 1987; Nelson & Burke, 2000), other data find no differences in coping behaviors when women and men occupy similar jobs. See chapter 6 for a more detailed discussion of coping strategies.

ORGANIZATIONAL RESTRUCTURING

In this section I draw on existing research to develop a view of organizational restructuring as a stressful life event, and develop arguments outlining why it may be particularly stressful for women, given their unique personal and professional roles. While much of the early work on organizational restructuring explored the impact of layoffs in the context of blue collar work (Brockner, 1988; Leana & Feldman, 1992), research attention has now shifted to white collar and professional work (Armstrong-Stassen, 1998; Havlovic, Bouthillette, & Van der Wal, 1998) and the relative effectiveness of alternative forms of restructuring (Burke & Greenglass, 2000). Some of these studies have primarily male respondents (Armstrong-Stassen, 1998), others have primarily female respondents (Burke & Greenglass, 2000), but specific attention rarely is paid to the effects of gender on responses to restructuring.

Most of the research on organizational restructuring points out that the process of restructuring is inherently chaotic, unpredictable, and painful. Organizations often put off restructuring until they are in crisis. Once the crisis is observed, there is little time and few resources available to organize a response. Organizations must attempt long-term change, knowing that the long term is irrelevant if they cannot survive the short term. That may lead to the short-term cost-cutting that was so popular in the past decade, with disastrous long-term implications (Gordon, 1996). For individuals in failing organizations, this short-sighted approach has translated into living in a constant state of crisis with no clear vision of what may lie ahead (Cascio, 1993). While such uncertainty is likely to be stressful for both men and women, for women it is yet another roadblock to career success, and may affect them in unique ways (Karambayya, 1998).

Structural or Functional Issues

During restructuring there is an almost exclusive focus on the "bottom line" and a discounting of anyone and anything that does not directly contribute to it. Therefore, a disproportionate amount of the downsizing tends to take place in white collar jobs and in support functions (Cascio, 1993). Women tend to be overrepresented in these areas, relative to their general representation in the paid workforce, and therefore bear the brunt of the downsizing. Paradoxically, organizations discover that the workload does not decrease in these functional areas (Cascio, 1993), in fact it often increases. In human resources, for example, emphasis may shift from hiring and performance evaluation to design of termination packages, retraining, and career counseling. Women, who make up the majority of the employees in support functions, are often exposed to the "double whammy" of losing friends and colleagues while being required to work extra long and hard to cope with the increased workload (Karambayya, 1998).

In organizations in which downsizing reflects seniority patterns, women are particularly vulnerable because they are later entrants into managerial ranks, and have not yet achieved positions of power. When organizations resort to cutting the "bulge in the middle," women are likely to be hard hit, because they comprise the majority of these positions. Being in the middle also means that women managers have to contend with the dilemmas and paradoxes facing middle managers during restructuring. Middle managers are faced with conflicting and contradictory messages from the top of the organization about what is expected of them. They are asked to be warriors and healers, take risks without failing, work longer and promote balance, shrink the workforce and grow the profits, survive the short term but think long term, maintain stability, and embrace change (Ambrose, 1996). These paradoxes underlying restructuring set performance standards for middle managers that are almost impossible to achieve.

Women who have fought long and hard to "be heard" find that they have lost their voice, and are unable to make a difference. It is not always clear to them whether they are being silenced because they are women and lack access to the top, or because the organization, threatened as it is from the outside, has no capacity for internal dissent (Karambayya, 1998). They are often stuck with delivering the bad news, and facing those who are most affected by it, while not having the clout to influence strategy or direction for the organization.

Gendered Cultures

Restructuring efforts in organizations often have a powerful impact on the culture of the organization. As Maddock and Parkin (1994) point out in their analysis of gendered cultures, "at work, women have to manage gender, as well as do their job." In her analysis of the public sector in Britain, Maddock (1999) demonstrates that restructuring facilitates the emergence of a culture that values competition over cooperation, connections over competence, and compliance over challenge. The metaphors used by organizational members to describe such cultures reflect fear, danger, and macho posturing. These include "banana republic," "cowboy management," and a constant threat of a "bullet in the brain" (Karambayya, 1998). While such a culture may be incompatible with one's personal values whether one is male or female, women may be doubly disadvantaged. They are expected to fill social expectations of nurturing, supportive behavior, while advancing their career interests in a context that is suddenly hostile and intensely competitive. Meanwhile, their support networks are disintegrating, and as the later entrants into the organization or managerial ranks, they are particularly vulnerable to job loss or demotion.

These gendered cultures pose impossible dilemmas for women (Ely, 1994; Maddock & Parkin, 1994). As Kanter (1977, p. 123) pointed out: "Women are measured by two yardsticks—how as women they carried out the management role, and how as managers they lived up to the images of womanhood." When they attempt to resist the cultural change, women risk being dismissed as "whining victims," and when they adapt and attempt to assimilate they are seen as "aggressive bitches" (Karambayya, 1998).

As would be expected under the predictions of the threat–rigidity model (Staw, Sandelands, & Dutton, 1981), organizations in the midst of restructuring become rigid and less responsive to inside forces while attempting to deal with external threat. In attempts to adopt "post-bureaucratic" practices they often become more bureaucratic (Maile, 1999), establishing strict and limited performance criteria, rigorous procedures for tolerating flexible hours, sickness, and absence. Women who have fought for and gained flexibility from employers in regard to working hours and conditions, find such flexibility is either severely restricted or withdrawn altogether (Karambayya, 1998). During restructuring, organizations appear to adopt a regressive, intolerant view of work, demanding almost total commitment to the job, ignoring any other facets of life. Such a view, while unpopular with most employees, may affect women the most because it ignores their family and community commitments. Despite their time-consuming natures, these roles are very important parts of women's identities. Organizations that do not have much to offer women in terms of career opportunities during restructuring may also be depriving them of what sustains them in other spheres of their lives. For example, Karambayya (1998) found that initiatives originally designed to retain women, such as part-time or job sharing options and extended parental leaves, were withdrawn during restructuring because they were seen as unfair to men, or incompatible with the "work harder and longer" culture that emerged.

Career Models

There is some evidence that men and women engage in patterns of career involvement that are qualitatively different. Goffee and Nicholson (1994) point out that women exhibit career patterns that reflect frequent employment changes, often in response to family needs or a spouse's career. They suggest that having been denied access to the top echelons of organizations, women are more likely to be motivated by intrinsic features of their jobs, while men are more driven by extrinsic characteristics such as pay and prestige.

Women, having faced serious challenges to their progression in organizations, may have become more self-reliant in their career planning, never expecting their careers to reflect the orderly progression and organizational loyalty characterizing the careers of men. Goffee and Nicholson (1994) suggest that women, accustomed to facing a difficult organizational environment, have developed better strategies for dealing with the uncertainty and threat of job loss than men, who are used to experiencing organizational life as a predictable series of moves up the corporate ladder. However, there is no empirical evidence to support that thesis.

Mary Dean Lee (1994) has developed models of women's careers reflecting shifting patterns of engagement in work and family depending on major life events. Her models propose that, unlike men, women have various models for combining work and family, some reflecting concurrent involvement in both spheres of life, others reflecting sequencing of work and family in several different ways. Women may periodically reassess their involvement in various spheres of their lives in response to major changes in their work and family life. Such reevaluation may occur after the birth of a child, a spouse's career or job change, or a crisis at their own workplace (Marshall, 1995). Organizational restructuring, if it is perceived to have major implications for the woman involved, may be one such trigger for a reevaluation of life and career priorities (Karambayya, 1998).

Relational Practice

Recent work by Joyce Fletcher (1998, 1999) draws attention to the fact that women view their contexts, including work, through a relational lens. Their models for performance and success include dimensions of interpersonal connections and facilitation. In her study of female engineers, Fletcher demonstrates the ways in which those relational assumptions influence the day-to-day interactions in which these women engage. Fletcher (1999) presents typology of relational work consisting of four categories based on the intent of the behavior: preserving, mutual empowering, self-achieving and creating team. Each of these types of behaviors involves nurturing, supportive activities intended to benefit relationships, colleagues, the team or the work of the team.

Fletcher suggests that organizations suffer from a male bias in that the only performance measures of consequence are those that value independence over interdependence, and self-reliance over relatedness. Organizations do not appear to value relational work because it is considered to have little or no impact on the "bottom line," so it seems to "get disappeared" and devalued. Huff (1990) makes a similar argument that women in organizations seem to carry the burden of emotional and relationship-oriented work, becoming in essence "wives of the organization."

In the context of restructuring, not only is relational work more necessary because the work environment is more unstable, chaotic and "toxic" (Frost & Robinson, 1999), but also it can be more dangerous because it can cost individuals their jobs. Under these circumstances relational work is often more burdensome because the impact of restructuring can be emotionally and physically exhausting. In the light of pressure to achieve short-term results during restructuring, relational work is more likely than ever to be discounted and undervalued. As the practitioners of relational work, women may find themselves engaging in increasing levels of relational maintenance work that is ignored by the institutional power holders, at greater risk to their own well-being and careers.

Psychological Contracts

A *psychological contract* is defined as "individual beliefs, shaped by the organization, regarding terms of an exchange agreement between individuals and their organization" (Rousseau, 1995, p. 9). The perceptual and idiosyncratic nature of psychological contracts has been emphasized and is significant (Morrison & Robinson, 1997). Restructuring efforts, because they involve changes to the nature of work or to career opportunities within the organization, often involve violations of psychological contracts.

Morrison and Robinson (1997) distinguish between contract breach and violation. They define *perceived breach* as a cognitive recognition by an employee that the terms of the psychological contract are not being honored by the organization. They use *violation* to describe the affective reactions that accompany perceived breach of contract. Violations of psychological contracts often involve anger and disappointment, outward signs of distress, which sometimes result in physiological and psychological responses. Such an experience of violation may be more acute when the organization is perceived as unwilling, rather than unable, to fulfill the terms of its contract with employees, and when the breach of contract is perceived to be intentional, rather than accidental.

Rousseau (1995) proposes three kinds of contract change: drift, accommodation, and transformation. *Drift* refers to internally motivated changes to the contract that are gradual and sometimes fail to be noticed until they reach a threshold level. *Accommodation* and *transformation* are externally induced with the former being a less radical, adaptive response to external conditions and the latter being a rethinking of the nature and basis of the relationship.

There are several ways in which organizational practices during restructuring affect the psychological contract of employees, and are perceived as a breach of contract. First, the changes that result from restructuring often involve an increase in work levels without any concurrent increase in compensation. The changes that are introduced are perceived to be the result of unilateral decision making in a context of reduced trust and increased uncertainty. Even in circumstances in which the organization has not resorted to involuntary job loss, restructuring is seen as a set of changes that requires individuals to make a greater investment in the employment relationship with no promise of any additional return, and sometimes the threat of dire consequences.

Women may be especially susceptible to stress arising out of violations of psychological contracts during restructuring. They are asked to produce and commit more in return for fewer personal rewards. On the one hand, they are being asked to work longer and harder, while on the other, benefits directed at making the workplace more hospitable to them are gradually disappearing. Meanwhile the social support networks that they relied on are no longer available to them, but their social and nonwork obligations do not change in any way (Karambayya, 1998).

COPING STRATEGIES

This section describes a set of strategies that emerged from an earlier study on women's careers in the context of restructuring (Karambayya, 1998) that cut across the categories of problem-focused and emotion-focused coping behaviors. This section then is somewhat speculative, and is intended to suggest interesting avenues for future research.

Reevaluation of Work in the Context of Life

Stressful events may sometimes have the effect of inspiring people to "take stock" of their lives. A significant part of that process may be a reevaluation of work in the context of life. Such a process of reflection and reassessment may be triggered by external events such as an awareness of life stage (a midlife crisis, for example), or a significant event in one's personal life (such as divorce, or the birth of a child) or career life (such as loss of a job). Several researchers have made mention of such a period of reflection including Marshall (1995) and Lee (1994). An organizational restructuring, because it calls for a major shift in energies devoted to work, may trigger such a reassessment. Karambayya (1998) points out that when organizations offer voluntary severance packages to employees, the employees' need to respond to the package may call for such a reevaluation.

Such personal reflection may include an assessment of the significance of work in the person's life, the personal price that is considered necessary for a full commitment to work, resources and energy available to the person, and the short- and long-term benefits that may be obtained. The result of this process may be a decision to alter personal or professional life in a way that is more closely aligned with the individual's needs and energies. One such strategy may be what Hertz (1986) referred to as *work restructuring*, consisting of behaviors that represent cutting back on work commitments to adapt to nonwork demands. These behaviors may include changing arrival or departure times for work, cutting down on travel, or working from home when possible. Other changes may include changing one's job, employer, or even career. What is significant about this type of coping mechanism is that it is directed at changing the behavior of the focal individual or the people around her, not at the organization or the source of the stress.

Separation of Work From the Rest of Life

A strategy related to work restructuring is an attempt to set boundaries between work and other aspects of one's life. Women have often reported feeling alienated from the prevailing values in an organization, or feeling that there is no longer a "good fit" between their personal values and those enacted by the organization (Bell, 1990; Karambayya, 1998; Marshall, 1995). Sometimes the employee's response to such a clash of cultural values is to leave the organization in the hopes of finding another workplace that might be more compatible with personal values. However, when corporate values are seen as pervasive, transcending a particular workplace, the response may be to segment one's life. In her study of African American women, Bell (1990) referred to one such method of segmentation as living a "bicultural life"—changing one's expectations and persona temporarily to fit organizational demands, while reverting to another set of values and behavior outside the workplace. This approach takes the cultural incompatibility as a given and adapts to it. It does not attempt to address the incompatibility or to change it. Clearly such a bicultural life comes with its own set of stresses and problems, and may not be sustainable for any length of time. As with work restructuring, this approach is directed at changing the behavior of the target individual and is likely to have no effect on the organization or its culture.

Social Support

One coping strategy women facing the stress and demands of restructuring may adopt is to seek social support within or outside the organization. Such support may offer two types of opportunities: it may lead to concrete changes in the person's life that alleviate the stress she is under, or it could offer an opportunity to "vent," a safe way to express frustration. For example, an individual who is aware of his or her spouse's work-related stress may take on more of the home or childcare responsibilities, to some extent alleviating the time-based pressure that the employee is under. A colleague who is familiar with the work context and recognizes the level of overload may take on additional responsibilities, easing the work burden a little. Colleagues and peers may be able to offer suggestions on career management or job options.

This approach to coping does have the potential to alter the nature of the stress encountered by reallocating work, but most often does so without formal organizational intervention or resources. So although this approach may indirectly target the source of the stress, it uses personal resources to do so, and does not ensure organizational awareness of the stressors. This strategy may be compatible with women's general tendency to seek support during crises, and to view organizational life through a communal, rather than an individualistic, lens (Hobfoll, 1988; see also chapter 6).

Exit, Voice, Loyalty, and Neglect

Research on gender and stress may benefit from an examination of existing research on the effectiveness of various responses to dissatisfaction in organizations. Hirschman (1970) proposed that responses to dissatisfaction with firms, organizations, and states (nations or political entities) may take one of three primary forms: exit, voice, and loyalty. *Exit*, which involves permanent withdrawal from the organization, and *voice*, which involves expression of the employee's discontent, are both directed at encouraging change and preventing decline in the system. *Loyalty*, which involves staying with the organization and supporting it, favors stability rather than change. Hirschman's framework has since been expanded to include *neglect* (Farrell, 1983), which involves psychological withdrawal from a relationship, and may include behaviors such as merely doing enough to get by, and spending less time and effort at work.

Robinson (1993) found that dissatisfaction with an employer is expressed in one of five ways: temporary escape, permanent escape, changing the situation, doing nothing, or venting. The first two reflect withdrawal behaviors and were labeled "retreat." Changing the situation usually involved behaviors similar to voice. Another response, labeled "silence," was to just wait passively for the organization or supervisors to take action. The final category was a set of destructive behaviors including sabotage and argumentative behavior that gave expression to discontent. These behavioral responses to dissatisfaction have been differentiated along two dimensions: active–passive and constructive–destructive. While temporary or permanent retreat from the organization may offer the employee a respite from the sources of stress in the workplace, it may do little to address those stressors directly. Voice is the response most clearly directed at encouraging change in the organization. Passive behaviors such as silence leave change to the discretion of the organization, and may in fact masquerade as satisfaction and therefore go undetected. There is no research that examines gender differences in responses to dissatisfaction. However, extension of the findings in the area of gender and coping strategies may suggest that women would be more likely to use indirect, self-directed means of responding to their dissatisfaction. There is some evidence that women, in larger proportions than their representation in organizations would predict, choose exit as their mechanism for dealing with dissatisfaction, sometimes after trying other alternatives such as voice (Karambayya, 1998).

Voice would appear to be the most functional response to dissatisfaction from the perspective of both the individual and the organization. Unfortunately, organizations in decline, particularly those in the midst of restructuring, do not have mechanisms for "listening" or responding to voice. Women in restructuring organizations report going "unheard," and attribute that to their lack of status and power in the organization, and to the inability of the organization to handle dissent while it is in crisis (Karambayya, 1998). While the former may have something to do with the gender diversity in top management, the latter may reflect a threat–rigidity response.

CONCLUSION

Working women have had to face unique stressors in their work and nonwork lives. In their work lives they have endured inhospitable organizational environments, careers limited by the glass ceiling, and jobs that do not lend themselves to personal control. On the nonwork front they have managed to carry the bulk of family responsibilities, most significantly child-care and eldercare. These dual pressures have contributed to work overload and time pressure, as well as the need to live with irreconcilable work and nonwork roles. Women have typically responded with emotion-focused behaviors, adapting their own behaviors and feelings without changing the situational antecedents of stress, resulting in lower levels of well-being and self-esteem (Davidson & Fielden, 1999).

Preliminary research on organizations undergoing restructuring now suggests that women may be exposed to additional stressors in such organizations. They are particularly vulnerable to job loss and loss of career opportunities during restructuring because they do not have the option or the desire to devote themselves exclusively to their work, and lack the resources and the credibility to challenge organizational norms that make excessive demands of their time and/or energy. Organizational cultures may become less tolerant during restructuring and become more gendered in subtle ways. Meanwhile, women who choose to exercise "voice" and dare to raise dissenting views are less likely to be heard or to have an impact.

Quite often the response to these organizational stressors has been to adapt to changing demands or to assume that the problem calls for personal tradeoffs. Such responses only contribute to silencing the issues, turning an organizational issue into a private one. Organizations often are not called on to address the sources of stress, and may not even notice the personal sacrifices that must be made to accommodate them. Both men and women can gain from a more open exploration of the short- and long-term consequences of organizational restructuring. Some organizations have already recognized that the quiet exodus of their most valuable employees poses a threat to their competitiveness.

There is a growing need to develop more complete models of the antecedents and consequences of organizational restructuring for organizations and individuals. Those models need to recognize the impact of an organization's changes on the professional and personal lives of its employees. Ideally those models would need to look at cross-level effects, gender effects, and longitudinal effects of organizational decisions to restructure.

REFERENCES

Amabile, T. A., & Conti, R. (1999). Changes in the work environment for creativity during downsizing. *Academy of Management Journal, 42*, 630–640.

Ambrose, D. (1996). *Healing the downsized organization.* New York: Harmony Books.

Armstrong-Stassen, M. (1998). Downsizing the federal government: A longitudinal study of managers' reactions. *Canadian Journal of Administrative Sciences, 15*, 310–321.

Barnett, R. C., Beiner, L., & Baruch, G. K. (1987). *Gender and stress*. New York: The Free Press.

Bedeian, A. G., & Armenakis, A. A. (1998). The cesspool syndrome: How dreck floats to the top of declining organizations. *Academy of Management Executive, 12,* 58–67.

Bell, E. (1990). The bicultural life experience of career-oriented Black women. *Journal of Organizational Behaviour, 11,* 459–477.

Belle, D. (1987). Gender differences in the social moderators of stress. In R. C. Barnett, L. Beiner, & G. K. Baruch (Eds.), *Gender and stress* (pp. 257–277). New York: The Free Press.

Brockner, J. (1988). The effects of work layoffs on survivors: Research, theory and practice. In B. M. Staw, & L. L. Cummings (Eds.), *Research in organizational behaviour,* Vol 10 (pp. 213–255). Greenwich, CT: JAI Press.

Burke, R. J., & Greenglass, E. R. (2000). Organizational restructuring: Identifying effective hospital processes. In R. J. Burke, & C. L. Cooper (Eds.), *The organization in crisis: Downsizing, restructuring and privatization.* Oxford, UK: Blackwell.

Cascio, W. F. (1993). Downsizing: What do we know? What have we learned? *Academy of Management Executive, 7,* 95–104.

Davidson, M. J., & Fielden, S. (1999). Stress and the working woman. In G. N. Powell (Ed.), *Handbook of gender and work* (pp. 413–426). Thousand Oaks, CA: Sage.

Dunahoo, C. L., Geller, P. A., & Hobfoll, S. E. (1996). Women's coping: Communal vs. individualistic orientation. In M. J. Schabracq, J. A. M. Winnubst, & C. L. Cooper (Eds.), *Handbook of work and health psychology* (pp. 183–204). London: Wiley.

Ely, R. J. (1994). The effects of organizational demographics and social identity on relationships among professional women. *Administrative Science Quarterly, 39,* 203–238.

Farrell, D. (1983). Exit, voice, loyalty, and neglect as responses to job dissatisfaction: A multi-dimensional scaling study. *Academy of Management Journal, 26,* 596–607.

Fletcher, J. K. (1998). Relational practice: A feminist reconstruction of work. *Journal of Management Inquiry, 7,* 163–186.

Fletcher, J. K. (1999). *Disappearing acts: Gender, power and relational practice at work.* Cambridge, MA: MIT Press.

Folger, R., & Skarlicki, D. P. (1998). When tough times make tough bosses: Managerial distancing as a function of layoff blame. *Academy of Management Journal, 41,* 79–87.

Freeman, S. J., & Cameron, K. S. (1993). Organizational downsizing: A convergence and reorientation framework. *Organizational Science, 4,* 10–29.

Frost, P., & Robinson, S. (1999). The toxic handler: Organizational hero—and casualty. *Harvard Business Review, July–August,* 97–106.

Goffee, R., & Nicholson, N. (1994). Career development in male and female managers: Convergence or collapse? In M. J. Davidson, & R. J. Burke (Eds.),

Women in management: Current research issues (pp. 80–92). London: Paul Chapman Publishing.

Gordon, D. M. (1996). *Fat and mean: The corporate squeeze of working Americans and the myth of managerial "downsizing"*. New York: The Free Press.

Havlovic, S. J., Bouthillette, F., & Van der Wal, R. (1998). Coping with downsizing and job loss: Lessons from the Shaughnessy Hospital closure. *Canadian Journal of Administrative Sciences, 15*, 322–332.

Hertz, R. (1986). *More equal than others: Women and men in dual-career marriages*. Berkeley, CA: University of California Press.

Hirschman, A. (1970). *Exit, voice and loyalty: Responses to dissatisfaction in firms, organizations and states*. Cambridge, MA: Harvard University Press.

Hobfoll, S. E. (1988). *The ecology of stress*. New York: Hemisphere.

Hochschild, A. R. (1989). *The second shift*. New York: Avon Books.

Huff, A. (1990, May). *Wives—of the organization*. Paper presented at the Women and Work Conference, Dallas, TX.

Kanter, R. M. (1977). *Men and women of the corporation*. New York: Basic Books.

Karambayya, R. (1998). Caught in the crossfire: Women and corporate restructuring. *Canadian Journal of Administrative Sciences, 15*, 333–338.

Leana, C. R., & Feldman, D. C. (1992). *Coping with job loss: How individuals, organizations and communities respond to layoffs*. New York: Lexington Books.

Lee, M. D. (1994). Variations in career and family involvement over time: Truth and consequences. In M. J. Davidson, & R. J. Burke (Eds.), *Women in management: Current research issues* (pp. 29–40). London: Paul Chapman Publishing.

Maddock, S. (1999). *Challenging women: Gender, culture and organization*. Thousand Oaks, CA: Sage.

Maddock, S., & Parkin, D. (1994). Gender cultures: How they affect men and women at work. In M. J. Davidson, & R. J. Burke (Eds.), *Women in management: Current research issues* (pp. 29–40). London: Paul Chapman Publishing.

Maile, S. (1999). Intermanagerial rivalries, organizational restructuring and the transformation of management masculinities. In S. Whitehead, & R. Moodley (Eds.), *Transforming managers: Gendering change in the public sector* (pp. 145–165). London: UCL Press.

Marshall, J. (1995). *Women managers moving on: Exploring career and life choices*. London: Routledge.

McKinley, W., Sanchez, C. M., & Schick, A. G. (1995). Organizational downsizing: Constraining, cloning, learning. *Academy of Management Executive, 9*, 32–42.

Mone, M. A., McKinley, W., & Barker, V. L. (1998). Organizational decline and innovation: A contingency framework. *Academy of Management Review, 23*, 115–132.

Morrison, E. W., & Robinson, S. L. (1997). When employees feel betrayed: A model of how psychological contract violation develops. *Academy of Management Review, 22*, 226–256.

Nelson, D. L., & Burke, R. J. (2000). Women, work stress and health. In M. J. Davidson, & R. J. Burke (Eds.), *Women in management: Current research issues*, Vol. II (pp. 177–191). Thousand Oaks, CA: Sage.

Noer, D. M. (1993). *Healing the wounds: Overcoming the trauma of layoffs and revitalizing downsized organizations*. San Francisco, CA: Jossey-Bass.

Robinson, S. L. (1993). Retreat, voice, silence and destruction: A typology of employees' behavioural responses to dissatisfaction. *Proceeding of the Administrative Sciences Association of Canada*. Lake Louise, Alberta.

Rousseau, D. M. (1995). *Psychological contracts in organizations: Understanding written and unwritten agreements*. Thousand Oaks, CA: Sage.

Staw, B. M., Sandelands, L. E., & Dutton, J. E. (1981). Threat-rigidity effects in organizational behaviour: A multi-level analysis. *Administrative Science Quarterly, 26*, 501–524.

Wethington, E., & McLeod, J. D. (1987). The importance of life events for explaining sex differences in psychological distress. In R. C. Barnett, L. Beiner, & G. K. Baruch (Eds.), *Gender and stress* (pp. 144–158). New York: The Free Press.

5

ASSESSING THE ROLE OF NEGATIVE AFFECTIVITY IN OCCUPATIONAL STRESS RESEARCH: DOES GENDER MAKE A DIFFERENCE?

STEVE M. JEX, GARY A. ADAMS, AND MICHELE L. EHLER

An implicit assumption in the study of occupational stress is that stable individual differences impact both the perception of workplace stressors, as well as the manner in which people respond to such stressors. In fact, the impact of individual differences is acknowledged in the vast majority of the theoretical models that have guided occupational stress research (e.g., see Jex, 1998 for a summary of models). Thus, occupational stress researchers largely acknowledge the importance of individual differences, and in fact, much occupational stress research has been focused on the impact of individual differences (e.g., Jex, Bliese, Buzzell, & Primeau, 2001).

Despite the wide range of individual difference variables that have been examined in occupational stress research, the one that has perhaps captured the greatest attention recently is *negative affectivity*. Watson and Clark (1984) defined negative affectivity as a mood-dispositional dimension reflecting stable individual differences in the propensity to experience negative affective states. In other words, individuals with high levels of negative affectivity tend to experience negative emotionality and distress *regardless of the characteristics of the situations they are in*.

This chapter explores an issue that has largely been ignored in the extant negative affectivity literature, namely whether the impact of negative affectivity depends on gender. We begin by providing an overview of the literature on the role of negative affectivity in occupational stress research. Following this, we describe gender-based differences in both the propensity for negative affect, as well as affect intensity. The chapter concludes with a discussion of the ways that gender can be incorporated into future negative affectivity research. Our major objective in this chapter is to show that the inclusion of gender in future research may yield important new insights into the negative affectivity construct.

AN OVERVIEW OF NEGATIVE AFFECTIVITY AND OCCUPATIONAL STRESS

The timing of Watson and Clark's 1984 article explicating the negative affectivity construct was significant for those in the organizational sciences. More specifically, this was a time when many were rejecting what might be described as "situational determinism" and advancing dispositional explanations of variables such as job satisfaction (e.g., Staw, Bell, & Clausen, 1986; Staw & Ross, 1985). Today there is general consensus that dispositions play an important role in many organizational processes (e.g., Judge & Larsen, 2001).

The first study on negative affectivity to generate widespread interest among occupational stress researchers was conducted by Brief, Burke, George, Robinson, and Webster (1988). These researchers examined the impact of statistically controlling stressor–strain correlations for the effects of negative affectivity through the use of first-order partial correlations (Cohen & Cohen, 1983). The findings from this study showed that many correlations were reduced substantially by this statistical partialing procedure. This led Brief et al. to conclude that stressor–strain correlations based on same source data may be substantially inflated. The seriousness of this finding is reflected in the following statement: "It would appear that we cannot rely confidently on the job stress literature as currently constituted for estimates of stressor–strain relationships" (p. 196).

In addition to pointing out the potential impact of negative affectivity, Brief et al. (1988) also proposed ways to address the issue of negative affectivity in further occupational stress research. They essentially proposed two strategies for dealing with the negative affectivity "problem." First, they recommended that occupational stress researchers measure negative affectivity and statistically partial its effects from stressor–strain correlations. Second, they recommended that researchers consider incorporating the use of non-self-report measures of stressors, strains, or both. On the stressor side, this might include the use of archival data (e.g., Spector & Jex, 1991), or perhaps perceptions of supervisors (e.g., Spector, Dwyer, & Jex, 1988). Objective measures of strain might include physiological indices (e.g., Fox, Dwyer, & Ganster, 1993), or performance output (Beehr, Jex, Stacy, & Murray, 2000).

Given researchers' reliance on self-report measures of both stressors and strains, the Brief et al., (1988) study had a very strong impact on occupational stress research. Given these implications, several studies were conducted that were designed essentially to replicate the impact of negative affectivity on stressor–strain relations (e.g., Chen & Spector, 1991; Jex & Spector, 1996; Parkes, 1990; Schaubroeck, Ganster, & Fox, 1992; Spector, Chen, & O'Connell, 2000;). While the specific findings did vary somewhat, the overall conclusion of all these studies was essentially consistent with Brief et al.; namely that controlling negative affectivity *does* reduce the magnitude of stressor–strain correlations. However, where several of these studies have diverged from Brief et al. is in their analysis of the magnitude of such effects. The general consensus is that although negative affectivity does inflate stressor–strain correlations, the magnitude of this effect is not great enough to change the substantive conclusions of occupational stress research based on self-report measures.

While initial negative affectivity research focused primarily on the biasing or methodological nuisance properties of negative affectivity, more recent research has begun to show that the impact of negative affectivity is also *substantive* in nature. By the term "substantive" we mean that the impact of negative affectivity goes beyond merely that of a methodological nuisance that biases self-report measures of stressors and strains. For example, Moyle (1995) proposed that in addition to being a methodological nuisance variable, negative affectivity may impact strain through both *mediational* processes and as a *moderator* variable. As can be seen in Figure 5.1, if negative affectivity impacts strain through mediation, this implies that stressors mediate the relation between negative affectivity and strains. This may be due to that fact that those with high levels of negative affectivity simply *perceive* high levels of stressors, or perhaps because they self-select themselves into more stressful work environments. Of course, it is also possible that being in a stressful work environment for a long period of time leads to higher levels of negative affectivity, which in turn lead one to perceive higher levels of strain. However, given that negative affectivity is a dispositional construct (e.g., Watson & Clark, 1984), this seems unlikely.

While mediational models of negative affectivity have not been tested explicitly, many of the findings in the negative affectivity literature are supportive of it because negative affectivity is consistently correlated with self-reported stressors (e.g., Brief et al., 1988; Chen & Spector, 1991; Spector et al., 2000). There is also some evidence of self-selection effects (e.g., Spector, Jex, & Chen, 1995).

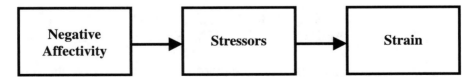

Figure 5.1. A mediational model of the impact of negative affectivity on strain.

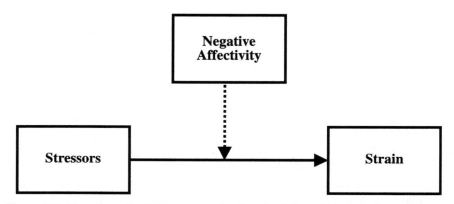

Figure 5.2. Negative affectivity as a moderator of relations between stressors and strain.

The other major role played by negative affectivity, that of a moderator variable, is illustrated in Figure 5.2. As can be seen, conceptualizing negative affectivity as a moderator variable means that stressor–strain relations differ as a function of negative affectivity. More specifically, this explanation proposes that high negative affectivity will increase reactivity to stressors such that stressor–strain relations are strongest among those who have high levels of negative affectivity. Like mediational effects, studies examining moderating effects have been much less prevalent than those examining methodological nuisance effects. However, there is evidence that negative affectivity moderates the effect of both work (e.g., Parkes, 1990) and life stressors (e.g., Bolger & Schilling, 1991).

More recently, Wofford and Daly (1997) have proposed that negative affectivity is one component of a broader cognitive-affective stress propensity construct. These authors propose that this broader construct both mediates the relationships between stressor stimuli and subjective stress *and* that it moderates the relationships of affective and physiological reactions with subjective stress and strains. This model is important because it highlights the shift from viewing negative affectivity only as a methodological nuisance, to the recognition that negative affectivity may enhance individuals' vulnerability for distress and strain, and may impact the way in which people react to stressors.

GENDER, NEGATIVE AFFECTIVITY, AND OCCUPATIONAL STRESS

Despite recent progress in the study of negative affectivity, one variable that has been conspicuously absent from this research domain is gender. We feel this absence is unfortunate for a number of reasons. First, there is evidence of important gender differences in the occupational stress process (chapter 1). These gender differences are consistent with evidence that gender differences impact other important organizational processes such as upward mobility (e.g., Lyness & Thompson, 2000), the adoption of new technology (Venkatesh, Morris, & Ackerman, 2000), and organizational restructuring (chapter 4).

A more compelling reason for incorporating gender into the study of negative affectivity has to do with gender-based differences in affect. Specifically, it is well documented that the incidence of unipolar depression, as well as other forms of negative affect, are consistently higher for women as compared to men (e.g., Nolen-Hoeksema, 1987). There is also considerable evidence of gender differences in *affect intensity* (e.g., Diener, Sandvik, & Larsen, 1985). Put simply, evidence suggests that women tend to both experience and report emotions at a higher level of *intensity* than do men. We believe, and will attempt to show, that both of these gender-based differences in affect may have important implications for negative affectivity research.

In the sections that follow, we expand on the gender-based differences in affect, which suggest that gender should be incorporated into the study of negative affectivity. We then conclude the chapter with several recommendations for specific ways in which gender can be incorporated into future negative affectivity research. Although we are focusing on gender differences in these sections, it is important to be mindful of the considerable differences that likely are present within groups. That is, while there may be average between-gender differences on the variables we discuss, there are also important differences among those of the same gender on these variables.

GENDER-BASED DIFFERENCES IN NEGATIVE AFFECT

It has been shown repeatedly that women tend to report and experience higher levels of unhappiness, unipolar depression, and other forms of negative affect than do men (Fujita, Diener, & Sandvik, 1991). For example, community-based epidemiological studies have shown that women typically exhibit nearly twice the incidence of clinical depression than do men (Nolen-Hoeksema, 1987). It has also been shown, as discussed earlier, that on average women consistently report higher levels of psychological strain than do men (Jick & Mitz, 1985).

While gender differences in negative affect, and depression in particular, have been well documented, it is less clear *why* these differences exist. Given that depression is often treated with medication, it is tempting to explain these observed differences in terms of known biochemical differences between males and females. However, according to Nolen-Hoeksema (1987), gender-based biochemical differences cannot account for the degree of gender-based differences in the incidence of depression. Jick and Mitz (1985) echo this point in attempting to explain gender-based differences in other forms of negative affect and psychological strain.

If gender differences in negative affect cannot be explained biochemically, what then might account for them? Although some have argued that such differences simply reflect reporting biases (e.g., Joiner, Schmidt, Lerew, Cook, & Gencoz, 2000), other likely reasons have to do with cognitive processes and socialization. With respect to cognitive processing, gender differences have been found in attributions for success and failure (e.g., Deaux, 1979). Specifically, women are more likely than men to attribute success to luck or other external factors they do not control. Unfortunately, women are also more likely than men to attribute failure to internal factors such as lack of ability. Thus, women may be more predisposed to depression because they tend to dismiss their successes and personalize their failures (Seligman, 1975).

Another consistent gender-based cognitive difference that may impact the propensity for depression is the capacity for *ruminative coping*. Ruminative coping is simply dwelling on a problem or the negative emotions surrounding the problem. It has been found consistently that women, as compared to men, have a much greater tendency to ruminate on the reasons for negative emotions as well as the negative emotions themselves. According to Nolen-Hoeksema, Larson, and Grayson (1999), rumination sets up what is essentially a self-defeating cycle that leads to greater levels of depression. They found, in a community-based sample, that depressive symptoms lead to greater levels of rumination, which in turn lead to reduced feelings of mastery and greater subsequent depression.

In this same study, men exhibited a greater tendency than women did to engage in activities that served to divert attention from the reasons for the negative emotion or the negative emotion itself. For example, one way to cope with feeling down about a poor test grade would be to go for a five-mile run in order to divert attention from the event and the negative emotions associated with it. In the short term at least, this would appear to be an adaptive response to negative emotionality. In the long run, however, men may pay a price for this response as evidenced by higher rates of severe physical illness than women in response to stressors (Jick & Mitz, 1985).

Another gender-based cognitive difference that may account for differences in negative affect is the feeling of powerlessness. Women tend to exhibit a greater tendency than men to feel that they are powerless to change stressful situations (Nolen-Hoeksema, 1987). To some extent this is due to the positions that women occupy in society, and in the workplace in particular. Also, as Nolen-Hoeksema et al. (1999) noted, such feelings result from a tendency to ruminate about negative events and emotions. In the workplace, for example, if one were to receive a substandard raise, ruminating about this negative event would likely lead to feelings of being powerless to do anything about it.

Given that women exhibit higher levels of negative affect such as depression, and there appear to be some well-documented reasons for this, the issue then becomes determining how this may impact negative affectivity research. One possibility is that because women are more prone to negative affect in general, a disposition such as negative affectivity may be less informative in explaining the affect of women in comparison to men. In statistical terms, there may be a ceiling effect when attempting to use negative affectivity to explain negative emotionality in women. Since there is no reason to believe that negative affectivity is differentially distributed by gender, negative affectivity may tell us less about females than males, at least in terms of its main effect on psychological strain.

This issue, however, is complicated by the fact that women do exhibit higher levels of negative affect *in general*, and that this difference holds up with respect to reactivity to stressors. That is, the preferred way that females tend to *react* to job-related stressors is through negative emotions such as depression, anxiety, etc. (Jick & Mitz, 1985). Note that this is a different issue than gender-based differences in absolute levels of negative affect. Therefore, since negative affectivity also has been proposed to moderate reactions to at least some stressors (e.g., Moyle, 1995; Parkes, 1990), the combination of a high level of negative affectivity among females may lead to very high levels of reactivity. Stated differently, the moderating effects of negative affectivity may be dependent, at least to some degree, on gender (Heinisch & Jex, 1997). This proposition becomes even more plausible when one considers the greater salience of negative emotions such as depression for women in comparison to men.

GENDER-BASED DIFFERENCES IN AFFECT INTENSITY

Another consistent gender difference that may have an influence on negative affectivity research is *affect intensity*. Specifically, there is considerable evidence that women tend to feel and report emotions at a more intense level than do men. That is, when women are happy, they experience this emotion more intensely than do men. Conversely, when women experience negative emotions such as sadness, fear, or anxiety, these are also experienced more intensely as compared to men.

What accounts for these differences in affect intensity? According to Diener et al. (1985), gender-based differences in affect intensity may be due largely to gender-based societal norms. All cultures have what might be described as "display rules" for emotional expression that signal members of that culture as to what is and what is not appropriate. In most Western cultures, for example, emotional display rules decree that males are expected to maintain a reserved demeanor, and therefore it is seen as socially unacceptable for men to experience emotions intensely, at least in terms of outward appearance. Women, on the other hand, are typically given much more latitude in the public expression of both positive and negative emotions.

Another reason for differences in affect intensity offered by Diener et al. (1985) has to do with gender-based differences with regard to interpersonal relationships. Compared to men, women tend to place greater importance on interpersonal relationships and see them as providing different benefits than do men. For example, studies have shown that women tend to view marriage primarily in terms of emotional intimacy. Men, on the other hand, show a greater tendency to view marriage (and one would assume other close relationships) in terms of companionship and camaraderie. Given these gender-based differences, one might conclude that women place a much greater investment in the interpersonal aspects of relationships in comparison with men. Thus, when relationships go well, women tend to react more positively than do men. In contrast, when relationships do not go well, this greater emotional investment on the part of women leads to more intense negative feelings in comparison to men.

Given these well-documented gender differences in affect intensity, what are the implications for negative affectivity research? One possibility, which is similar to the previous discussion of the differences of gender on the propensity for negative emotions, is that negative affectivity has a greater impact among women. Since women appear to exhibit a greater range of both positive and negative emotions, it stands to reason that an affect-based disposition such as negative affectivity would have a greater impact in this group as compared to males. Note, however, that among women, the greatest impact of negative affectivity may be in terms of *reactivity* to stressors, rather than simply the experience of negative emotions such as depression and anxiety. In statistical terms, this is akin to saying that negative affectivity may operate primarily as a main effect variable among men, yet function as both a main effect and moderator variable among women.

While these propositions are plausible, there unfortunately has been little research examining the differential impact of negative affectivity by gender. In fact, this issue has been explored in only one study that we are aware of in the occupational stress literature. Heinisch and Jex (1997) examined the impact of negative affectivity on relations between role stressors, workload, and interpersonal conflict and depression. They also explored whether these effects were impacted by gender. The findings of this study showed, as predicted, that for males, negative affectivity functioned only as a main effect variable in all statistical tests. That is, negative affectivity was associated with higher reported levels of depression regardless of the level of perceived stressors.

The pattern of findings for females was different, however. Specifically, negative affectivity moderated the relations between two of the stressors (role conflict and workload) and depression. As expected, these stressors were positively related to depression only among those females reporting high levels of negative affectivity. For females low on negative affectivity, stressors actually were associated *negatively* to depression, suggesting that stressors may have a positive impact on women with a low level of negative affectivity. The authors speculated that for these women, stressors might be viewed as a challenge or opportunity for mastery.

INCORPORATING GENDER INTO NEGATIVE AFFECTIVITY RESEARCH

To this point we have described what are some fairly well-documented gender differences in both the propensity for negative emotionality and affect intensity. Furthermore, we have attempted to explain the implications of these gender differences for negative affectivity research. While such information is clearly useful, it is also important to provide some guidance and recommendations as to how gender may be incorporated into future negative affectivity research. In this section we offer a number of such recommendations.

At the most general level, we recommend that future studies of negative affectivity at least employ statistical controls for the impact of gender. While this has been done in some investigations of negative affectivity (e.g., Decker & Borgen, 1993; Parkes, 1990), there are many studies in which the impact of gender has been ignored completely (e.g., Brief et al., 1988; Chen & Spector, 1991; Jex & Spector, 1996; Moyle, 1995). Whether failure to control statistically for gender has skewed the results of past negative affectivity research is obviously open to question. However, considering that the vast majority of negative affectivity studies have employed mixed-gender samples, the potential certainly exists. This may at least partially explain the high level of inconsistent findings that has plagued this research area since Brief et al.'s (1988) study.

A second way that gender can be incorporated into negative affectivity research is to examine it as a predictor variable and model its effects. This not only includes examining its effects on strain (e.g., Jick & Mitz, 1985), but (more important for the present discussion) also examining whether the impact of negative affectivity differs by gender. This could be done, for example, simply by examining methodological nuisance effects separately for men and women. Based on the affect-based gender differences noted earlier in the chapter, such effects may differ depending on the stressor–strain combination examined. Thus far, occupational stress researchers investigating negative affectivity have not taken this step.

Another way to model the effect of gender in negative affectivity research is to examine whether moderator effects differ by gender. Heinisch and Jex (1997), for example, investigated the three-way interaction between stressors, negative affectivity, and gender in predicting depression. If there are gender-based differences in how negative affectivity impacts reactivity to stressors, such differences should be examined in a moderator framework. The failure to do so may explain why negative affectivity research has been relatively disappointing with respect to uncovering moderator effects.

If researchers incorporate gender into negative affectivity research and explore higher order interactive effects, there are important methodological issues that must be taken into consideration. For example, much has been written in the literature about statistical tests of moderator effects (e.g., Cohen & Cohen, 1983; James & Brett, 1984), and low statistical power associated with such tests has been highlighted. This is due, to a great extent, to the small effect sizes that are often associated with higher order interactions (e.g., Heinisch & Jex, 1997, explained 1% of the variance by their three-way interactions). Obviously, some ways to remedy this situation are to employ large sample sizes (see Cohen, 1992 for a guide), to use measures that are relatively free from error (Nunnally & Bernstein, 1994), and to consider adopting an alpha level that is more liberal than the conventional .05 level.

An equally important methodological issue, specifically when examining gender as a moderator variable, is the proportion of males and females in the sample. Using simulated data, Aguinis and Stone-Romero (1997) have shown quite clearly that the statistical power to detect moderator effects is optimal when the proportion on a dichotomous variable is 50–50, and drops dramatically when the proportion deviates from this value. In some situations researchers may not have control over the gender distributions of their samples. However, when conditions permit, sampling should be designed to increase the chances that the distribution of males and females will be as even as possible.

Another potentially important consideration for researchers is the investigation of how gender differences influence the manifestation of negative affectivity. Although Watson and Clark (1984) claimed that negative affectivity was a "higher order" factor responsible for intercorrelations of a wide variety of measures of negative emotionality, recent evidence has cast some doubt on this claim. For example, it has been shown that specific measures of negative affectivity may differ with respect to whether they produce methodological nuisance effects (e.g., Fortunato, Jex, & Heinisch, 1999; Fortunato & Stone-Romero, 1999). This suggests that perhaps all measures of negative emotionality are not equally representative markers of the higher order negative affectivity trait, as originally claimed by Watson and Clark (1984).

Along this same line, there also is recent evidence that males and females may differ in the manifestation of the negative affectivity trait. For example, Smith and Reise (1998) recently employed Item Response Theory

(IRT) to examine gender differences in characteristics of items from the Stress Reaction Scale (Tellegen, 1982). This study found that women were more likely than men to endorse items on this scale that reflected emotional vulnerability and sensitivity. Men, on the other hand, were more likely than women to endorse items that reflected tension, irritability, and being easily upset. These findings are important because they suggest that there may be differences in currently used negative affectivity measures in the extent to which they are able to capture true levels of this trait for males and females. On a more substantive level, these findings suggest that men and women may differ in the manner in which the negative affectivity trait is manifest.

CONCLUSION

Gender essentially has been ignored in studies of negative affectivity detailed in the occupational stress literature. In this chapter we have attempted to show this may be an important oversight in light of gender differences in the stress process, in the propensity for negative emotionality, and in affect intensity. By ignoring gender, occupational stress researchers may be failing to account for a variable that could impact the results of empirical findings. Ignoring gender may also represent a missed opportunity to learn more about this important mood-dispositional construct.

In addition to describing the theoretical rationale for incorporating gender into negative affectivity research, we also discussed the various ways in which this might be accomplished. This may include simply statistically controlling for the effects of gender; investigating the methodological nuisance properties of negative affectivity separately for men and women; investigating the higher order interaction between stressors, negative affectivity, and gender; and finally, investigating gender differences in the manifestation of negative affectivity.

A clear limitation of this chapter is that it is long on theory, and short on actual empirical data. This simply is due to the fact that gender has been examined in so few occupational stress studies of negative affectivity. While acknowledging this limitation, we also point out that considerable empirical data exists outside of the occupational stress research domain to support the importance of affect-based gender differences. Furthermore, the consistency of these findings makes it clear that occupational stress researchers investigating the impact of negative affectivity no longer can afford to ignore them. Future research can provide empirical data relevant to many of the questions we have proposed in this review.

In conclusion, we return to the question posed in the title of this chapter, namely "Assessing the Role of Negative Affectivity in Occupational Stress Research: Does Gender Make a Difference?" Given the current state of negative affectivity research, this is clearly an empirical question. Unfortunately, in any scientific field, not all empirical questions are worthy of being answered. Based on the evidence presented in this chapter, we believe that this is most certainly a question worthy of being answered in future negative affectivity research. In doing so, researchers potentially may develop a much greater understanding of negative affectivity, greater insight into the impact of gender, and perhaps ultimately a greater general understanding of stress in organizations.

REFERENCES

Aguinis, H., & Stone-Romero, E. F. (1997). Methodological artifacts in moderated multiple regression and their effects on statistical power. *Journal of Applied Psychology, 82,* 192–206.

Beehr, T. A., Jex, S. M., Stacy, B. A., & Murray, M. A. (2000). Work stressors and coworker support as predictors of individual strain and job performance. *Journal of Organizational Behavior, 21,* 391-405.

Bolger, N., & Schilling, E. A. (1991). Personality and the problems of everyday life: The role of neuroticism in exposure and reactivity to daily stressors. *Journal of Personality, 59,* 355–386.

Brief, A. P., Burke, M. J., George, J. M., Robinson, B. S., & Webster, J. (1988). Should negative affectivity remain an unmeasured variable in the study of job stress? *Journal of Applied Psychology, 73,* 193–198.

Chen, P. Y., & Spector, P. E. (1991). Negative affectivity as the underlying cause of correlations between stressors and strains. *Journal of Applied Psychology, 76,* 398–408.

Cohen, J. (1992). A power primer. *Psychological Bulletin, 112,* 155–159.

Cohen, J., & Cohen, P. (1983). *Applied multiple regression/correlation for the behavioral sciences.* Hillsdale, NJ: Erlbaum.

Deaux, K. (1979). Self-evaluations of male and female managers. *Sex Roles, 5,* 571–580.

Decker, P. J., & Borgen, F. H. (1993). Dimensions of work appraisal: Stress, strain, coping, job satisfaction, and negative affectivity. *Journal of Counseling Psychology, 40,* 470–478.

Diener, E., Sandvik, E., & Larsen, R. J. (1985). Age and sex effects for emotional intensity. *Developmental Psychology, 21,* 542–546.

Fortunato, V. J., Jex, S. M., & Heinisch, D. A. (1999). An examination of the discriminant validity of the Strain-Free Negative Affectivity Scale. *Journal of Occupational & Organizational Psychology, 72,* 503–522.

Fortunato, V. J., & Stone-Romero, E. F. (1999). Taking the strain out of negative affectivity: Development and initial validation of scores on a strain-free measure of negative affectivity. *Educational & Psychological Measurement, 59,* 77–97.

Fox, M. L., Dwyer, D. J., & Ganster, D. C. (1993). Effects of stressful job demands and control on physiological and attitudinal outcomes in a hospital setting. *Academy of Management Journal, 36*, 289–318.

Fujita, F., Diener, E., & Sandvik, E. (1991). Gender differences in negative affect and well-being: The case for emotional intensity. *Journal of Personality and Social Psychology, 61*, 427–434.

Heinisch, D. A., & Jex, S. M. (1997). Negative affectivity and gender as moderators of the relationship between work-related stressors and depressed mood at work. *Work & Stress, 11*, 46–57.

James, L. R., & Brett, J. M. (1984). Mediators, moderators, and tests for mediation. *Journal of Applied Psychology, 69*, 307–321.

Jex, S. M. (1998). *Stress and job performance: Theory, research, and implications for managerial practice*. Thousand Oaks, CA: Sage.

Jex, S. M., Bliese, P. D., Buzzell, S., & Primeau, J. (2001). The impact of self-efficacy on stressor–strain relations: Coping as an explanatory mechanism. *Journal of Applied Psychology, 86*, 401–409.

Jex, S. M., & Spector, P. E. (1996). The impact of negative affectivity on stressor-strain relations: A replication and extension. *Work & Stress, 10*, 36–45.

Jick, T. D., & Mitz, L. F. (1985). Sex differences in work stress. *Academy of Management Review, 10*, 408–420.

Joiner, T. E., Schmidt, N. B., Lerew, D. R., Cook, J. H., & Gencoz, F. (2000). Differential roles of depression and anxious symptoms and gender in defensiveness. *Journal of Personality Assessment, 75*, 200–211.

Judge, T. A., & Larson, R. J. (2001). Dispositional affect and job satisfaction: A review and theoretical extension. *Organizational Behavior and Human Decision Processes, 86*, 67–98.

Lyness, K. S., & Thompson, D. E. (2000). Climbing the corporate ladder: Do male and female executives follow the same route? *Journal of Applied Psychology, 85*, 86–101.

Moyle, P. (1995). The role of negative affectivity in the stress process: Test of alternative models. *Journal of Organizational Behavior, 16*, 647–668.

Nolen-Hoeksema, S. (1987). Sex differences in unipolar depression: Evidence and theory. *Psychological Bulletin, 101*, 259–282.

Nolen-Hoeksema, S., Larson, J., & Grayson, C. (1999). Explaining the gender differences in depressive symptoms. *Journal of Personality and Social Psychology, 77*, 1061–1072.

Nunnally, J. C., & Bernstein, I. H. (1994). *Psychometric theory* (3rd ed.). New York: McGraw-Hill.

Parkes, K. R. (1990). Coping, negative affectivity, and the work environment: Additive and interactive predictors of mental health. *Journal of Applied Psychology, 75*, 399–409.

Schaubroeck, J., Ganster, D. C., & Fox, M. L. (1992). Dispositional affect and work-related stress. *Journal of Applied Psychology, 77*, 322–335.

Seligman, M. E. (1975). *Helplessness: On depression, development, and death.* San Francisco: Freeman.

Smith, L. L., & Reise, S. P. (1998). Gender differences on negative affectivity: An IRT study of differential item functioning on the Multidimensional Personality Questionnaire Stress Reaction scale. *Journal of Personality and Social Psychology, 75,* 1350–1362.

Spector, P. E., Chen, P. Y., & O'Connell, B. J. (2000). A longitudinal study of the relations between job stressors and job strains while controlling for prior negative affectivity and strains. *Journal of Applied Psychology, 85,* 211–218.

Spector, P. E., Dwyer, D. J., & Jex, S. M. (1988). Relations of job stressors to affective, health, and performance outcomes: A comparison of multiple data sources. *Journal of Applied Psychology, 73,* 11–19.

Spector, P. E., & Jex, S. M. (1991). Relations of job stressors, job characteristics, and job analysis ratings with affective and health outcomes. *Journal of Applied Psychology, 76,* 46–53.

Spector, P. E., Jex, S. M., & Chen, P. Y. (1995). Personality traits as predictors of job characteristics. *Journal of Organizational Behavior, 16,* 59–65.

Staw, B. M., Bell, N. E., & Clausen, J. A. (1986). The dispositional approach to job attitudes: A lifetime longitudinal test. *Administrative Science Quarterly, 31,* 56–77.

Staw, B. M., & Ross, J. (1985). Stability in the midst of change: A dispositional approach to job attitudes. *Journal of Applied Psychology, 70,* 469–480.

Tellegen, A. (1982). *Brief manual of the Multidimensional Personality Questionnaire.* Unpublished manuscript, University of Minnesota. Minneapolis, MN.

Venkatesh, V., Morris, M. G., & Ackerman, P. L. (2000). A longitudinal field investigation of gender differences in individual technology adoption decision making processes. *Organizational Behavior and Human Decision Processes, 83,* 33–60.

Watson, D., & Clark, L. A. (1984). Negative affectivity: The disposition to experience aversive emotional states. *Psychological Bulletin, 96,* 465–490.

Wofford, J. C., & Daly, P. S. (1997). A cognitive-affective approach to understanding individual differences in stress propensity and resultant strain. *Journal of Occupational Health Psychology, 2,* 134–147.

6

WORK STRESS, COPING, AND SOCIAL SUPPORT: IMPLICATIONS FOR WOMEN'S OCCUPATIONAL WELL-BEING

ESTHER R. GREENGLASS

The purpose of this chapter is to examine the implications of work for women's psychological well-being, and particularly their occupational well-being. With increasing numbers of women holding multiple roles, including employee, wife, mother, and daughter, it is important to examine the impact of those roles on women's health. Considerable research indicates that multiple roles have positive effects on women's well-being. At the same time, research indicates that role conflict is more likely to occur when women hold multiple roles. The conflict between work and family roles has received considerable research attention. Data indicate psychological consequences of role conflict for both women and men. As women and men increasingly share employment responsibilities, they may also begin to share more family-related stress. Research findings compare role conflict in women and men, the stress it engenders, and the ways in which the sexes deal with this stress. The implications of research findings for women's occupational well-being and their health in general are examined in this chapter.

WORK STRESS AND HEALTH IN WOMEN

Considerable research has been conducted on the relationship between work stress and health in women. Previous research identifies stressors on women in the workforce that transcend education, occupation, and

Grateful acknowledgment is due to Lesley Goldstein for her assistance in the preparation of this chapter.

marital status. Despite little or no difference in the traits, abilities, education, and motivation of managerial and professional women and men (Powell, 1990), women have fewer higher status positions in the workforce, are less upwardly mobile, and in general have lower salaries than their male counterparts. This may indicate the presence of sex bias. Women are more likely than men to face pay inequities (Institute for Women's Policy Research, 1999), underutilization of skills, and sex discrimination in performance (Cox & Harquail, 1991), all of which have been positively associated with a variety of stress symptoms (Greenglass, 1985a, 1985b, 1991). The reader is referred to chapter 1 for further discussion of these stressors.

Other stressors associated with poor health in women relate to the socioeconomic conditions associated with many women's lives. As a result of their disadvantaged economic position in society, many women are poor. The "feminization of poverty" refers to the fact that the majority of people who are poor, worldwide, are women and their children. Statistics continue to show that women are overly represented among the poor. More than 75% of the poor in the United States are women and children (U.S. Census Bureau, 2000). Poverty is related to malnutrition, inadequate shelter, less access to adequate health care, higher infant mortality, greater disability from chronic disease, greater exposure to violence, and increased risk of depression (McGrath, Keita, Strickland & Russo, 1990). Individuals at lower socioeconomic levels also have fewer coping resources and are more vulnerable to depression and psychophysiological symptoms (McLeod & Kessler, 1990).

Multiple Roles and Health

Since the 1960s, there has been a dramatic increase in the number of married women who have entered the paid labor force. In particular, there has been an increase in the number of employed, married women with small children. Women's workforce participation has doubled in the past 30 years, and 6 out of every 10 women in North America are in the paid labor force (Spain & Bianchi). At the same time, society continues to expect that women will take responsibility for the majority of childcare and work in the home (Long & Cox, 2000). See chapter 1 for a discussion of the implications of multiple roles.

Role Conflict, Stress, and Health in Women

Work–family conflict has been associated with several dysfunctional psychological outcomes, including burnout (Bacharach, Bamberger, & Conley, 1991), upleasant moods (Williams & Alliger, 1994), decreased family and occupational well-being (Kinnunen & Mauno, 1998), psychological and physical complaints (Frone, Russell, & Cooper, 1992), and job and life dissatisfaction (Netemeyer, Boles, & McMurrian, 1996). A meta-analysis reviewing the relationship between work–family conflict and job–life satisfaction found a consistent negative relationship among all types of work–family conflict and job–life satisfaction (Kossek & Ozeki, 1998). As individuals experience conflict within their family and work roles, satisfaction in both their job and life domains decreases. Also, there is evidence that occupational well-being decreases with an increase in work–family conflict. Chapter 1 further discusses role conflict.

STRESS, COPING, AND GENDER DIFFERENCES

Given that role conflict is associated with increased distress in both women and men, it is important to inquire into how individuals cope with stress. Effective coping has implications not only for alleviating role conflict but also for improving occupational well-being. Typically, research in the area of stress has distinguished between problem-focused and emotion-focused coping. While problem-focused coping is directed towards managing the source of stress, emotion-focused coping is aimed at regulating emotional responses elicited by the situation (Folkman & Lazarus, 1980). Investigators generally agree that problem-focused coping is an effective individual coping strategy, given research findings that it is negatively related to distress symptoms (Billings & Moos, 1984; O'Neill & Zeichner, 1985). Greenglass (1988) reports negative relationships in managers between job anxiety and problem-focused coping, and in particular, *internal control*, the perception that one's own efforts can change a situation. The same research also found significantly negative correlations between job anxiety and preventive coping. Additional findings indicate that palliative coping, including wishful thinking and self-blame, are positively correlated with psychological distress such as job anxiety, depression and somatization, and negatively associated with job satisfaction (Greenglass, 1993), thus suggesting that palliative coping itself may be a distress symptom.

Researchers have studied gender-related effects on the coping strategies people use to deal with stress. Men have been reported to be more likely than women to engage in coping that alters a stressful situation (Folkman & Lazarus, 1980; Stone & Neale, 1984). However, research shows that when education, occupation, and position are controlled, few gender differences are found in coping strategies. McDonald and Korabik (1991) found that most male and female managers reported coping with stressful job situations by taking direct action to solve problems. Long (1990) and Greenglass (1988) found no gender differences in their studies of coping in managers. These data indicate that when women and men occupy jobs equivalent in decision-making latitude, access to resources, and control, or when they both occupy managerial positions, men and women utilize problem-solving coping strategies to the same extent. The type of coping employed to deal with stress is often related to the status, resources, and power associated with one's position. Many more women than men hold lower level jobs offering less opportunity to use problem-solving and direct-action strategies (Folkman & Lazarus, 1980). Women are also more likely than men to experience high levels of demands in the workplace with low control over those demands (Piechowski, 1992).

Typically, coping research has used individual behavior as the focal point for analysis and considers autonomous, agentic, and independent behavior to be synonymous with effective coping (Banyard & Graham-Bermann, 1993). However, research shows that coping is highly specific to both the individual and the context (Lazarus & Folkman, 1984). The social milieu in which a particular stressor is experienced should be incorporated into research paradigms examining the relationship between gender and coping. Unger (1990) suggests that gender will be associated with different coping outcomes in different situations.

Other data from the work–stress literature highlight the part played by gender role expectations in people's reactions to stress. Several studies have found that men score significantly higher than women on *depersonalization*, one of the three job burnout subscales of the Maslach Burnout Inventory (MBI; Greenglass & Burke, 1988; Maslach & Jackson, 1985; Maslach & Jackson, 1986; Ogus, Greenglass, & Burke, 1990; Schwab & Iwanicki, 1982). Depersonalization refers to a callous and cynical response toward others who may be one's clients, students or patients. Because the masculine gender role stresses strength, independence, and separation (Greenglass, 1982; Pleck, 1980), depersonalization may be regarded as a consequence of men's repressed emotionality. Viewed in this way, depersonalization may be seen as an ineffective coping form that allows men to continue to work with people yet remain distant from their problems (Greenglass, 1991). Depersonalization is likely related to the concept of emotional inexpressiveness discussed by Eisler and Blalock (1991), who argue that the strict prohibition against emotional expressiveness in men is one of the most powerful mental mandates influencing men and their behavior. Male inexpressiveness is the result of gender role socialization that begins early in childhood. Males are taught that emotional expressiveness is a feminine trait and they learn to distance themselves from their femininity (Greenglass, 1982).

GENDER DIFFERENCES IN SOCIAL SUPPORT

There is substantial research evidence that social support has a positive effect on physical and mental health (Belle, 1987; Cohen & Syme, 1985; Greenglass, Fiksenbaum, & Burke, 1996; Hobfoll, Dunahoo, Ben-Porath, &

Monnier, 1994; Waldron & Jacobs, 1989). Prospective research shows that the extent to which people are embedded in socially supportive relationships and networks is a strong predictor of health and morbidity (Oakley, 1992). While women and men have strong needs for friendship, their friendships differ in the extent to which they provide emotional intimacy. Research indicates that male friendships tend to be less close and less intimate than female friendships (Claes, 1992). Enduring friendships between women have been well documented as forming an important support system for women (Lapsley, 1999). Further studies suggest that there are gender differences in both the elicitation and provision of social support. In general, women have been reported to engage in more intimate, emotional, and self-disclosing relationships than men (Luckow, Reifman, & McIntosh, 1998; Ptacek, Smith, & Dodge, 1994; Shumaker & Hill, 1991). These gender differences are thought to be due to gender-specific socialization experiences. The feminine gender role allows, and even encourages, the display of dependence on others, while the masculine gender role puts a premium on strength and individuality.

When dealing with work stress, women are more likely than men to seek advice, information, practical assistance, and emotional support from others with whom they have relationships (Greenglass, Schwarzer, Jakubiec, Fiksenbaum, & Taubert, 1999a). These findings also were reported in recent research where the Proactive Coping Inventory (PCI; Greenglass, Schwarzer, & Taubert, 1999b) was employed to assess individuals' coping strategies. The PCI consists of seven scales to assess strategies for coping with stress. *Proactive coping* is distinguished by three main features:

1. It integrates planning and preventive strategies with proactive self-regulatory goal attainment.
2. It integrates proactive goal attainment with identification and utilization of social resources.
3. It utilizes proactive emotional coping for self-regulatory goal attainment.

Two of the seven scales on the PCI are *Instrumental Support Seeking,* aimed at obtaining advice, information, and feedback from people in one's social network; and *Emotional Support Seeking,* which regulates emotional distress by disclosing feelings to others, evoking empathy, and seeking companionship from one's social network. Research shows that proactive coping promotes occupational well-being. In a study of employed men and women, proactive coping was significantly and positively related to professional efficacy and perception of fair treatment at work, and was negatively related to emotional exhaustion and cynicism (Greenglass, 2000).

Further research shows that women score significantly higher than men on the Instrumental Support Seeking and Emotional Support Seeking scales of the PCI (Greenglass et al., 1999a; Greenglass, 2000). Thus, when dealing with stress, women are more likely than men to seek advice, information, practical assistance, and emotional support from others with whom they have relationships. These results were found in student samples as well as employed adult samples. The findings are consistent with other research suggesting that women, more than men, utilize social support when coping with stress. Close relationships can help a person cope with stress. In such relationships people can disclose and discuss problems, share concerns, and receive advice that is keyed to their needs (Solomon & Rothblum, 1986). These relationships can also provide useful information, practical advice, and morale boosting, all of which can assist individuals in dealing with their stressors (Greenglass, et al., 1996). The fact that women, more than men, seek support is consistent with feminine gender role socialization since women are expected to be more interdependent and sensitive to others (Greenglass, 1982).

LINKING SOCIAL SUPPORT AND COPING

In the past, research on coping has tended to be separate from research on social support, conceptually and empirically. Effective coping has been seen as instrumental coping and internal control, both of which have been regarded as individually based. Increasingly, however, research is focusing on linking coping and social support in order to evolve an interpersonal theory of coping with stress. For example, DeLongis and O'Brien (1990), in their treatment of how families cope with Alzheimer's disease, discuss how interpersonal factors may be important as predictors of an individual's ability to cope with a given situation. They talk about the importance of drawing on the resources of others when coping with difficult situations. In their research, Hobfoll (1986, 1988) and Hobfoll et al., (1994) also discuss the interpersonal, interactive nature of coping and social resource acquisition, as well as the importance of drawing on the resources of others for coping with difficult situations.

There are several advantages to linking social support with coping. First, in viewing social support as a form of coping, one can theoretically link areas that have been previously viewed as conceptually distinct. This allows for the elaboration of traditional constructs using theoretical developments in the area of social support and coping. Second, the conceptualization of social support as a coping behavior broadens the traditional definition of coping to include interpersonal and relational skills. Third, the consideration of interpersonal and relational behaviors as coping entails the positive valuation of behaviors that have been rewarded and expected traditionally in women. Relationship behaviors and concern for the interpersonal sphere have traditionally been relegated to the dependency field, and thus have not been highly valued. However, according to the present reformulation, interpersonal strength and relational skills are conceptualized as positive coping strengths, which can be developed in both sexes.

Norcross, DiClemente, and Prochaska (1986) report that women employ more coping forms involving interpersonal relationships. Other research findings suggest that women use support from others through talking with one another. According to Etzion and Pines (1981) women are able to make more effective use of their support networks since they talk more as a way of coping with stress. Hobfoll's (1988) model of social support may be useful in understanding the development of psychopathology in women. He has put forth a model of ecological congruence to predict the effectiveness of specific resources to buffer the effects of stressful life events. The model emphasizes the person–situation fit of social support and other coping resources; biological, cultural, need, time, and perception dimensions should be considered in order to understand and predict the potential effect of natural or professional intervention—the application of resources. The model suggests that lack of congruence among gender-related attributes, attitudes and values of the person, the meanings of the coping responses, and the expected consequences and meaning of the coping processes, may contribute to increased risk of psychopathology in women.

A study examining coping strategies in male and female students found that males reported using more physical recreation and females used more social support seeking, including sharing the problem with others and enlisting support in managing their problem (Frydenberg & Lewis, 1993). Research indicates that women tend to incorporate social support resources into their coping strategies at work more than men. Greenglass (1993) examined the role of social support in the development of coping forms used by women and men managers. In this study, perceived support from one's supervisor, friends, and family was assessed as were instrumental, preventive, and emotion-focused coping. Results were that supervisor support positively and significantly predicted preventive coping and instrumental coping in women only. Additional results were that friend and family support predicted lower use of emotion-focused coping, including wishful thinking and self-blame in women. That is, to the extent that women reported support from their friends and families, they were less likely to use wishful thinking and self-blame as coping strategies. These data suggest that women were able to use support from friends and family members to lessen their reliance on coping forms such as wishful thinking and self-blame, strategies which have been associated with greater job anxiety, depression, somatization, and drug taking (Greenglass, 1993). In contrast, in men, only friend and family support positively predicted preventive coping.

Thus, women, compared to men, are better able to incorporate interpersonal support into the construction of other cognitive coping forms and to use social support to lessen their reliance on less effective strategies. Similar results were reported in a recent study examining the contribution of social support to coping strategies in a sample of male and female govern-ment employees (Fiksenbaum & Greenglass, 2000). Three types of social support (practical, emotional, and informational) from three different sources (supervisor, coworkers, and family and friends) were assessed, as were a variety of coping strategies (instrumental, internal control, preventive, palliative, wishful thinking, and self-blame). Results indicated that social support was a major contributor to coping, and that this effect was mediated by gender. Specifically, coworker support contributed positively to instru-mental coping, internal control, and preventive coping in women. In men, coworker support did not significantly predict instrumental coping. The data indicate that women were benefiting more from social support, partic-ularly from their coworkers, since the more effective types of coping increased with social support, and less effective coping (wishful thinking) decreased with greater social support. This is likely due to socialization asso-ciated with the feminine gender role, which places greater value on inter-personal relationships and allows for seeking social support to a greater extent than does the masculine gender role.

CONCLUSION

The work sphere is a primary source of stress for women. Given the conditions that characterize much of women's work, they are more likely than men to face pay inequities, sex discrimination, and underutilization of skills, all of which have been positively associated with stress. Other stres-sors for women derive from their socioeconomic disadvantage and their greater likelihood of being poor. At the same time, women are more likely to be primarily responsible for children than are men, regardless of their employment status. Added to their responsibilities is the care of the elderly, which also is more likely seen to be the domain of women. This chapter tends to focus on the issues confronting educated professional women who are predominantly white. Additional stressors relating to sex and racial dis-crimination have been documented among Hispanic women and Black women. Research has documented that conflict between home and work roles is prevalent and may be observed in women as well as men. Work–family conflict has been identified as a stressor associated with several dysfunc-tional outcomes, resulting in lower occupational well-being and decreased job satisfaction. Research shows that for both men and women, the quality of their experiences at home and at work mediate the effect of these roles on their occupational well-being. At the same time, individuals' coping strategies can alleviate their work stress. Use of social support is another means by which stress can be lowered. Effective coping with work stress and role conflict depends on the effective utilization of social support and cop-ing. Moreover, additional insight is gained by incorporating gender into the interpretation of the relationship between occupational well-being, work stress, and role conflict.

REFERENCES

Bacharach, S. B., Bamberger, P., & Conley, S. (1991). Work–home conflict among nurses and engineers: Mediating the impact of role stress on burnout and satisfaction at work. *Journal of Organizational Behavior, 12,* 39–53.

Banyard, V. L., & Graham-Bermann, S. A. (1993). Can women cope? A gender analysis of theories of coping with stress. *Psychology of Women Quarterly, 17,* 303–318.

Belle, D. (1987). Gender differences in the social moderators of stress. In R. Barnett, L. Biener, & G. Bauch (Eds.), *Gender & stress* (pp. 257–277). New York: Free Press.

Billings, A. G., & Moos, R. H. (1984). Coping, stress and social resources among adults with unipolar depression. *Journal of Personality and Social Psychology, 46,* 877–891.

Claes, M. E. (1992). Friendship and personal adjustment during adolescence *Journal of Adolescence, 15,* 39–55.

Cohen, S., & Syme, S. L. (1985). Issues in the study and application of social support. In S. Cohen, & S. L. Syme (Eds.), *Social support and health.* New York: Academic Press.

Cox, T. H., & Harquail, C. V. (1991). Career paths and career success in the early career stages of male and female MBAs. *Journal of Vocational Behavior, 39,* 54–75.

De Longis, A., & O' Brien, T. (1990). An interpersonal framework for stress and coping: An application to the families of Alzheimer's patients. In M. A. P. Stephens, J. H. Crowther, S. E. Hobfoll, & D. L. Tennenbaum (Eds.), *Stress and coping in later life families* (pp. 221–239). New York: Hemisphere.

Eisler, R. M., & Blalock, J. A. (1991). Masculine gender role stress: Implications for the assessment of men. *Clinical Psychology Review, 11,* 45–60.

Etzion, D., & Pines, A. (1981). *Sex and culture as factors explaining reported coping behavior and burnout of human service professionals: A social psychological perspective.* Tel Aviv: Tel Aviv University, The Israel Institute of Business Research.

Fiksenbaum, L., & Greenglass, E. (2000). Interpersonal Predictors of Coping: Gender Differences. Manuscript submitted for publication.

Folkman, S., & Lazarus, R. S. (1980). An analysis of coping in a middle-aged community sample. *Journal of Health and Social Behavior, 21,* 219–239.

Frone, M., Russell, M., & Cooper, M. (1992). Antecedents and outcomes of work–family conflict: Testing a model of the work–family interface. *Journal of Applied Psychology, 77,* 65–75.

Frydenberg, E., & Lewis, R. (1993). Boys play sport and girls turn to others: Age, gender and ethnicity as determinants of coping. *Journal of Adolescence, 16,* 252–266.

Greenglass, E. R. (1982). *A world of difference: Gender roles in perspective.* Toronto: Wiley

Greenglass, E. R. (1985a). An interactional perspective on job-related stress in managerial women. *Southern Psychologist, 2,* 42–48.

Greenglass, E. R. (1985b). Psychological implications of sex bias in the workplace. *Academic Psychology Bulletin, 7,* 227–240.

Greenglass, E. R. (1988). Type A behavior and coping strategies in female and male supervisors. *Applied Psychology: An International Review, 37,* 271–288.

Greenglass, E. R. (1991). Burnout and gender: Theoretical and organizational implications. *Canadian Psychology, 32,* 562–572.

Greenglass, E. R. (1993). The contribution of social support to coping strategies. *Applied Psychology: An International Review, 42,* 323–340.

Greenglass, E. R., & Burke, R. J. (1988). Work and family precursors of burnout in teachers: Sex differences. *Sex Roles, 18,* 215–229.

Greenglass, E. R., Fiksenbaum, L., & Burke, R. J. (1996). Components of social support, buffering effects and burnout: Implications for psychological functioning. *Anxiety, Stress, and Coping, 9,* 185–197.

Greenglass, E. R., Schwarzer, R., Jakubiec, D., Fiksenbaum, L., & Taubert, S. (1999a, July). *The Proactive Coping Inventory (PCI): A multidimensional research instrument.* Paper presented at the 20th International Conference of the Stress and Anxiety Research Society (STAR), Cracow, Poland.

Greenglass, E. R., Schwarzer, R., & Taubert, S. (1999b). *The Proactive Coping Inventory (PCI): A multidimensional research instrument.* Retrieved from http://userpage.fu-berlin.de/~health/greenpci.htm.

Hobfoll, S. E. (1986). *Stress, social support, and women.* Washington: Hemisphere Pub. Co.

Hobfoll, S. E. (1988). *The ecology of stress.* New York: Hemisphere.

Hobfoll, S. E., Dunahoo, C. L., Ben-Porath, Y., & Monnier, J. (1994). Gender and coping: The dual-axis model of coping. *American Journal of Community Psychology, 22,* 49–82.

Institute for Women's Policy Research (1999). *Employment, earnings and economic change.* Retrieved from http://www.iwpr.org/RESEARCH.HTM.

Kinnunen, U., & Mauno, S. (1998). Antecedents and outcomes of work–family conflict among employed women and men in Finland. *Human Relations, 51,* 157–177.

Kossek, E., & Ozeki, C. (1998). Work–family conflict, policies, and the job–life satisfaction relationship: A review and directions for organizational behavior–human resources research. *Journal of Applied Psychology, 83,* 139–149.

Lapsley, H. (1999). *Margaret Mead and Ruth Benedict: The kinship of women.* Amherst, MA: University of Massachusetts Press.

Lazarus, R. S., & Folkman, S. (1984). Personal control and stress and coping processes: A theoretical analysis. *Journal of Personality and Social Psychology, 46,* 839–852.

Long, B. C. (1990). Relation between coping strategies, sex-typed traits and environmental characteristics: A comparison of male and female managers. *Journal of Counseling Psychology, 37*, 185–194.

Long, B. C., & Cox, R. S. (2000). Women's ways of coping with employment stress: A feminist contextual analysis. In P. Dewe, M. Leiter, & T. Cox (Eds.), *Coping, health and organizations* (pp. 109–123). London: Taylor & Francis.

Luckow, A. E., Reifman, A., & McIntosh, D. N. (1998, August). *Gender differences in coping: A meta-analysis.* Poster presented at the Annual Meeting of the American Psychological Association, San Franscisco, CA.

Maslach, C., & Jackson, S. E. (1985). The role of sex and family variables in burnout. *Sex Roles, 12*, 837–851.

Maslach, C., & Jackson, S. E. (1986). *Maslach Burnout Inventory Manual* (2nd ed.). Palo Alto, CA: Consulting Psychologists Press.

McDonald, L. M., & Korabik, K. (1991). Sources of stress and ways of coping among male and female managers. In P. L. Perrewé, (Ed.), Handbook on job stress [Special Issue]. *Journal of Social Behavior and Personality, 6*, 185–198.

McGrath, E., Keita, G. P., Strickland, B. R., & Russo, N. F. (1990). *Women and depression: Risk factors and treatment issues.* Washington, DC: American Psychological Association.

McLeod, J. D., & Kessler, R. C. (1990). Socioeconomic status differences in vulnerability to undesirable life events. *Journal of Health and Social Behavior, 31*, 162–172.

Netemeyer, R., Boles, J., & McMurrian, R. (1996). Development and validation of work–family conflict and family–work conflict scales. *Journal of Applied Psychology, 81*, 400–410.

Norcross, J. C., DiClemente, C. C., & Prochaska, J. O. (1986). Self-change of psychological distress: Laypersons' vs. psychologists' coping strategies. *Journal of Clinical Psychology, 42*, 834–840.

Oakley, A. (1992). *Social support and motherhood: The natural history of a research project.* Oxford: Basil Blackwell.

Ogus, E. D., Greenglass, E., & Burke, R. J. (1990). Gender-role differences, work stress and depersonalization. *Journal of Social Behavior and Personality, 5*, 387–398.

O'Neill, C. P., & Zeichner, A. (1985). Working women: A study of relationships between stress, coping and health. *Journal of Psychosomatic Obstetrics and Gynaecology, 4*, 105–116.

Piechowski, L. D. (1992). Mental health and women's multiple roles. *Families in Society, 73*, 131–139.

Placek, J., Smith, R., & Dodge, K. (1994). Gender differences in coping with stress: When stressor and appraisals do not differ. *Personality and Social Psychology Bulletin, 20*, 421–430.

Pleck, J. H. (1980). *Male sex role identity: Fact or fiction?* (Working Paper). Boston, MA: Wellesley College.

Powell, G. N. (1990). One more time: Do male and female managers differ? *Academy of Management Executive, 4,* 68–75.

Schwab, R. L., & Iwanicki, E. F. (1982). Who are our burned out teachers? *Educational Research Quarterly, 7,* 5–16.

Shumaker, S. A., & Hill, D. R. (1991). Gender differences in social support and physical health. *Health Psychology, 10,* 102–111.

Solomon, L. J., & Rothblum, E. D. (1986). Stress, coping, and social support in women. *The Behavior Therapist, 9,* 199–204.

Spain, D., & Bianchi, S. M. (1996). *Balancing act: Motherhood, marriage and employment among American women.* New York: Russell Sage Foundation.

Stone, A. A., & Neale, J. M. (1984). New measure of daily coping: Development and preliminary results. *Journal of Personality and Social Psychology, 46,* 892–906.

Unger, R. (1990). Imperfect reflections of reality: Psychology constructs gender. In R. Hare-Mustin, & J. Marecek (Eds.), *Making a difference: Psychology and the construction of gender* (pp. 102–149). New Haven, CT: Yale University Press.

U.S. Census Bureau, Special Populations Branch, Population Division (2000). *Poverty status of the population in 1999 by age and sex.* Washington, DC: Author.

Waldron, I., & Jacobs, J. A. (1989). Effects of multiple roles on women's health: Evidence from a national longitudinal study. *Women & Health, 15,* 3–19.

Williams, J., & Alliger, M. (1994). Role stressors, mood spillover, and perceptions of work–family conflict in employed parents. *Academy of Management Journal, 37,* 837–868.

II

STRESS AND FAMILY
DYNAMICS

INTRODUCTION:
STRESS AND FAMILY DYNAMICS

The next two sections of the book, along with the conclusion, represent where we need to go in terms of our research. In this section, we examine the underresearched area of stress and the family. Previous research has tended to focus solely on work roles. The family is a complex dynamic that has important implications for work stress and health, and these chapters represent leading-edge investigations. Chapter 7 casts social support within the family framework to ascertain whether men and women benefit from this resource in the same ways. Chapter 8 examines gender as it relates to time spent in work versus family roles, and the way this time breakdown affects stress and health. Crossover, a form of stress contagion, is a new topic in the stress literature, and chapter 9 explores not only negative crossover but also suggests that we need to study positive crossover as well.

7

DO MEN AND WOMEN BENEFIT FROM SOCIAL SUPPORT EQUALLY? RESULTS FROM A FIELD EXAMINATION WITHIN THE WORK AND FAMILY CONTEXT

PAMELA L. PERREWÉ AND DAWN S. CARLSON

Interest in the study of work–family constructs has intensified during the past 2 decades due, in part, to the significant changes in workplace demographics as well as the evolving nature of the balance between work and family responsibilities (Edwards & Rothbard, 2000; Kinnunen & Mauno, 1998). The negative consequences from the work–family interplay, particularly work–family conflict, have been well documented. Strain resulting from conflicts between work and family include decreased family and occupational well-being (Kinnunen & Mauno, 1998), value attainment and job–life satisfaction (Kossek & Ozeki, 1998; Perrewé, Hochwarter, & Kiewitz, 1999), and increased reports of depression, somatic complaints, and cholesterol levels (Thomas & Ganster, 1995).

Despite the proliferation of research in this area, there have been relatively few well-orchestrated research efforts examining gender-based relationships of social support in the work and family contexts. Further, while social support has been established as playing a key role in the stressor–strain relationship, very few studies have clearly examined how social support differs for men and women. Although there has been a tremendous influx of women into the workforce during the past several decades, the expectations of society regarding men and women in work and family roles has not changed significantly (Greenhaus & Parasuraman, 1999). Thus, attention to the role of gender in research on work–family linkages is important if we are to begin to understand the complexities that lie within the work–family framework.

Given that it is difficult, if not impossible, to eliminate many work and family stressors, examining individuals' personal mechanisms for coping, such as social support, is important. Researchers have examined the effects of social support in diverse settings, from daycare centers and schools (Jackson, Schwab, & Schuler, 1986; Russell, Altmaier, & Van Velzen, 1987) to social workers and hospitals (Constable & Russell, 1986). In general, social support is associated with lower reported levels of strain (Carlson & Perrewé, 1999; Eastburg, Williamson, Gorsuch, & Ridley, 1994). It is not clear, however, whether social support differentially affects the experiences of men and women (Greenhaus & Parasuraman, 1999). Further, it is not clear if men or women perceive more social support from their family and work domains. This chapter describes a study that examines the interaction of gender and social support as they impact both the work and family domains in terms of conflict and satisfaction.

WORK AND FAMILY CONFLICT

Work–family conflict is a form of interrole conflict in which role demands from the work and family domains are mutually incompatible, so that meeting demands in one domain makes it difficult to meet demands in the other (Greenhaus & Beutell, 1985). Role demands often originate from the values held by the person as well as from the expectations expressed by work and family role senders (Katz & Kahn, 1978). For example, if the organization culture continually encourages employees to work overtime on the job, conflict could arise if a simultaneous objective is to maintain a strong presence at home.

Work–family conflict can take two distinct forms of interrole conflict: work interference with family (WIF) and family interference with work (FIW). WIF conflict occurs when the tasks at work prohibit individuals from attending to tasks at home. Conversely, FIW conflict surfaces if family requirements keep individuals from giving their desired contribution at work. This chapter describes both types of conflict as outcomes in relation to gender and social support.

WORK AND FAMILY SATISFACTION

Beyond simply considering conflict, satisfaction from both the work and family context should be examined. Locke (1976) argued that satisfaction is an emotional response resulting from individuals' estimates of how well life factors (e.g., work stressors, family stressors) either enhance or frustrate their values. Every emotional response reflects two estimates: the discrepancy between what is wanted versus what is obtained and the importance of the value to the individual. Thus, work satisfaction is an emotional response representing how well one's values are met in the workplace, while family satisfaction is an emotional response representing how well one's values are met in the family domain.

SOCIAL SUPPORT

Social support is defined as the amount of emotional and instrumental assistance received from another (Beehr, 1985; House, 1981). *Instrumental support* refers to the tangible or direct assistance received from others. *Emotional support* is the perceived availability of thoughtful, caring individuals with whom one can share personal thoughts and feelings, and is considered by some to be the most important form of support (House, 1981). The notion that social support can reduce experienced stress not only offers much appeal, but has empirical support as well (see chapter 6).

Although the types and specific effects of social support may vary across studies, research has demonstrated the general stress-reducing benefits of social support (Cohen & Wills, 1985; Fenlason & Beehr, 1994). Research consistently has demonstrated the positive consequences of social support and recent research presents evidence that social support is, perhaps, best viewed as an antidote to reducing perceived stress (Carlson & Perrewé, 1999). Specifically, social support was shown to directly reduce perceived role stressors, time demands, and work–family conflict. The stress-reducing effects of social support have, for the most part, been found to be domain-specific. Namely, social support from the family has its greatest stress-reducing effects on family strain and social support from work has its greatest stress-reducing effects on work strain (e.g., Ayree & Luk, 1996; Frone, Yardley & Markel, 1997; Parasuraman, Greenhaus, & Granrose, 1992).

The positive benefits from social support are not limited to reducing perceived stress. Social support has been found to increase satisfaction and contribute to the well-being of dual career couples (Parasuraman et al., 1992). Indeed, research indicates that social support may influence mortality through changes in the cardiovascular, endocrine, and immune systems (Uchino, Cacioppo, & Kiecolt-Glaser, 1996). Although the positive consequences from social support are evident, gender differences in the benefits from utilizing social support have not been examined extensively. We believe gender may very well play a role in the *extent* to which social support is associated with reduced work and family conflict and increased work and family satisfaction.

Social Support From Work

Social support from work can be viewed as a resource that enhances both performance and well-being. Specifically, work social support can help reduce the stress that workers experience from work–family conflict.

Research has demonstrated that employees who receive social support from their coworkers and supervisors are more likely to experience less work–family conflict (Erdwins, Buffardi, Casper, & O'Brian, 2001; Frone et al., 1997; Thomas & Ganster, 1995).

Recent research demonstrates the positive associations between social support and satisfaction (e.g., Carlson & Perrewé, 1999) and, more specifically, coworker and supervisor social support have been found to facilitate employee work satisfaction (Dunseath, Beehr, & King, 1995; Parasuraman et al., 1992; Thomas & Ganster, 1995). Therefore, the beneficial effects of social support in the work domain often are associated with lower work interference with family conflict and greater work satisfaction.

Social Support From the Family

Research on the life-enriching benefits of social support suggests support from the family reduces individuals' work–family conflict (Aryee, 1992; Aryee, Luk, Leung, & Lo, 1998; Greenberger & O'Neil, 1993). Both instrumental and emotional sources of social support have been found to reduce family interference with work conflict (Adams, King, & King, 1996; Parasuraman, Purohit, Godshalk, & Beutell, 1996). In addition, research has demonstrated that employees who receive social support from their spouses and family are less likely to experience family interference with work conflict (Frone et al., 1997).

Furthermore, family social support has been found to lead to greater overall life satisfaction (Adams et al., 1996; Lim, 1996) and greater family satisfaction (Carver & Jones, 1992). More specifically, both spouse and family support are positively related to greater family satisfaction (Frone et al., 1997). This combined research would suggest that social support from the family domain would have a negative impact on family interference with work conflict, and a positive impact on family satisfaction.

INTERACTIVE EFFECTS OF GENDER AND SOCIAL SUPPORT

Much of the gender research has focused on differences in regard to work–family conflict. Pleck (1977) argued that men and women would differ in their interrole conflict domain. Specifically, Pleck argued that because men are considered the primary financial providers, their work would interfere with their family life more than would be the case for women. Women, on the other hand, are considered to have the primary responsibilities for the home. Thus, women should perceive more conflict from the family into the work domain. Empirical research in this area, however, has not been supportive of Pleck's (1977) assertions. According to Greenhaus and Parasuraman (1999), research has either found that men and women perceive about the same amount of conflict (e.g., Duxbury & Higgins, 1991) or women perceive more conflict than do men (e.g., Williams & Alliger, 1994). Greenhaus and Parasuraman (1999) argue that women generally spend more total time on work and family activities than do men; thus, findings that suggest women perceive more conflict than men are not surprising.

Given that women spend more total time on work and family duties, Greenhaus and Parasuraman (1999) note that those studies that fail to find gender differences in work–family conflict are difficult to explain. They do, however, offer a plausible explanation: women may be better than men at adopting coping strategies that reduce work–family conflict. We find this idea intriguing and examine the differential gender effects of adopting social support as a coping strategy on work–family conflict and work–family satisfaction. If women do, in fact, adopt effective coping strategies such as social support, it follows that social support may be an effective means of reducing work–family conflict—at least for women.

Work Domain

Research suggests that women may receive more social support from coworkers than do men; however, women and men receive similar levels of support from their supervisors (Parasuraman & Greenhaus, 1994). Although there is no consistent evidence that women benefit more or less than men from support provided by their supervisors or coworkers (Parasuraman et al., 1992), some support exists for the notion that women receive more combined social support at work. Based on this discussion, we expect that women will benefit more in terms of reduced *work* interference with family conflict and increased *work* satisfaction than men will experience when social support is high. This proposition is examined in our field study.

Family Domain

In regard to gender differences, there is some research that suggests husbands receive more instrumental support from their wives, but that men and women seem to give the same amount of emotional social support to each other (see Greenhaus & Parasuraman, 1999 for a review). In addition, studies have found that women tend to have more supportive relationships and more family support networks than do men (Leavy, 1983). In a recent study that included the health of employees as an outcome, the difference between men and women receiving family social support was examined (Walters et al., 1996). The finding suggested that, for women, social support was a significant variable in reducing health concerns. However, for males, social support did not have a significant effect. Based on this discussion, we expect that women will benefit more in terms of reduced *family* interference with work conflict and increased *family* satisfaction than men when social support is high. The following field study examines this proposition.

THE FIELD STUDY

The respondents were more than 500 members within three organizations in the areas of real estate, insurance, and the department of revenue. The total sample was 50% male with an average age of 42 years and average organizational tenure of 7.3 years. Further, 68% of the respondents indicated they were married and 61% had children. In order to ensure that there were no differences in the group by gender (a critical variable in this study), *t*-tests were conducted on marital status, children, tenure, and age. Marital status, number of children, and tenure with the organization all showed no significant difference between men and women. The only variable that showed a significant difference was age, with men being older than were women. Therefore, age was included as a control variable in the analysis.

Consistent with past research in this area, data were collected using a survey instrument. Most research on work–family conflict has been performed using self-report questionnaire items under the assumption that self-reports accurately reflect objective circumstances (Near, Rice, & Hunt, 1980). To increase the accuracy of the responses, respondents were guaranteed anonymity.

Measures

Gender. Gender was recorded such that women were coded as 1 and men were coded as 0. All of the scales described below were responded to using a 7-point Likert-type scale, unless otherwise indicated. Response anchors varied from "strongly agree" (7) to "strongly disagree" (1).

Work Social Support. This scale consists of six items developed by Etzion (1984). The six items correspond to support features to which subjects responded by noting the degree to which each is present in their work. Example items include the degree to which appreciation, sharing of duties, and emotional support are present. The Cronbach's alpha for this scale was .85.

Family Social Support. A scale identical to the work social support scale was adapted by Etzion (1984) to measure family social support. However, in this case, the six items correspond to the degree to which each is present in the subject's family life. Example items included the degree to which appreciation, sharing of duties, and emotional support are present. The Cronbach's alpha for this scale was .88.

Work Interference With Family Conflict. This scale consists of five items that address work interference with family conflict (e.g., My work often interferes with my family responsibilities.) The first four questions came from Gutek, Searle, and Klepa's (1991) work–family conflict scale. The final item was adapted from the work–family conflict research of Frone, Russell, and Cooper (1992). This scale was created to measure work interference with family as well as family interference with work. The Cronbach's alpha for this scale was .81.

Family Interference With Work Conflict. This scale consists of five items that address family interference with work conflict (e.g., My family often interferes with my responsibilities at work). The first four questions came from Gutek, et al.'s (1991) work–family conflict scale. The final item was adapted from the work–family conflict research of Frone et al. (1992). The Cronbach's alpha for this scale was .87.

Work Satisfaction. The work satisfaction scale was an overall measure of the degree to which an individual is satisfied or happy with his or her job. The three-item measure of work satisfaction was from Camman, Fichman, Jenkins, and Klesh (1979) and Seashore, Lawler, Mirvis and Camman (1982). An example item is "All in all, I am satisfied with my job." The Cronbach's alpha for this scale was .85.

Family Satisfaction. The family satisfaction scale measured the degree to which an individual was satisfied or happy with the family aspects of his or her life. The family satisfaction scale consisted of three items and was developed by Staines and Pleck (1984). An example item is "How satisfied are you with your family life?" The Cronbach's alpha for this scale was .93.

Analyses

The hypotheses were tested using hierarchical moderated regression. Separate regression equations were run for each of the four dependent variables (work interference with family, work satisfaction, family interference with work, family satisfaction). In each equation, organizational membership and age were controlled for in the first step. In the second step, the main effects of gender and domain-specific social support were entered prior to entering the multiplicative interaction terms of gender and social support.

RESULTS

The means, standard deviations, and intercorrelations for the variables of interest are provided in Table 7.1. An examination of the correlation matrix indicates that women were less likely than were men to report social support from the family domain. Further, women were more likely to report conflict stemming from work interference with family. In addition, work and family social support were significantly correlated and work and family satisfaction were significantly correlated. Interactive effects for gender and social support on work–family conflict and satisfaction can be found in Tables 7.2 and 7.3. As can be seen, there was no interactive effect found for gender and work

TABLE 7.1
Means, Standard Deviations, and Correlations

Variables	Mean	Std.	1	2	3	4	5	6
1. Gender	.50	.50	1.00					
2. Work social support	4.61	1.33	.04	1.00				
3. Family social support	5.25	1.31	−.14*	.15*	1.00			
4. Work interference w/family conflict	3.32	1.28	.17*	−.14*	−.23*	1.00		
5. Family interference w/family conflict	2.25	.97	.01	−.09*	−.29*	.38*	1.00	
6. Work satisfaction	5.41	1.47	.01	.48*	.03	−.13*	−.20*	1.00
7. Family satisfaction	5.70	1.17	−.02	.15*	.58*	−.23*	−.34*	.15

Note. *$p < .05$.
$n = 511$.

TABLE 7.2
Hierarchical Regression Results Predicting
Work–Family Conflict and Work Satisfaction

Variables	β	R²	ΔR²	F (Δ)	df
Work interference w/family					
Step 1:					
Organizational membership	.182				
Age	−.035	.036		8.91**	2,477
Step 2:					
Gender	.10*				
Work social support	−.19**	.080	.044	11.33**	2,475
Step 3:					
Gender × Work social support	.11	.083	.003	1.61	1,474

Variables	β	R²	ΔR²	F (Δ)	df
Work satisfaction					
Step 1:					
Organizational membership	.224**				
Age	.177**	.071		18.47**	2,482
Step 2:					
Gender	.06				
Work social support	.46**	.275	.204	67.67**	2,480
Step 3:					
Gender × Work social support	.37*	.282	.006	4.20*	1,479

Note. *$p < .05$ (one-tailed test) **$p < .01$.

TABLE 7.3
Hierarchical Regression Results Predicting
Family–Work Conflict and Family Satisfaction

Variables	β	R^2	ΔR^2	$F (\Delta)$	df
Family interference w/work					
Step 1:					
Organizational membership	.019				
Age	−.152**	.024		5.91**	2,476
Step 2:					
Gender	−.045				
Family social support	−.28**	.103	.078	20.70**	2,474
Step 3:					
Gender × Family social support	−.43*	.109	.006	3.24	1,473

Variables	β	R^2	ΔR^2	$F (\Delta)$	df
Family satisfaction					
Step 1:					
Organizational membership	.044				
Age	.140**	.020		4.89**	2,482
Step 1:					
Gender	.07*				
Family social support	.57**	.340	.321	116.7**	2,480
Step 2:					
Gender × Family social support	.71**	.357	.016	12.09**	1,479

Note. *$p < .05$ (one-tailed test)   **$p < .01$.

social support on work interference with family. However, an interactive effect was found for gender and work social support on work satisfaction. Specifically, as work social support increased, work satisfaction increased more for women than for men. The interactive effect of gender and social support from family was examined as to its impact on family interference with work. An interactive effect was found for gender and family social support on family interference with work conflict, such that as family social support increased, family interference with work conflict decreased more for women.

Finally, the interactive effect of gender and family social support on family satisfaction also was examined. An interaction effect for gender and family social support on family satisfaction was found and the findings suggest that as family social support increased, family satisfaction increased more for women.

CONCLUSION

While social support has been established as playing a key role in the stressor–strain relationship, very few studies have clearly examined how social support differs for men and women. This chapter describes a field examination of the moderating role of gender in the relationship of social support with conflict and satisfaction in both the work and family context.

The findings from this study suggest several general conclusions. First, men are more likely to perceive social support in their family environment than are women. Second, women are more likely to perceive conflict stemming from their work domain into their family domain. Finally, women seem to benefit more than do men from both work and family social support.

In regard to the family domain, it is interesting that men perceive more social support than do women and women perceive more conflict from work into the family domain than do men. Perhaps women are giving more social support to their spouses than they are receiving, although it is also possible that women simply desire more social support from their family domain than do men. Regardless, these findings support earlier research (e.g., Thomas & Ganster, 1995) that suggests women continue to perceive themselves to be responsible primarily within the family domain. If women are continuing to shoulder the bulk of the family responsibilities, it is not surprising that they perceive less family social support than do men and perceive more conflict stemming from work into the family. These findings support the notion that women still perceive themselves primarily to be responsible for the welfare of the family and need more social support from the family.

Examining the interactions between gender and social support on work and family outcome variables yields some interesting findings. First, the impact of work social support on work interference with family conflict did not differ for men and women. While social support had a strong main effect and is important in reducing conflict, this appears to be important for both genders. Thus, social support stemming from work did not have differential effects on men and women in regard to work–family conflict. Second, work social support did lead to higher increases in work satisfaction for women than for men. Thus, women are more satisfied with their work and work environment when they perceive social support stemming from the workplace.

In regard to family social support, females appear to reap greater benefits from family social support in regard to family interference with work conflict. As family social support increased, family interference with work decreased for women while slightly increasing for men. Perhaps women are simply more adept than men at adopting effective family social support coping mechanisms (Greenhaus & Parasuraman, 1999). Another plausible explanation, however, is that women may be more susceptible to the positive outcomes associated with family social support. In other words, when family social support is present, women may benefit the most.

Supporting this statement is the finding that family social support had differential effects for men and women on family satisfaction. Specifically, family satisfaction increased more for women than men when family social support was high. Two plausible conclusions can be deduced from these findings. First, women may be more sensitive to support factors in the family domain. If women still have a stronger sense of responsibility for the family than men, it makes sense that they would benefit most from social support if it effectively helps them to cope with family strain.

Second, women seem to be better able to effectively utilize social support. Although men may perceive more social support stemming from the family (perhaps because women shoulder the bulk of the responsibilities), women benefit the most from social support. As we have seen, women report more work satisfaction, more family satisfaction, and less family interference with work when social support is high. Clearly, additional research is needed before definitive statements about how well women utilize social support can be made.

Based on our discussion and research findings, women seem to benefit the most from social support. Clearly, additional research is needed, however, to fine-tune these relationships. We first recommend studying gender in relation to specific dimensions of social support. Not only should instrumental and emotional social support be examined separately, but these two categories may also be dimensionalized. For example, at a global level, emotional social support includes talking, listening, and expressing concern for the distressed individual. Nevertheless, because conversations can vary in content (Beehr, King, & King, 1990), the global label "emotional support" remains insufficient and vague. For example, conversations with coworkers may focus on either positive or negative aspects of one's job, leading to optimism or a deepening pessimism.

Second, no research has focused attention on gender and how different sources of social support (e.g., supervisor, coworkers, subordinates, spouse, and children) may differentially effect men and women. Thus, examining the *type* of social support as well as the *source* of social support for men and women might tease out the complexities that lie within the gender, social support, and conflict relationships. Given that research has supported the influential role of social support (see chapter 6), it is important for organizations and families to provide support. Continued research in gender and social support is clearly needed, however, before specific recommendations about how to provide support is warranted.

REFERENCES

Adams, G., King, L., & King, D. (1996). Relationships of job and family involvement, family social support, and work–family conflict with job and life satisfaction. *Journal of Applied Psychology, 81*, 411–420.

Aryee, S. (1992). Antecedents and outcomes of work–family conflict among married professional women. Evidence from Singapore. *Human Relations, 45*, 813–837.

Ayree, S., & Luk, V. (1996). Work and nonwork influences on the career satisfaction of dual-earner couples. *Journal of Vocational Behavior, 49*, 38–52.

Ayree, S., Luk, V., Leung, A., & Lo, S. (1998). Role stressors, interrole conflict, and well-being: The moderating influence of spousal support and coping behaviors among employed parents in Hong Kong. *Journal of Vocational Behavior, 54*, 259–278.

Beehr, T. A. (1985). The role of social support in coping with organizational stress. In T. A. Beehr, & R. S. Bhagat (Eds.), *Human stress and cognition in organizations: An integrated perspective* (pp. 375–398). New York: Wiley.

Beehr, T. A., King, L. A., & King, D. W. (1990). Social support and occupational stress: Talking to supervisors. *Journal of Vocational Behavior, 36*, 61–81.

Camman, C., Fichman, M., Jenkins, D., & Klesh, J. (1979). *The Michigan organizational assessment questionnaire.* Ann Arbor, MI: University of Michigan.

Carlson, D. S., & Perrewé, P. L. (1999). The role of social support in the stressor–strain relationship: An examination of work–family conflict. *Journal of Management, 25*, 513–540.

Carver, M. C., & Jones, W. H. (1992). The family satisfaction scale. *Social Behavior and Personality, 20,* 71–84.

Cohen, S., & Wills, T. A. (1985). Stress, social support and the buffering hypothesis. *Psychological Bulletin, 92*, 257–310.

Constable, J. F., & Russell, D. W. (1986). The effect of social support and the work environment upon burnout among nurses. *Journal of Human Stress, Spring,* 20–26.

Dunseath, J., Beehr, T. A., & King, D. W. (1995). Job stress–social support buffering effects across gender, education and occupational groups in a municipal workforce: Implications for EAPs and further research. *Review of Public Personnel Administration, 15*, 60–83.

Duxbury, L. E., & Higgins, C. A. (1991). Gender differences in work–family conflict. *Journal of Applied Psychology, 76*, 60–74.

Eastburg, M. C., Williamson, M., Gorsuch, R., & Ridley, C. (1994). Social support, personality and burnout in nurses. *Journal of Applied Psychology, 24*, 1233–1250.

Edwards, J., & Rothbard, N. (2000). Mechanisms linking work and family: Clarifying the relationship between work and family constructs. *Academy of Management Review, 25*, 178–199.

Erdwins, C., Buffardi, L. C., Casper, W. J., & O'Brian, A. (2001). The relationship of women's role strain to social support, role satisfaction, and self-efficacy. *Family Relations, 50*, 230–238.

Etzion, D. (1984). Moderation effect of social support on the stress–burnout relationship. *Journal of Applied Psychology, 69*, 615–622.

Fenlason, K. J., & Beehr, T. A. (1994). Social support and occupational stress: Effects of talking to others. *Journal of Organizational Behavior, 15*, 157–175.

Frone, M. R., Russell, M., & Cooper, M. L. (1992). Antecedents and outcomes of work–family conflict: Testing a model of the work–family interface. *Journal of Applied Psychology, 77*, 65–75.

Frone, M. R., Yardley, J. K., & Markel, K. S. (1997). Developing and testing an integrative model of the work–family interface. *Journal of Vocational Behavior, 50*, 145–167.

Greenberger, E., & O'Neil, R. (1993). Spouse, parent, worker: Role commitments and role-related experiences in the construction of adults' well-being. *Developmental Psychology, 29*, 181–197.

Greenhaus, J. H., & Beutell, N. J. (1985). Sources of conflict between work and family roles. *Academy of Management Review, 10*, 76–88.

Greenhaus, J. H., & Parasuraman, S. (1999). Research on work, family, and gender: Current status and future directions. In G. N. Powell (Ed.), *Handbook of gender & work* (pp. 391–412). London: Sage.

Gutek, B., Searle, S., & Klepa, L. (1991). Rational versus gender role–explanations for work–family conflict. *Journal of Applied Psychology, 76*, 560–568.

House, J. S. (1981). *Work stress and social support.* MA: Addison-Wesley.

Jackson S. E., Schwab, R. L., & Schuler, R. S. (1986). Toward an understanding of the burnout phenomenon. *Journal of Applied Psychology, 71*, 630–640.

Katz, D., & Kahn, R. (1978). *The social psychology of organizations* (2nd ed.). New York: Wiley.

Kinnunen, U., & Mauno, S. (1998). Antecedents and outcomes of work–family conflict among employed women and men in Finland. *Human Relations, 51*, 157–177.

Kossek, E., & Ozeki, C. (1998). Work–family conflict, policies, and the job–life satisfaction relationship: A review and directions for organizational behavior–human resources research. *Journal of Applied Psychology, 83*, 139–149.

Leavy, R. L. (1983). Social support and psychological disorder: A review. *Journal of Community Psychology, 11*, 3–21.

Lim, V. K. (1996). Job insecurity and its outcomes: Moderating effects of work-based and nonwork-based social support. *Human Relations, 49*, 171–194.

Locke, E. (1976). The nature and causes of job satisfaction. In M. D. Dunnette (Ed.), *Handbook of industrial and organizational psychology* (pp. 1297–1349). Chicago: Rand McNally.

Near, J. P., Rice, R. W., & Hunt, R. G. (1980). The relationship between work and nonwork domains: A review of empirical research. *Academy of Management Review, 5*, 415–429.

Parasuraman, S., & Greenhaus, J. H. (1994). Determinants of support provided and received by partners in two-career relationships. In L. A. Helsop (Ed.), *The ties that bind* (pp. 121–145). Canadian Consortium of Management Schools: Calgary, Alberta.

Parasuraman, S., Greenhaus, J. H., & Granrose, C. S. (1992). Role stressors, social support and well-being among two-career couples. *Journal of Organizational Behavior, 13*, 339–356.

Parasuraman, S., Purohit, Y. S., Godshalk, V. M., & Beutell, N. J. (1996). Work and family variables, entrepreneurial career success, and psychological well-being. *Journal of Vocational Behavior, 48*, 275–300.

Perrewé, P. L., Hochwarter, W. A., & Kiewitz, C. (1999). Value attainment: An explanation for the negative effects of work–family conflict on job and life satisfaction. *Journal of Occupational Health Psychology, 4*, 318–326.

Pleck, J. H. (1977). The work–family role system. *Social Forces, 24*, 417–427.

Russell, D. W., Altmaier, E., & Van Velzen, D. (1987). Job-related stress, social support, and burnout among classroom teachers. *Journal of Applied Psychology, 72*, 269–274.

Seashore, S. E., Lawler, E. E., Mirvis, P., & Camman, C. (1982). *Observing and measuring organizational change: A guide to field practice.* New York: Wiley.

Staines, G. L., & Pleck, J. H. (1984). Nonstandard work schedules and family life. *Journal of Applied Psychology, 69*, 515–523.

Thomas, L., & Ganster, D. (1995). Impact of family-supportive work variables on work–family conflict and strain: A control perspective. *Journal of Applied Psychology, 80*, 6–15.

Uchino, B. N., Cacioppo, J. T., & Kiecolt-Glaser, K. G. (1996). The relationships between social support and physiological processes: A review with emphasis on underlying mechanisms and implications for health. *Psychological Bulletin, 119*, 488–531.

Walters, V., Lenton, R., French, S., Eyles, J., Mayr, J., & Newbold, B. (1996). Paid work, unpaid work and social support: A study of the health of male and female nurses. *Social Science Medicine, 43*, 1627–1636.

Williams, J., & Alliger, M. (1994). Role stressors, mood spillover, and perceptions of work–family conflict in employed parents. *Academy of Management, 37*, 837–868.

8

THE ALLOCATION OF TIME TO WORK AND FAMILY ROLES

JEFFREY H. GREENHAUS AND SAROJ PARASURAMAN

Time plays a crucial role in the evolution of individual careers (Parasuraman, Greenhaus, & Linnehan, 2000). In the context of the work–family interface, the significance of time derives from the fact that it is finite. Thus, time traditionally has been regarded as a valuable but scarce resource (Buck, Lee, MacDermid, & Smith, 2000). Moreover, the zero-sum nature of time implies that the greater the number of hours that are devoted to the work role, the less time that is available to fulfill family responsibilities and vice versa. Therefore, a substantial time commitment to one role (work *or* family) can produce an "energy drain" that may conflict with the requirements of the other role (Edwards & Rothbard, 2000). Furthermore, extensive conflict between work and family roles can impair an individual's psychological well-being (Greenhaus & Parasuraman, 1999).

Because of these linkages among time allocations, work–family conflict, and well-being, it is important to understand the factors that influence time allocation decisions, especially for partners in dual-earner relationships, which are quickly becoming the norm in American society. Yet, there has been relatively little research on the determinants of time allocated to work and family roles. Moreover, this limited research has for the most part focused only on individual variables as predictors of employees' time commitment to work and family. Viewing a dual-earner couple as an interdependent social unit, it becomes important to examine cross-partner influences on each partner's time allocation decisions. An open systems view of dual-earner couples suggests that each partner's time allocation decisions could be influenced by the other partner's involvement and time commitment to his or her work and family roles.

This chapter seeks to expand our knowledge of the factors related to dual-earner partners' allocation of time to work and family. A number of theoretical perspectives are relevant to understanding the factors that influence the time allocated to work and family roles. According to the *rational view*, the time and energy devoted to a particular role depend on the objective demands of the role and the other claims on the individual's time and attention (Gutek, Searle, & Klepa, 1991; O'Driscoll, Ilgen, & Hildreth, 1992). The *social psychological view* posits that the psychological importance or salience of a particular role to the individual's social identity is also an important determinant of the time invested in that role relative to other roles (Greenhaus & Powell, 2000; Lobel, 1991). A third perspective suggests that the time allocated to work and family may be a function of early socialization, internalized beliefs, and normative expectations of gender-appropriate role behavior.

Although previous research has provided some direct or indirect support for all of these theoretical explanations for the time individuals allocate to work and family, they have been assumed to be mutually exclusive, and treated as competing models of the choice behavior of employed men and women. The possibility of multiple explanations for a given behavior—in this case the time allocated to work and family roles—remains relatively unexplored. Also unexplored is the *effect* of work and family time allocations on psychological well-being.

In response to these gaps in the literature, this chapter examines (a) the effect of work and family role pressures on the amount of time allocated to work and family by dual-earner men and women; (b) the effect of work and family identity salience on the time spent on work and family; (c) the effect of partners' involvements in work and family activities on individuals' time allocations; (d) the presence of gender differences in the predictors of time allocated to work and family activities; and (e) the effect of time allocations on the psychological health and well-being of dual-earner men and women. The specific variables included in the study and the hypothesized relationships among them also are described in this chapter.

WORK AND FAMILY ROLE PRESSURES AS DETERMINANTS OF TIME ALLOCATIONS

The amount of time an individual devotes to a particular role is at least partially due to the pressures experienced within the role. Role senders within a given domain exert pressure on individuals to participate in the role and meet performance expectations (Kahn, Wolfe, Quinn, Snoek, & Rosenthal, 1964). These pressures arouse forces within the individual to meet the demands of the role and the expectations of role senders (Greenhaus & Powell, 2000).

In the work domain, job stressors represent role pressures that increase the amount of time one devotes to work (Aryee, 1992; Greenhaus, Bedeian, & Mossholder, 1987; Judge, Boudreau, & Bretz, 1994). In particular, *work overload*, described as "too much work to do in the time available," has been found to be related to the number of hours per day or week that an individual spends on work activities (Aryee, 1992; Frone, Yardley, & Markel, 1997; Parasuraman, Purohit, Godshalk, & Beutell, 1996). Therefore, Hypothesis 1a predicts a positive relationship between work overload and the amount of time allocated to work.

In the family domain, the demands associated with parenthood and the presence of young children have been found to increase the amount of time devoted to the family role (Frone et al., 1997; Parasuraman et al., 1996). Additionally, extensive parental responsibilities have been associated with work–family conflict (Aryee, Luk, Leung, & Lo, 1999; Carlson, 1999; Hammer, Allen, & Grigsby, 1997; Matsui, Ohsawa, & Onglotco, 1995; Netemeyer, Boles, & McMurrian, 1996), presumably because parental responsibilities increase the allocation of time to family activities, which subsequently interferes with the work role. Therefore, Hypothesis 1b predicts a positive relationship between parental responsibilities and the amount of time allocated to family.

A spouse or partner's level of involvement in work and family activities also represents a role pressure that can affect an individual's time allocations. We expect that individuals whose partners identify strongly with the family and spend a great deal of time in family activities are free to devote more time to their own work. The partner's extensive involvement with family enables an individual to reallocate his or her time from the family role to the work role. On the other hand, partners who place substantial importance on their own work and spend extensive time at work are likely to put pressure on individuals to allocate their time to home and family activities (Parasuraman et al., 1996). In other words, we predict that individuals devote extensive time to work when their partners are highly involved in the family (Hypothesis 2a) and that individuals devote extensive time to family when their partners are highly involved in work (Hypothesis 2b).

WORK AND FAMILY IDENTITY SALIENCE AS DETERMINANTS OF TIME ALLOCATIONS

Social identity theory posits that social roles form the basis of an individual's identity (Burke, 1991; Frone, Russell, & Cooper, 1995), and individuals who participate in multiple roles organize their social identities in a hierarchy of salience or centrality (Thoits, 1991). According to social identity theory, the more salient a particular role identity, the more meaning one derives from participation in the role (Thoits, 1991), and therefore the more time one invests in that role (Burke & Reitzes, 1991; Lobel, 1991; Stryker & Serpe, 1994).

Consistent with social identity theory, various indicators of *work identity* salience (e.g., job involvement, work commitment) have been related to the amount of time or effort devoted to work (Dwyer, Fox, & Ganster, 1993; Greenberger & O'Neil, 1993; Lobel & St. Clair, 1992), and *family identity* salience has been associated with the amount of time spent in the family role (Greenberger & O'Neill, 1993). We therefore predicted that work salience is positively related to the amount of time allocated to work (Hypothesis 3a) and that family salience is positively related to the amount of time allocated to family (Hypothesis 3b).

GENDER DIFFERENCES IN THE PREDICTION OF TIME ALLOCATIONS

Men and women often experience their work and family lives in substantially different ways (Friedman & Greenhaus, 2000). Despite full-time employment, dual-earner women still bear the primary responsibility for nurturing and assuring the well-being of the family. The persistent gendered division of responsibility for housework and childcare reflects the strength of traditional gender-based role expectations and normative beliefs about appropriate role behavior.

Although men and women are likely to differ in their allocation of time to work and family activities, it is not clear whether the *process* by which men and women make time allocation decisions is different. Given the lack of theory to guide the development of specific predictions, we did not develop hypotheses regarding gender differences in the determinants of time allocations. Instead, we posed the following questions to explore in this research. Do family variables (parental responsibilities and family salience) have a differential effect on the time allocations of men and women? Do work variables (work overload and work salience) have a differential effect on the time allocations of men and women? Do partner variables (spousal involvements in work and family) have a differential effect on the time allocations of men and women? It is our hope that an examination of these questions will clarify the similarities and differences in the ways that men and women react to cues from the work and family environments in making time allocation decisions.

THE IMPACT OF TIME ALLOCATIONS ON LIFE STRESS

Stress is experienced when individuals appraise a situation as potentially harmful or threatening because it exceeds their coping resources (Lazarus & Folkman, 1984). Although men and women who devote extensive time to their work and family roles might be expected to experience high levels of stress because they feel overwhelmed, fatigued, irritable, and anxious, the evidence linking time allocations to stress-related outcomes is inconsistent. Judge et al. (1994) found that the amount of time devoted to work was inversely related to life satisfaction, whereas time spent with children was unrelated to life satisfaction. On the other hand, Frone et al. (1997) observed no relationship between work time and work distress, but found a positive relationship between parenting time and family distress.

To continue investigation in this area, we examined the impact of work and family time allocations on stress. However, we simultaneously examined the effect of two other factors on stress: (a) the role pressures of work overload and parental responsibilities, which we believe influence time allocation decisions; and (b) work–family conflict, which is often a consequence of extensive time allocations (Greenhaus & Parasuraman, 1999). Given the findings of prior research (Frone et al., 1997; Greenhaus & Parasuraman, 1999; Judge et al., 1994; Parasuraman et al., 1996), we predict that life stress is positively related to work overload and parental responsibilities (Hypothesis 4a), time allocations to work and family (Hypothesis 4b), and work–family conflict (Hypothesis 4c).

Moreover, our inclusion of role pressures, time allocations, and work–family conflict in the same analysis enables us to assess the relative impact of these variables on stress. In particular, because there is reason to believe that role pressures influence time allocations and extensive time allocations produce work–family conflict, we examine whether the effects of role pressures or time allocations on stress are mediated by work–family conflict.

RESEARCH PROCESS

Sample

This study was part of a larger research project on the work and family life of small business owners (Parasuraman et al., 1996). Study participants were contacted in continuing professional education courses for small business owners in two eastern U.S. universities. They were asked to participate in the study if they were married or living with a partner, and if they and their spouse or partner each worked at least 20 hours per week. Each person who met these criteria was given two copies of a survey entitled "Work and Family Research Study," one for the participant to complete and the other for his or her spouse or partner to complete. Partners were instructed to complete the survey independently and mail the completed surveys back to the researchers in separate prepaid envelopes.

The present sample consisted of 73 matched pairs of men and women in dual-earner relationships. In 26 of the couples, both partners were business owners, and in 47 couples, only one partner was a business owner. The men in the sample (M = 42.6 years) were slightly older than the women (M = 40.5 years) and averaged about two more years in their current employment setting than the women (M = 9.2 years for men; 5.9 years for women). The couples were married or living together for an average of 14 years at the time of the study, and approximately 70% of the couples had at least one child living at home. Four fifths of the men and approximately 75% of the women had completed a bachelor's degree or higher level of education.

Measures

Time allocation to work was measured by the following item: "How many hours would you say you work in an average week? Include time spent at the office, time spent traveling, and time spent working at home." Response categories were 1 (20–29 hours), 2 (30–39 hours), 3 (40–49 hours), 4 (50–59 hours), and 5 (60 hours or more). Time allocation to family was measured by the following item: "On average days when you are working, about how much time do you spend on housework and/or child-care?" Response categories were 1 (less than one hour), 2 (1–2 hours), 3 (3–4 hours), and 4 (more than four hours).

Work overload was measured by a four-item scale adapted from Caplan, Cobb, French, Harrison, and Pinneau (1975). Responses to each item were made on a five-point scale ranging from 1 (strongly disagree) to 5 (strongly agree). Responses were averaged to produce a total work overload score (α = .77 for men; α = .82 for women). Parental responsibilities were assessed through the presence of children living at home. Individuals who had one or more children living at home were coded 1, and those who had either no children or had children not living at home were coded 0.

Work salience was assessed with four items from Lodahl and Kejner's (1965) job involvement scale with the word "work" substituted for "job." Responses to each item in the present scale were made on a five-point scale from (1) strongly disagree to (5) strongly agree. Responses were averaged to produce a total work salience score (α = .73 for men; α = .81 for women). Family salience was assessed with three of the work involvement items with the word "family" substituted for "work." (The fourth work involvement item was not thought to be appropriate for translation into a family involvement item.) Responses were averaged to produce a total family salience score (α = .86 for both men and women). A third indicator of identity salience was the relative priority of an individual's career compared to the career of his or her spouse. Respondents indicated on a five-point scale the relative importance of their career and their partner's career. The response was coded such that the higher the score, the greater the priority of the individual's career relative to the spouse's career (Greenhaus, Parasuraman, Granrose, Rabinowitz, & Beutell, 1989).

Work–family conflict was measured by 14 items taken or adapted from the literature. Responses to each item were made on a five-point scale ranging from 1 (strongly disagree) to 5 (strongly agree). Responses were averaged to produce a total work–family conflict score (α = .82 for men; α = .86 for women). A 10-item scale (Parasuraman, Greenhaus, & Granrose, 1992) was used to assess life stress. The items asked individuals to indicate the extent to which they experienced various feelings about things in their life such as being upset, feeling blue, or feeling jumpy and nervous. Responses to each item were made on a five-point scale ranging from 1 (almost never) to 5 (almost all the time) and were averaged to produce a total life stress score (α = .92 for men; α = .93 for women).

Because we matched the surveys of the men and women partners in our sample, women's scores on the work involvement and family involvement scales were used to assess men's spouses' identity salience, and men's scores on these scales were used to assess women's spouses' identity salience. Similarly, women's time spent in work and family activities was used to assess men's spouses' time allocations, and men's time spent in work and family activities was used to assess women's spouses' time allocations.

FINDINGS

Preliminary analyses revealed that men allocated more time to work than did women, whereas women allocated more time to the family than did men. Similarly, work salience and relative career priority were higher for men than for women, and family salience was higher for women than for men. In addition, women experienced a higher level of life stress than did men. Unexpectedly, time allocation to work was unrelated to time allocation to family for men or women.

Tables 8.1 and 8.2 present the results of the multiple regression analyses predicting time allocations to work and family respectively. Consistent with Hypothesis 1a, work overload was positively related to the amount of time allocated to work for dual-earner men and women. Moreover, in support of Hypothesis 1b, parental responsibilities were positively associated with the amount time allocated to family by both men and women.

The findings provided very limited support for Hypothesis 2a. Women whose spouses' family salience was strong allocated more time to work than did women whose spouses' family salience was weak. However, spouses' time allocations to family were unrelated to work time allocations for men or women. Moreover, the data fail to support Hypothesis 2b. Spouses' work salience and work time allocations were unrelated to family time allocations for men or women. The only spouse variable that significantly predicted

TABLE 8.1
Multiple Regression Analyses Predicting
Time Allocation to Work for Men and Women

Step	Predictors	β for Men	β for Women
1.	Role pressures		
	Work overload	.37**	.55**
	Parental responsibilities	.14	−.14
2.	Identity salience		
	Work salience	−.06	.18
	Family salience	−.01	.00
	Relative career priority	.17	.16
3.	Spouse identity salience		
	Spouse work salience	−.08	.23*a
	Spouse family salience	−.20	.29**b
4.	Spouse time allocation to		
	Work	.22	.14
	Family	.15	.15

Note. For men, ΔR^2s are: Step 1 (.16, $p < .01$), Step 2 (.03, ns), Step 3 (.04, ns), Step 4 (.05, ns); for women ΔR^2s are: Step 1 (.31, $p < .01$), Step 2 (.08, $p < .10$), Step 3 (.10, $p < .01$), Step 4 (.03, ns); β weights are shown for the step in which the variable initially entered the regression equation.

* $p < .05$.

** $p < .01$.

[a] Difference between β weights for men and women is marginally significant at $p < .10$.

[b] Difference between β weights for men and women is significant at $p < .01$.

TABLE 8.2
Multiple Regression Analyses Predicting
Time Allocation to Family for Men and Women

Step	Predictors	β for Men	β for Women
1.	Role pressures		
	Work overload	−.15	−.20†
	Parental responsibilities	.22†	.35**
2.	Identity salience		
	Work salience	−.35*a	.08
	Family salience	−.17	−.04
	Relative career priority	−.19	−.24†
3.	Spouse identity salience		
	Spouse work salience	.07	.18
	Spouse family salience	−.07	−.01
4.	Spouse time allocation to		
	Work	.18	.16
	Family	.26*	.40**

Note. For men, ΔR^2s are: Step 1 (.06, ns), Step 2 (.11, $p < .10$), Step 3 (.01, ns), Step 4 (.08, $p < .10$); for women ΔR^2s are: Step 1 (.15, $p < .01$), Step 2 (.04, ns), Step 3 (.03, ns), Step 4 (.12, $p < .05$); β weights are shown for the step in which the variable initially entered the regression equation.

† $p < .10$.

* $p < .05$.

** $p < .01$.

[a] Difference between β weights for men and women is significant at $p < .05$.

TABLE 8.3
Multiple Regression Analyses Predicting Life Stress for Men and Women

Predictors	β for Men			β for Women		
	Step 1	Step 2	Step 3	Step 1	Step 2	Step 3
Step 1						
Work overload	.35**	.40**	.20	.32**	.32**	−.02
Parental responsibilities	.05	.10	.02	.11	.08	.08
Step 2						
Time allocation to work		−.18	−.21†		.04	−.04
Time allocation to family		−.12	−.08		.09	.03
Step 3						
Work-family conflict			.45**			.63**
ΔR²	.13*	.04	.14**	.12*	.01	.25**

Note. † $p < .10$.
  * $p < .05$.
  ** $p < .01$.

time allocations for both men and women was the spouse's time allocation to family. The more time one partner devotes to family life, the more time the other partner devotes to the family. The data provided no support for Hypothesis 3. Work salience and relative career priority were not associated with time spent working, and family salience was unrelated to time allocations to the family.

The effects of role pressures, spouse involvements, and identity salience generally were similar for men and women. However, the results did reveal three significant gender differences in the prediction of time allocations. Work salience detracted from family time more substantially for men than for women, and a spouse's work salience and family salience were more strongly associated with extensive time allocations to work for women than for men.

The results pertaining to the relative effects of role pressures, time allocations, and work–family conflict on life stress (Hypothesis 4) were highly consistent for men and women (Table 8.3). In Step 1 of the analysis, work overload was positively related to life stress. When time allocations to work and family were entered into the analysis in Step 2, work overload continued to predict life stress, and time allocations were unrelated to stress. In the final step of the analysis, work–family conflict emerged as a significant predictor of life stress and work overload was no longer a significant predictor. These results indicate that time allocations had no effect on life stress (providing no support for Hypothesis 4b), work–family conflict had a direct effect on stress (providing strong support for Hypothesis 4c), and work overload had an indirect effect on stress through work–family conflict (providing some support for Hypothesis 4a).

CONCLUSION

The findings of the present research provide insights into the determinants and consequences of time allocations to work and family roles for partners in dual-earner relationships. Our findings indicate that role pressures greatly influence time allocation decisions. Moreover, it is the conflict between work and family roles, rather than the time devoted to each role, that influences the amount of stress that individuals experience in their lives.

Consistent with a rational perspective, the time invested in work and family roles is a function of the demands of the roles. Work overload increased the time allocated to work by men and women alike. This finding, which is consistent with prior research (Aryee, 1992; Frone et al., 1997), demonstrates the behavioral consequences of overload within the work role, and suggests the limited degrees of freedom available to many individuals in not responding to work role demands. Our findings also showed that men and women increase the time allocated to family activities in response to their parental responsibilities, demonstrating the impact of the family environment on time allocation decisions (Frone et al., 1997; Parasuraman et al., 1996).

Contrary to expectations based on a social identity perspective (Burke & Reitzes, 1991; Lobel, 1991; Stryker & Serpe, 1994), work and family salience did not influence work time allocation decisions. However, identity salience was associated with family time allocations, although in a somewhat different way for men and women. For men, the greater the work salience, the less time spent on family activities. For women, the greater the priority of her career as compared to the husband's career, the less time spent on family activities. The explanation for these results, however, is unclear. It might be expected that a focus on work and career would increase the amount of time devoted to work which, in turn, would decrease the amount of time devoted to family activities. However, in the present sample, work identity salience was unrelated to work time allocations, and perhaps more surprisingly, the amount of time spent at work was unrelated to the time allocated to family life. Although speculative, it is possible that work- or career-oriented individuals devote considerable time to community work or to social interactions with colleagues outside of work, either of which could cut into the amount of time spent with the family.

We also found that spouses' involvements in work and family play a more complex role in determining individuals' time allocation decisions than anticipated. In contrast to our predictions, spouses' time involvement in work had no effect on individuals' allocation of time to their families, and spouses' time involvement in family did not influence individuals' allocation of time to their work. We did find, however, a relationship between each spouse's time allocation to family; the more time one spouse devotes to family, the more time the other spouse devotes to family. Of course, we don't know whether this reflects a norm of reciprocity between the partners or the tendency of men and women to choose partners who are similarly oriented to spending time with the family.

We also observed that the more strongly a husband identifies with his family, the more time a wife devotes to her work. Although this finding was consistent with Hypothesis 2a, our prediction was based on the notion that family-oriented spouses would spend more time with the family, which would enable their partners to spend more time at work. However, a spouse's level of family salience was unrelated to the amount of time he or she devoted to the family. Therefore, some other explanation needs to be sought.

The amount of time spent on work or family activities did not produce extensive life stress. Instead, it is the conflict between work and family roles that directly heightens stress. This finding suggests that individuals experience stress when they have difficulties managing the boundaries between different life roles (Friedman & Greenhaus, 2000). Although extensive time commitments produce some challenges for managing role boundaries, clearly time in and of itself is not the major culprit as a life stressor.

Therefore, it is likely that other aspects of the work–family interface determine life stress. Effectively managing role boundaries involves not only juggling time commitments but also learning to avoid transferring stress from one role to another, engaging fully in a role rather than being preoccupied with another role, and learning not to apply behaviors inappropriately from one role to the other (Friedman & Greenhaus, 2000). Our findings clearly highlight the importance of identifying effective ways for dual-earner partners to manage the boundaries between work and family roles.

In summary, the findings of the present study demonstrate the ways in which work and family role pressures, identity salience, and spouse involvements influence the amount of time an individual allocates to work and family roles. The study goes beyond previous research in that it examines within-person work–family variables as well as cross-partner determinants of time allocations. The study confirms the utility of examining relationships of work and family role pressures and identity salience with time allocation decisions. It also underscores the need for further research.

Although there are many different directions that future research may take, our findings suggest one particularly important avenue for additional inquiry—understanding the relationship between the investment of time in work and the investment of time in family. Prior research suggested a negative relationship between time spent at work and time spent with the family (Greenhaus & Parasuraman, 1999), and our predictions were often based on this premise. Yet we observed no relationship between these variables for men or for women.

Apparently, the men and women in our sample did not cut back on their investment in the work role or the family role as time in the other domain increased. Future research should seek to understand when time allocations to work and family roles are inversely related, when they are unrelated, and when, if at all, they are positively related. Such research ideally involves the collection of data from both partners in dual-earner relationships and necessitates the examination of the couple as the unit of study, at least for some of the analyses. We encourage researchers to gain a better understanding of the complex relationships among time allocation decisions to advance our understanding of the process by which individuals and couples respond to the challenges of balancing their work and family commitments.

REFERENCES

Aryee, S. (1992). Antecedents and outcomes of work–family conflict among married professional women: Evidence from Singapore. *Human Relations, 45*, 813–837.

Aryee, S., Luk, V., Leung, A., & Lo, S. (1999). Role stressors, interrole conflict, and well-being: The moderating influence of spousal support and coping behaviors among employed parents in Hong Kong. *Journal of Vocational Behavior, 54*, 259–278.

Buck, M. L., Lee, M. D., MacDermid, S. M., & Smith, S. (2000). Reduced-load work and the experience of time among professionals and managers: Implications for personal and organizational life. In C. L. Cooper, & D. M. Rousseau (Eds.), *Trends in organizational behavior*, Vol. 7 (pp. 13–35). West Sussex, UK: John Wiley & Sons.

Burke, P. J. (1991). Identity processes and social stress. *American Sociological Review, 56*, 836–849.

Burke, P. J., & Reitzes, D. C. (1991). An identity approach to commitment. *Social Psychology Quarterly, 54*, 239–251.

Caplan, R. D., Cobb, S., French, J. R. P., Harrison, R. V., & Pinneau, S. R. (1975). *Job demands and worker health: Main effects and occupational differences*. Washington, DC: Department of Health, Education and Welfare.

Carlson, D. S. (1999). Personality and role variables as predictors of three forms of work–family conflict. *Journal of Vocational Behavior, 55*, 236–253.

Dwyer, D. J., Fox, M. L., & Ganster, D. C. (1993, August). *The relationship of stress and the conflict between work and nonwork domains: An investigation of the effects of work and nonwork time and energy*. Paper presented at the Annual Meeting of the Academy of Management, Atlanta, GA.

Edwards, J. R., & Rothbard, N. P. (2000). Mechanisms linking work and family: Clarifying the relationship between work and family constructs. *Academy of Management Review, 25*, 178–199.

Friedman, S. D., & Greenhaus, J. H. (2000). *Work and family—Allies or enemies? What happens when business professionals confront life choices*. New York: Oxford University Press.

Frone, M. R., Russell, M., & Cooper, M. L. (1995). Job stressors, job involvement and employee health: A test of identity theory. *Journal of Occupational and Organizational Psychology, 68,* 1–11.

Frone, M. R., Yardley, J. K., & Markel, K. S. (1997). Developing and testing an integrative model of the work–family interface. *Journal of Vocational Behavior, 50,* 145–167.

Greenberger, E., & O'Neil, R. (1993). Spouse, parent, worker: Role commitments and role-related experiences in the construction of adults' well-being. *Developmental Psychology, 29,* 181–197.

Greenhaus, J. H., Bedeian, A. G., & Mossholder, K. W. (1987). Work experiences, job performance, and feelings of personal and family well-being. *Journal of Vocational Behavior, 31,* 200–215.

Greenhaus, J. H., & Parasuraman, S. (1999). Research on work, family, and gender: Current status and future directions. In G. N. Powell (Ed.), *Handbook of gender and work* (pp. 391–412). Newbury Park, CA: Sage.

Greenhaus, J. H., Parasuraman, S., Granrose, C. S., Rabinowitz, S., & Beutell, N. J. (1989). Sources of work–family conflict among two-career couples. *Journal of Vocational Behavior, 34,* 133–153.

Greenhaus, J. H., & Powell, G. N. (2000, August). *When work and family collide: Choices and conflict between competing roles demands.* Paper presented at the Annual Meeting of the Academy of Management, Toronto.

Gutek, B. A., Searle, S., & Klepa, L. (1991). Rational versus gender role explanations for work–family conflict. *Journal of Applied Psychology, 76,* 560–568.

Hammer, L. B., Allen, E., & Grigsby, T. D. (1997). Work–family conflict in dual-earner couples: Within-individual and crossover effects of work and family. *Journal of Vocational Behavior, 50,* 185–203.

Judge, T. A., Boudreau, J. W., & Bretz, R. D. (1994). Job and life attitudes of male executives. *Journal of Applied Psychology, 79,* 767–782.

Kahn, R. L., Wolfe, D. M., Quinn, R., Snoek, J. D., & Rosenthal, R. A. (1964). *Organizational stress.* New York: Wiley.

Lazarus, R. S., & Folkman, A. (1984). *Stress, coping, and adaptation.* New York: Springer.

Lobel, S. A. (1991). Allocation of investment in work and family roles: Alternative theories and implications for research. *Academy of Management Review, 16,* 507–521.

Lobel, S. A., & St. Clair, L. (1992). Effects of family responsibilities, gender, and career identity salience on performance outcomes. *Academy of Management Journal, 35,* 1057–1069.

Lodahl, T. M., & Kejner, M. (1965). Definition and measurement of job involvement. *Journal of Applied Psychology, 49,* 24–33.

Matsui, T., Ohsawa, T., & Onglotco, M. (1995). Work–family conflict and the stress-buffering effects of husband support and coping behavior among Japanese married working women. *Journal of Vocational Behavior, 47,* 178–192.

Netemeyer, R. G., Boles, J. S., & McMurrian, R. (1996). Development and validation of work–family conflict and family–work conflict scales. *Journal of Applied Psychology, 81,* 400–410.

O'Driscoll, M. P., Ilgen, D. R., & Hildreth, K. (1992). Time devoted to job and off-job activities, interrole conflict, and affective experiences. *Journal of Applied Psychology, 77,* 272–279.

Parasuraman, S., Greenhaus, J. H., & Granrose, C. S. (1992). Role stressors, social support, and well-being among two-career couples. *Journal of Organizational Behavior, 13,* 339–356.

Parasuraman, S., Greenhaus, J. H., & Linnehan, F. (2000). Time, person–career fit, and the boundaryless career. In C. L. Cooper, & D. M. Rousseau (Eds.), *Trends in organizational behavior,* Vol. 7 (pp. 63–78). West Sussex, UK: John Wiley & Sons.

Parasuraman, S., Purohit, Y. S., Godshalk, V. M., & Beutell, N. J. (1996). Work and family variables, entrepreneurial career success, and psychological well-being. *Journal of Vocational Behavior, 48,* 275–300.

Stryker, S., & Serpe, R. T. (1994). Identity salience and psychological centrality: Equivalent, overlapping, or complementary concepts? *Social Psychology Quarterly, 57,* 16–35.

Thoits, P. A. (1991). On merging identity theory and stress research. *Social Psychology Quarterly, 54,* 101–112.

9

GENDER ASYMMETRY
IN CROSSOVER RESEARCH

MINA WESTMAN

This chapter deals with the role of gender in crossover research. The first section defines the crossover concept and distinguishes it from other work–family approaches. The next section presents a model of crossover including its possible mechanisms. This is followed by a research review on crossover of stress and strain. Next, gender is introduced as a moderating variable in the stress–strain process, and we extrapolate its role in the crossover process.

WORK–FAMILY INTERFACE:
FROM SEGMENTATION TO CROSSOVER

Scholars in the work–family domain rely on constructs such as segmentation, compensation, and spillover to characterize the process by which work and family are linked (Piotrkowski, 1979; Zedeck, 1992). *Segmentation* postulates that the work and family domains are distinct, serve different functions, and exist side by side—a separation that allows compartmentalization of one's life (Dubin, 1973). The *compensation* notion is that there is an inverse relationship between work and family such that people make different investments in one in an attempt to make up for what is missing in the other (Staines, 1980). The *spillover* model assumes a similarity between what occurs in the work and family domains (Staines, 1980). The spillover model postulates that in spite of physical and temporal boundaries between work and family, emotions, attitudes, and behaviors carry over from one domain to the other (Piotrkowski, 1979).

Bolger, DeLongis, Kessler, & Wethington (1989) differentiated between two situations: *spillover*—stress experienced in one domain of life results in stress in the other domain for the same individual; and *crossover*—stress experienced in the workplace by the individual leads to stress being experienced by his or her spouse at home. Whereas spillover is an *intraindividual* transmission of stress, crossover is a dyadic, *interpersonal* transmission of stress or strain. Thus, crossover research is based on the propositions of the spillover model, recognizing the fluid boundaries between work and family life. It maintains that spillover is a necessary, but not a sufficient, condition for crossover. The crossover model adds another level of analysis to previous approaches by adding the interpersonal level and the dyad as an additional focus of research.

THE CROSSOVER MODEL: CORE CONSTRUCTS AND PATHS

Westman's crossover model (Westman, 2001) integrates crossover research into a job–stress model and anchors it in systems theory (Bronfenbrenner, 1977) and in role theory (Kahn, Wolfe, Quinn, Snoek, & Rosenthal, 1964). Using systems theory, Bronfenbrenner (1977) made the point that because components within any system tend to interrelate and affect each other, processes operating in different settings are not independent of each other. The usefulness of role theory (Kahn et al., 1964) as a basis for crossover research is that it underscores the interrelations between a focal person and his or her role senders in the work setting and in other settings where the individual functions.

With the accumulated findings of crossover research (Jones & Fletcher, 1993; Long & Voges, 1987; Westman & Etzion, 1995), it is reasonable to posit that variables reflecting job and family demands are antecedents of the crossover process. Therefore, the conceptual model of crossover classifies a selected array of stressors as antecedent influences of the crossover process. Furthermore, the model posits interpersonal variables and personal attributes as possible mediators and moderators.

Figure 9.1 distinguishes among five dimensions of the crossover process: job and family stress, life events, strain, personal attributes, and the interaction process. Starting at the left, the model shows that the received role of the individual may lead to strain of the same individual (Boxes A & B; Arrows 1a &1b). Job-related strains, according to Jex and Beehr (1991), are behavioral, psychological, or physical outcomes resulting from the experience of stress. Furthermore, the experienced stress and strain of one individual may cause stress and strain directly in the other individual (Arrows 2a & 2b).

Although research has identified several antecedent influences such as job demands on the crossover process, the psychological process mediating these linkages remains to be explored. Detecting the main underlying mechanisms of the crossover process is a basis for developing a systematic theoretical and empirical model in crossover research. In order to unravel these mechanisms, Westman's (2001) model includes mediators (interpersonal relations) and moderators (individual attributes) affecting the crossover process.

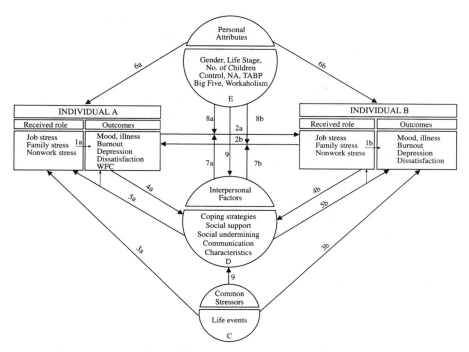

Individuals A & B act as focal persons interchangeably

Figure 9.1. Conceptual framework for crossover research.

PROPOSED MECHANISMS FOR THE CROSSOVER PROCESS

The crossover literature reveals no systematic theoretical and empirical model that distinguishes among the possible explanations of crossover effects. Few researchers have considered how workplace demands of job incumbents translate into the poor well-being of their spouses (Arrows 2a & 2b in the model). A better understanding of these processes will enable identification of effective strategies for coping with stress and strain crossover. Westman and Vinokur (1998) have specified three main mechanisms underlying the crossover process: empathy, common stressors, and an indirect process. The literature review (see Table 9.1), details empirical studies that investigated the crossover process from different angles. As can be seen from the literature review, role stressors are the main antecedents in the crossover process. Furthermore, most studies explored the direct crossover between spouses whereas only a few investigated the indirect one.

Direct Empathetic Crossover

The first proposed mechanism of the crossover process is that stress causes strain that crosses over *directly* from one partner to the other. The basis for this view is the finding that crossover effects appear between closely

TABLE 9.1

Summary of Characteristics and Findings of Crossover Studies

Study/Sample	Crossover of[a]	Direction of Crossover[a]	Mediating Variables[a]	Design/Data Collection/Analyses	Findings[a]
Barnett et al. (1995), 210 dual-earner couples	Distress	H to W and W to H	Commitment	Longitudinal, three waves data collection	Increase in one partner's distress over time was mirrored in the changes in distress of the other.
Beehr, Johnson, & Nieva (1995), 177 male and female police officers and their spouses	Coping strategies to spouses' well-being	Police officers to spouses		Cross-sectional, vignettes	Police officers' coping strategies were positively related to spouse's well-being.
Bolger et al. (1989), 166 married couples	Job stress to home stress	H to W		Longitudinal, daily diaries	One spouse's job stress affected the other spouse's stress at home.
Booth (1977), 560 couples	W's occupational status on H's marital satisfaction.	W to H	Tenure, division of labor	Cross-sectional	W's employment had no impact on H's well-being.
Burke, Weir, & DuWors (1980), 85 senior administrators of correctional institutes and their spouses	Occupational demands to strain	H to W	W's life demands W's received social support	Cross-sectional	H's job demands were related to wives' dissatisfaction, decreased social participation, and increased psychosomatic symptoms.
Eckenrode & Gore (1981), 356 women	Significant other's life event on women's health	Significant others to women	Demographic variables	Cross-sectional	Frequency of significant others' life events affected women's health status and health behavior.

Greenhaus & Parasuraman (1987), 425 couples	W's employment status on H's job satisfaction and quality of life	W to H	Cross-sectional	Wives' employment was positively related to husbands' job satisfaction and quality of life.
Hammer, Allen, & Grigsby (1997), 399 couples	Work–family conflict	W to H and H to W	Cross-sectional	Crossover effects of WFC from husbands to wives and vice versa.
Haynes, Eaker, & Feinleib (1983), 269 couples	W's profession—H's heart disease.	W to H	Longitudinal (10 years)	Hs of employed Ws in white-collar jobs were over 3 times more likely to develop CHD than those married to blue-collar workers or housewives.
Jackson & Maslach (1982), 142 police officers and their spouses	H's job stress on W's dissatisfaction and distress.	H to W	Cross-sectional	H's stress affected their coping and the distress, and dissatisfaction of W.
Jones & Fletcher (1993), 60 working couples	Job and domestic stresses to evening mood–mental well-being.	H to W and W to H	Cross-sectional	Spouses have accurate perceptions of their partners' jobs. Transmission of stress from H to W especially H in high-stress jobs.
Long & Voges (1987), 301 prison officers and their wives	H's job stress to well-being of W	H to W	Cross-sectional	H's stress is related to W's stress and strain.
Mitchell, Cronkite, & Moos (1983), 157 couples	Negative events and ongoing strain to partners' depression	H to W	Cross-sectional	Partners' events and strain were related to partners' depression.

(continued)

TABLE 9.1
(Continued)

Study/Sample	Crossover of[a]	Direction of Crossover[a]	Mediating Variables[a]	Design/Data Collection/Analyses	Findings[a]
Parasuraman, Greenhaus, & Granrose (1992), 119 couples	Role stressors and WFC to partners' family satisfaction	W to H		Cross-sectional. Moderated regression analysis	Females' family role stressors were negatively related to their spouses' family satisfaction. Males' work and family stressors and WFC did not affect their spouses' family satisfaction.
Riley & Eckenrode (1986), 314 women	H's life events to W's distress	H to W	Personal resources	Cross-sectional	Women with lower levels of personal resources were distressed by the life events of their significant others.
Roberts & O'Keefe (1981), 752 couples	W's occupational status on H's stress levels	W to H	Income, education, and occupation	Cross-sectional	W's employment status had little or no effect on H's stress experience.
Rook, Dooley, & Catalano (1991), 1,383 married females (a second interview with a subset of 92)	H's stress to W's psychological distress	H to W	Marital tension, social support, wives' life events	Longitudinal, telephone interviews	H's job stress was associated with W's distress.
Rosenfield (1980), 60 married couples	W's occupational status to H's distress	W to H		Cross-sectional	Ws' employment was positively related to Hs' distress.
Rosenfield (1992), 60 married couples	W's occupational status to H's well-being	W to H	Income, share in domestic labor	Cross-sectional	Ws' employment was negatively related to Hs' well-being only when Ws' employment decreased Hs' relative income and increased their share of domestic labor.

Study	Type of Outcome	Direction of Crossover[a]	Mediator/Moderator	Design	Findings
Staines, Pottic, & Fudge (1986), 408 husbands to housewives, 208 husbands to wives working for pay	W's employment status on H's job and life satisfaction	W to H	Husbands' adequacy as breadwinner	Cross-sectional	Hs of employed Ws registered lower job and life satisfaction than Hs of housewives.
Vinokur, Price, & Caplan (1996), 815 job-seekers and their spouses	Depression	H to W and W to H	Economic hardship, transactions between couples	Longitudinal, SEM	Partners' depression is affected by common stressors and nonsupportive and undermining transactions.
Westman & Etzion (1995), 101 career officers and their working wives	Burnout	W to H and H to W	Partner's job stress, sense of control, social support	Cross-sectional, SEM	Symmetric crossover effects of burnout from husbands to wives and vice versa.
Westman, Etzion, & Segev (2000), 420 females in the American Air Force and their spouses	Work–Family Conflict	H's to W and W's to H's	Social support	Cross-sectional	W's WFC affected H's WFC and H's WFC affected W's WFC
Westman, Etzion, & Danon (2001), 98 couples from a downsizing organization	Burnout	H's to W's and W's to H's	Social undermining, sense of control	Cross-sectional	H's burnout affected W's burnout.
Westman & Vinokur (1998), 232 couples	Depression	W to H and H to W	Social undermining	Longitudinal, SEM	Direct crossover of depression. Life events impacted the crossover process and social undermining mediated it.

Note. [a] H—husbands; W—wives.

related partners who care for each other and share the greater part of their lives together. Accordingly, strain in one partner produces an empathetic reaction in the other that increases his or her level of strain. This view is supported by social learning theorists (e.g., Bandura, 1969) who have explained the transmission of emotions as a conscious processing of information. They suggest that individuals imagine how they would feel in the position of another and thus come to experience and share their feelings.

This view is also supported by Eckenrode and Gore's (1981) findings that men's life events increased the amount of stress their wives experienced. They suggested that the effect of one's life events on the spouse's distress might be the result of empathy expressed in reports like "We feel their pain is our own" (p. 771).

Spuriousness—Common Stressors

The *common stressors* mechanism suggested by Westman and Vinokur (1998) is that the relationship between spouses' strain is spurious. What appears to be a crossover effect is the result of common stressors in a shared environment increasing the strain in both partners (Arrows 3a & 3b). Hobfoll and London (1986) suggested that many stressors make simultaneous demands on both individuals in a dyad. Vinokur, Price, and Caplan (1996) found that family financial strain had an impact on the crossover process and on the supportive and undermining transactions between the partners. Another common stressor that may affect both partners is stressful life events (e.g., divorce, job transfers).

Unfortunately, most crossover studies focus on job stress and do not include life events as possible common stressors that might affect both spouses. An exception is Rook, Dooley, & Catalano (1991), who used husbands' life events as their measure of stress, although these stressful events were reported by the wives. The validity of such a measure is questionable, but it is an indication of the way wives perceive and are affected by their husbands' life events. Westman and Vinokur (1998) found that common life events affected the crossover process by increasing each partner's depression.

CROSSOVER AS AN INDIRECT PROCESS

The explanation of crossover as an indirect process[1] posits a mediating effect that includes coping mechanisms, communication characteristics, social support, and social undermining, which have been widely identified

---

[1]As can be seen from Figure 9.1, the indirect process also relates to the communication characteristics and the social undermining process. However, as we did not find in the literature any impact of gender on these processes we did not relate to these variables in the current chapter.

as mediators of stress and strain responses (Coyne & Downey, 1991; Jones & Fletcher, 1993).

Coping Strategies

Numerous studies suggest that problem-focused strategies are positively related to well-being, whereas emotion-focused strategies are negatively related to well-being (Westman & Shirom, 1995). Ptacek, Smith, and Dodge (1994) propose that gender differences in coping arise from early socialization that promotes stereotypes of men as independent, instrumental, and rational, and women as emotional, supportive, and dependent. Most of the studies examined the direct effect of individuals' coping on their own well-being, or the moderating effects of coping on the relationship between stress and strain (Edwards, Baglioni, & Cooper, 1990). However, only a few studies examined the relationship between individuals' coping and their spouses' well-being. One's strain can affect one's own coping strategies as well as the partner's coping strategies. Therefore, coping can be viewed as either a predictor of one's strain and of the spouse's strain (Beehr, Johnson, & Nieva, 1995), or as a mediator of the relationship between one's stress and the spouse's stress or strain (Jackson & Maslach, 1982).

Certain coping strategies may enhance the well-being of the coper while resulting in worse outcomes for the partner. For example, withdrawal from stressful episodes may be functional for the individual adopting such a strategy, but may involve delegating responsibilities to a partner who is not prepared to assume the added burdens. The possibility that problem-focused coping may negatively affect those close to the focal respondent has been considered by Hobfoll, Dunahoo, Ben-Porath, and Monnier (1994).

Social Support

Social support refers to transactions with others that provide the recipient with support (House, 1981). An interpersonal interaction style that does not provide enough support, or demands support from a spouse unable to provide it, can produce a crossover effect and also affect the intensity of the crossover process.

According to Hobfoll et al. (1994), many researchers have demonstrated the beneficial effects of social support for the recipient, but have overlooked its impact on the donor. The role of the donor in the interaction may be one of the keys to the crossover process. Riley and Eckenrode (1986) found that couples are influenced by each other's distress indirectly, via the other's reduced social support. They noted that the demand for social support caused a drain in others in the dyad or in the social group. They underscored two processes to explain this finding: the transaction of support, whereby individuals share their resources with the needy, and a diminishing of resources experienced by the providers of social support as they share and empathetically experience the demands of the needy. These findings indicate that stress experienced by one partner creates a demand for support, and the other partner is apt to feel anxious or guilty when unable to meet this demand. Conversely, a crisis experienced by an individual may diminish the social support available to his or her partner. Similarly, Hobfoll and London (1986), studying Israeli women whose relatives were mobilized to serve in the military during wartime, found that social support aided the recipients but depleted the resources of the donors at a time when they also needed their stress resistance resources. The indications are that social support is a finite resource and that people compete for it in a zero-sum game. Therefore, expected donors experience strain either because of their inability to provide support or because of their depleted resources.

PERSONAL ATTRIBUTES AS MODERATING VARIABLES

There is no systematic empirical evidence on the contribution of personal attributes to the crossover process. They can influence stress and strain directly as exogenous variables (Arrows 6a & 6b) or indirectly (Arrows 8a & 8b) as moderators that interact with Person A's job stress and strain in explaining Person B's stress and strain. The most frequently investigated characteristics are gender, life stage, and number of children, and generally have been weakly related to crossover.

In order to relate to the role of gender in the crossover process we focus on the following issues:

1. Gender differences in the antecedents and outcomes of work stress
2. Gender and the crossover of stress and strain
3. Gender differences in the direction of crossover
4. Gender differences in the crossover process

GENDER DIFFERENCES IN STRESS RESEARCH: SOURCES AND OUTCOMES

The past 20 years have seen organizations undergo sweeping changes. The participation of women in the labor market has increased dramatically, as has the range of occupations in which women are employed. Women are now found at all levels of organizations. Nevertheless, only a few researchers have focused exclusively on the role of gender in the crossover process.[2] Because the literature review revealed a dearth of information on the rela-

---

[2] This topic is well covered in other chapters in this book; therefore, it is summarized here briefly.

tionship between gender and the crossover process, this chapter draws on research into gender and stress and strain. The following section discusses the gender differences in stress, strain, and the relationship between them. We begin by addressing the general impact of gender in stress research and move on to the unique role of gender in crossover research.

Reviewing stress research in organizations, some researchers have found little or no evidence of gender influences in perception of job stress and stress–strain relationships (Di Salvo, Lubbers, Rossi, & Lewis, 1995; Martocchio & O'Leary, 1989). On the other hand, Tuosignant, Brosseau, and Tremblay (1987) among others, indicated that one of the most consistent results in mental health research is that women report significantly more symptoms than men. Furthermore, recent studies suggest that the level of depressive symptoms in women continues to be higher than in men, despite women's substantial gains in education and career opportunity (Mirowski & Ross, 1995).

Similarly, Jick and Mitz (1985), who reviewed the empirical evidence for sex differences in work stress, found that women tend to report higher rates of psychological distress than do men. They suggested that the difficulty in identifying gender-related differences in workplace stress may be due to sampling bias—men are overrepresented in managerial positions and women are more frequently found in clerical and service jobs. This is well illustrated by Spielberger and Reheiser's (1994) findings, which indicated that gender-related differences in occupational stress are determined by differences in the perceived severity of specific stressors, and in the frequency that men and women experience these stressors. Spielberger and Reheiser's (1994) findings indicate that even though the number of men and women in their sample was similar, there were nearly twice as many men in the higher occupational level group, and more than twice as many women in the lower group. They concluded that gender is extremely important in determining how different workplace stressors are perceived, and that men and women experience different frequencies of various stressors, depending to some extent on their occupational level. A review conducted by Matuszek, Nelson, and Quick (1995) indicated that women experience greater stress and poorer mental health than do men. Similarly, Baruch, Biener, and Barnett (1987) observed that women tend to occupy organizational positions that are inherently low in control, and have less power and authority, and thus experience more strain. Barnett and Brennan (1997) and Parasuraman, Greenhaus, and Granrose (1992) highlighted another angle, maintaining that because of the inequality in response to home demands, women report higher levels of distress than do men.

The diversity in research methodology, sampling procedures, and measures employed in these studies may account for these contradictory results. The dispute on whether women experience unique forms of occupational stress is far from resolved and the research evidence is not clear-cut.

Nelson and Burke (2000), in summarizing the current research with regard to gender, indicated that while women may experience unique stressors and respond to them differently than do men, gender interacts with predictors of stress in such complex ways that trying to isolate the role of gender in stress may be almost impossible.

The remainder of this chapter will suggest the various roles gender plays in the stress and strain crossover process.

GENDER AND THE CROSSOVER OF STRESS AND STRAIN

The impact of gender in the crossover process can be detected at several junctions. Gender's impact on perceived stress and strain and their relationships is relevant to the first suggested mechanism of the crossover process—direct crossover between spouses. Gender is a potential moderator of the impact of one's stress on the spouse's strain because of differences in the traditional role demands and expectations for men and women (Lambert, 1990). There is some indication that women are more susceptible than men to the impact of stressors affecting their partners. Kessler and McLeod (1984) showed that events happening to significant others are more distressing for women than for men. They suggested that because of women's greater involvement in family affairs, they become more sensitive not only to the stressful events that they experience themselves, but also to those that affect their spouses.

Hobfoll and Shirom (1993) suggested that the increase in the number of women entering the workforce has resulted not only in a great increase in stress in the work–family interface for women, but also in a similar increase in stress for men, part of which may be a result of crossover. This increase has focused attention on the effects of wives' employment, but not on the effects that their job stress may have on their husbands' well-being. Despite the significant increase in the number of women who have joined the workforce at all job levels, no research has focused exclusively on the crossover of stress from wives to husbands. Some researchers have investigated the impact of women's employment status, but not their job stress, on husbands' well being (Booth, 1977; Burke & Weir, 1976; Greenhaus & Parasuraman, 1987; Haynes, Eaker, & Feinleib, 1983; Rosenfield, 1980, 1992; Staines, Pottic, & Fudge, 1986).[3]

Several studies found that females' employment status had significant negative effects on the well-being of their male partners. Focusing on whether having an employed wife affected a husband's well-being, Greenhaus and Parasuraman (1987) found that husbands of employed women displayed lower levels of job satisfaction and quality of life than husbands of

---

[3] Although these references are 15–20 years old and are not reflective of the situation today, they are important for the issue of the development of crossover research.

nonemployed women. This finding may reflect a status effect indicating that men of nonemployed women are employed at the top of the occupational ladder and therefore more satisfied with their jobs. Similarly, Burke and Weir (1976) found that husbands of employed wives experienced more job pressure, and lower job and marital satisfaction than husbands of housewives. Trying to replicate these findings, Booth (1977) found that husbands of employed women were in poorer health and less content with their marriages than husbands of housewives, although they did not experience more stress. An alternative explanation is that when men have poor health, their wives must work to make up for the husbands' lost income. Roberts and O'Keefe's (1981) results corroborated those of Booth (1977), that wives' employment had little or no relationship with the levels of stress experienced by their husbands.

However, Rosenfield (1980) corroborated the findings reported by Burke and Weir (1976) that men whose wives were employed reported more distress than those whose wives were not. A later study by Rosenfield (1992) found that it was not the wives' employment per se that affected the husbands' well-being, but the impact on the husbands' status in the family. Only when the wives' employment decreased the husbands' relative income and increased their share of domestic labor was women's employment negative for husbands' psychological well-being. Similarly, Staines, Pottic, and Fudge (1985) found that feeling inadequate as a breadwinner led to the lower job and life satisfaction detected among husbands of employed women.

Although researchers have inferred causal relationships from wives' employment to husbands' well-being, the findings are equivocal and the methodology inadequate to support the crossover hypothesis. The reviewed studies neither specified which element of the wives' employment caused husbands' strain, nor eliminated the possibility that it was the husbands' own job stress that was causing their strain. Considering the findings of crossover from wives' employment to husbands' job stress and strain, perhaps it is not the fact of employment, but rather wives' job stress that affects the crossover process of stress and strain from wives to their husbands. Adequate resolution of the question as to whether, and under what conditions, the employment status of wives constitutes a risk factor for depression for husbands requires a prospective research design in which wives' job stress is measured and controlled.

GENDER DIFFERENCES IN THE DIRECTION OF CROSSOVER

Evidence concerning gender differences in the crossover process is not consistent. The majority of crossover studies have examined the effects of men's job stress on their wives. Because men were (and still are) considered breadwinners, there is not enough research on bidirectional crossover. Only

8 of the 25 reviewed studies on crossover have investigated both spouses and examined bidirectional crossover of stress or strain (Barnett, Raudenbush, Brennan, Pleck, & Marshall, 1995; Hammer, Allen, & Grigsby, 1997; Jones & Fletcher, 1993; Parasuraman et al., 1992; Westman & Etzion, 1995; Westman, Etzion, & Danon, 2001; Westman, Etzion, & Segev, 2000; Westman & Vinokur, 1998). Although five of these studies found bidirectional crossover of stress and strain between spouses (Barnett et al., 1995; Hammer et al., 1997; Westman & Etzion, 1995; Westman & Vinokur, 1998; Westman et al., 2000), three found only unidirectional crossover from husband to wife. (Jones & Fletcher, 1993; Parasuraman et al. 1992; Westman et al., 2001).

Bidirectional Crossover

Westman and Etzion (1995) demonstrated a crossover of burnout from career army officers to their spouses and vice versa, after controlling for husband's and wife's own job stress. Hammer et al. (1997), who were the first to investigate crossover of work–family conflict (WFC), found a bidirectional crossover of WFC. After controlling for work salience, flexibility, and family involvement, husbands' WFC accounted for an additional percentage of the explained variance on wives' WFC, and wives' WFC accounted for an additional percentage of the explained variance of husbands' WFC. Similarly, Westman et al. (2000) investigated the crossover of WFC in a sample of women in the U.S. Air Force and their spouses. They found bidirectional crossover of WFC after controlling for each individual's job and life stress. Husbands' and wives' WFC accounted for an additional percentage of the explained variance in their spouses' WFC.

Although these three studies employed cross-sectional designs, the bidirectional nature of the crossover effect also was demonstrated in studies using longitudinal designs. In longitudinal studies, Barnett et al. (1995) and Westman and Vinokur (1998) found bidirectional crossover of distress and depression from husbands to wives and from wives to husbands. For example, Barnett et al.'s (1995) longitudinal study of dual-earner couples found that changes in the job experiences of one partner affected the psychological distress of the other partner. Similarly, Westman and Vinokur (1998) found a crossover of depression from husbands to wives and from wives to husbands. These findings indicate that over time, changes in employees' distress are not only a function of their own job stress, but also of their partners' job stress and distress.

Unidirectional Crossover

A few studies using bidirectional designs found only unidirectional crossover, however. Parasuraman et al., (1992), investigating dual-career couples, found that whereas men's work and family stressors and WFC did not affect their wives' family satisfaction, women's family role stressors had a significant negative relationship with their husbands' family satisfaction. Similarly, Galambos and Walters (1992) found that wives' long working hours were associated with husbands' anxiety and depression, whereas husbands' working hours were unrelated to the psychological well-being of their wives.

While these studies found a unidirectional crossover from wives to husbands, other studies found only a unidirectional crossover from husbands to wives. In a sample comprised of 98 couples working in the same organization, witnessing and anticipating downsizing, Westman et al. (2001) found crossover of burnout from husbands to wives, but not from wives to husbands. Similarly, Jones and Fletcher (1993) reported a crossover effect of men's job demands on wives' psychological health, but found no effect of women's job demands on husbands' psychological health. One explanation for these findings may be the wives' occupations. The wives in Jones and Fletcher's original study did not report high levels of job stress. However, when Jones and Fletcher analyzed a subsample in which both spouses were characterized by high stress, they did find a bidirectional crossover effect.

These findings indicate that the level of stress and strain is an important component in the crossover process (see Westman, 2001). Whether the crossover is from male to female or female to male is at least partially dependent on the relative job status of the respondents. In sum, although the literature demonstrates gender differences in stress and strain, the crossover literature does not demonstrate such differences in the direction of crossover when women hold high-stress jobs. Mean levels of stress and strain are thus very relevant to crossover research at both the individual and the occupation level.

GENDER DIFFERENCES IN THE CROSSOVER PROCESS: THE INTERACTION PROCESS

A well-documented explanation for the crossover process is that the interaction process focuses on coping and social support. Differences in coping strategies between husbands and wives and the impact of husbands' stress on wives' coping are notable. Furthermore, the salient role of the differences in the function and "price" of social support between males and females highlights the gender differences in the crossover process.

Gender Differences in Coping

Burke, Weir, and Duwors (1980) found that wives whose husbands reported high job demands used more emotion-focused coping strategies, such as distraction, explosive outbursts, and talking to others.[4] However,

---

[4]A general discussion of gender differences in coping can be found in chapter 6.

women used problem-focused coping strategies when their husbands reported lower job demands. Kahn et al.'s (1985) findings that spouses of depressed persons used more aggressive strategies support this direction. The results supporting the second perspective may imply that women who use less constructive coping strategies experience greater crossover of stress from their husbands than do women using problem-focused strategies.

Gender Differences in Social Support

Research on social support has increasingly characterized support seeking, giving, and utilization of various sources of support as processes that involve men and women differently.[5] Kunkel and Burleson (1998) indicate that the general conclusion of the research examining gender differences in social support is that women tend to be more affectively oriented, whereas men tend to be more instrumentally oriented. Summarizing studies concerning social support, they assert that women are more willing to inquire about upsetting situations, provide emotional support, seek support, and employ supportive strategies that directly confront emotions. Women also focus on emotion when providing support. They conclude that men and women clearly differ in their propensity to provide and seek support, as well as in the strategies they employ when attempting to provide support. All these issues are relevant to the crossover process, emphasizing the role of women as donors of social support.

Similarly, Kessler and McLeod (1984) found that caring for a wide network of people was an additional burden for women, and this support translated into transmission of stress from their network to themselves. Furthermore, Wethington and McLeod (1987) found that women are likely to be embedded in family and community networks and tend to suffer from other people's problems.

Recent research on women's responses to stress has focused on their "tend-and-befriend" reaction, as opposed to men's "fight-or-flight" response (Taylor et al., 2000).[6] *Tending* involves nurturing activities designed to protect the self and the offspring, promote safety, and reduce stress; *befriending* is the creation and maintenance of social networks that may add to this process. Taylor et al. (2000) maintain that women's responses to stress are characterized by patterns that involve joining social groups and developing social grouping for the exchange of resources. Thus, they act as donors and are more susceptible to the crossover process.

---

[5] For a detailed discussion of gender differences in social support research, see chapter 6.
[6] For a more full description of the "tend-and-befriend" issue, see chapter 1.

CONCLUSION

The major social change driving research in recent decades has been the growth of women's participation in all areas of the labor market, and the associated changes in families. The reviewed literature indicates that gender differences in the perception of stress and strain, and in the relationship between stress and strain do exist. Furthermore, gender may affect one's vulnerability to stress and the possession and use of resources such as coping strategies and social support. Therefore, gender may be a crucial issue in crossover. However, neither theory nor empirical evidence gives adequate guidance on how gender differences may be expected to affect the impact of the crossover process. Research results concerning the relationships between gender and the crossover process are inconclusive.

Reviewing the gender differences literature, it is apparent that some researchers are interested primarily in gender differences in the relations among the variables in the model. Some researchers, however, mix and confuse the results on gender differences in relations and gender differences in mean levels, which are distinct issues. Gender differences in the level of the model's variables provide no evidence of the possibility of gender differences in the relationships among the variables. The opposite is also true. Gender differences in relationships between variables are not directly relevant to the issue of gender differences in the means. In sum, subgroup differences in means and subgroup differences in relations among variables are independent of each other. One can not use research in one issue to inform or formulate hypotheses regarding the other. Therefore, we have to be very careful in extrapolating existing findings concerning gender differences to crossover research.

However, some of the crossover findings indicate that the crossover process is unidirectional, or at least stronger from husbands to wives, who are more frequently the recipients of the husbands' stress and strain. There are at least three groups of findings that support this contention.

1. Women experience higher levels of distress and therefore are less resilient when facing the stress and strain of their husbands. This issue is affected by the accepted idea of men as breadwinners.
2. Women are more empathetic to the stress of their husbands and therefore more vulnerable to the crossover process.
3. Women are more vulnerable to the crossover process because of their role as providers of social support.

Several aspects of the relationship between gender and crossover merit further research because of their societal implications. One such implication is the impact of stress on gender roles and the impact of the crossover process on the entire family. As the number of women affected by stress, strain, and the crossover process increases, the need for a thorough study of its effects becomes urgent. Information about the contribution of gender will enrich our knowledge of the crossover process and facilitate preventive measures for the individual and for the family.

REFERENCES

Bandura, A. (1969). *Principles of behavior modification*. New York: Holt, Rinehart, & Winston.

Barnett, R. C., & Brennan, R. T. (1997). Change in job conditions, change in psychological distress, and gender: A longitudinal study of dual earner couples. *Journal of Organizational Behavior, 18*, 253.

Barnett, R. C., Raudenbush, S. W., Brennan, R. T., Pleck, J. H., & Marshall, N. L. (1995). Changes in job and marital experience and change in psychological distress: A longitudinal study of dual-earner couples. *Journal of Personality and Social Psychology, 69*, 839–850.

Baruch, G. K., Biener, L., & Barnett, R. C. (1987). Women and gender in research on work and family stress. *American Psychologist, 42*, 130–136.

Beehr, T. A., Johnson, L. B., & Nieva, R. (1995). Occupational stress: Coping of police and their spouses. *Journal of Organizational Psychology, 16*, 3–25.

Bolger, N., DeLongis, A., Kessler, R., & Wethington, E. (1989). The contagion of stress across multiple roles. *Journal of Marriage and the Family, 51*, 175–183.

Booth, A. (1977). Wife's employment and husband's stress: A replication and refutation. *Journal of Marriage and the Family, 39*, 645–650.

Bronfenbrenner, U. (1977). Toward an experimental ecology of human development. *American Psychologist, 32*, 513–531.

Burke, R. J., & Weir, T. (1976). Relationship of wives' employment status to husband, wife, pair satisfaction and performance. *Journal of Marriage and the Family, 38*, 279–287.

Burke, R. J., Weir, T., & Duwors, R. E. (1980). Work demands on administrators and spouse well-being. *Human Relations, 33*, 253–278.

Coyne, J. C., & Downey, G. (1991). Social factors and psychopathology: Stress, social support, and coping processes. *Annual Review of Psychology, 42*, 401–425.

Di Salvo, V., Lubbers, C., Rossi, A. M., & Lewis, J. (1995). Unstructured perceptions of work-related stress: An exploratory qualitative study. In C. Crandall, & P. Perrewé (Eds.), *Occupational stress: A handbook* (pp. 39–50). Philadelphia, PA: Taylor & Francis.

Dubin, R. (1973). Work and nonwork: Institutional perspectives. In M. D. Dunnette (Ed.), *Work and nonwork in the year 2001* (pp. 53–68). Belmont, CA: Wadsworth.

Eckenrode, J., & Gore, S. (1981). Stressful events and social support: The significance of context. In B. Gottlieb (Ed.), *Social networks and social support* (pp. 43–68). Beverly Hills, CA: Sage.

Edwards, J. R., Baglioni, A. J., & Cooper, C. L. (1990). Stress, Type-A, coping, and psychological and physical symptoms: A multi-sample test of alternative models. *Human Relations, 43,* 919–956.

Galambos, N. L., & Walters, B. J. (1992). Work hours, schedule inflexibility and stress in dual earner spouses. *Canadian Journal of Behavioral Sciences, 24,* 290–302.

Greenhaus, J. H., & Parasuraman, S. (1987). A work–nonwork interactive prospective of stress consequences. *Journal of Organizational Behavior Management, 8,* 37–60.

Hammer, L. B., Allen, E., & Grigsby, T. D. (1997). Work–family conflict in dual-earner couples: Within individual and crossover effects of work and family. *Journal of Vocational Behavior, 50,* 185–203.

Haynes, S. G., Eaker, E. D., & Feinleib, M. (1983). Spouse behavior and coronary heart disease in men: Prospective results from the Framingham heart study. *American Journal of Epidemiology, 118,* 1–22.

Hobfoll, S. E., Dunahoo, C. L., Ben-Porath, Y., & Monnier, J. (1994). Gender and coping: The dual-axis model of coping. *American Journal of Community Psychology, 22,* 49–82.

Hobfoll, S. E., & London, J. (1986). The relationship of self concept and social support to emotional distress among women during war. *Journal of Social Clinical Psychology, 12,* 87–100.

Hobfoll, S. E., & Shirom, A. (1993). Stress and burnout in the workplace: Conservation of resources. In T. Golombiewski (Ed.), *Handbook of organizational behavior* (pp. 41–61). New York: Marcel Dekker.

House, J. (1981). *Work stress and social support.* Reading, MA: Addison-Wesley.

Jackson, S. E., & Maslach, C. (1982). After-effects of job-related stress: Families as victims. *Journal of Occupational Behavior, 3,* 63–77.

Jex, S. M., & Beehr, T. A. (1991). Emerging theoretical and methodological issues in the study of work-related stress. *Research in Personnel and Human Resources Management, 9,* 311–365.

Jick, T. D., & Mitz, L. F. (1985). Sex differences in work stress. *Academy of Management Review, 10,* 408–420.

Jones, F., & Fletcher, B. (1993). An empirical study of occupational stress transmission in working couples. *Human Relations, 46,* 881–902.

Kahn, R. L., Wolfe, D. M, Quinn, R. P., Snoek, J. D., & Rosenthal, R. A. (1964). *Organizational stress.* New York: Wiley.

Kessler, R. C., & McLeod, J. D. (1984). Sex differences in vulnerability to undesirable life events. *American Sociological Review, 49,* 620–631.

Kunkel, A. W., & Burleson, B. R. (1998). Social support and emotional lives of men and women: An assessment of the different culture perspective. In D. Canary, & K. Dindia (Eds.), *Sex differences and similarities in communication.* London: Erlbaum.

Lambert, S. J. (1990). Processing linking work and family: A critical review and research agenda. *Human Relations, 43,* 239–257.

Long, N. R., & Voges, K. E. (1987). Can wives perceive the source of their husbands' occupational stress? *Journal of Occupational Psychology, 60,* 235–242.

Martocchio, J. J., & O'Leary, A. M. (1989). Sex differences in occupational stress: A meta-analytic review. *Journal of Applied Psychology, 74,* 495–501.

Matuszek, P. A., Nelson, D. L., & Quick, J. C. (1995). Gender differences in distress: Are we asking all the right questions? *Journal of Social Behavior and Personality, 10,* 99–120.

Mirowski, J., & Ross, C. E. (1995). Sex differences in distress: Real or artifact? *American Sociological Review, 60,* 449–468.

Nelson, D. L., & Burke, R. (2000). Women executives: Health, stress, and success. *Academy of Management Executive, 14,* 107–121.

Parasuraman, S., Greenhaus, J. H., & Granrose, C. S. (1992). Role stressors, social support and well-being among two-career couples. *Journal of Organizational Behavior, 13,* 339–356.

Piotrkowski, C. (1979). *Work and the family system: A naturalistic study of the working-class and lower-middle-class families.* New York: The Free Press.

Ptacek, J. T., Smith, R. E., & Dodge, K. L. (1994). Gender differences in coping with stress: When stressors and appraisals do not differ. *Personality and Social Psychology Bulletin, 20,* 421–430.

Riley, D., & Eckenrode, J. (1986). Social ties: Costs and benefits within different subgroups. *Journal of Personality and Social Psychology, 51,* 770–778.

Roberts, R., & O'Keefe, S. J. (1981). Sex differences in depression reexamined. *Journal of Health and Social Behavior, 22,* 394–400.

Rook, S. K., Dooley, D., & Catalano, R. (1991). Stress transmission: The effects of husbands' job stressors on the emotional health of their wives. *Journal of Marriage and the Family, 53,* 165–177.

Rosenfield, S. (1980). Sex differences in depression: Do women always have higher rates? *Journal of Health and Social Behavior, 22,* 394–400.

Rosenfield, S. (1992). The cost of sharing: Wives' employment and husbands' mental health. *Journal of Health and Social Behavior, 33,* 213–225.

Spielberger, C. D., & Reheiser, E. C. (1994). The job stress survey: Measuring gender differences in occupation stress. *Journal of Social Behavior and Personality, 9,* 199–218.

Staines, G. L. (1980). Spillover versus compensation: A review of the literature on the relationship between work and nonwork. *Human Relations, 33,* 111–129.

Staines, G. L., Pottic, K. G., & Fudge, D. A. (1986). Wives' employment and husbands' attitudes toward work and life satisfaction. *Journal of Applied Psychology, 71,* 118–128.

Taylor, S. E., Klein, L. C., Lewis, B. P., Gruenewald, T. L., Gurung, R. A. R., & Updegraff, J. A. (2000). Biobehavioral responses to stress in females: Tend-and-befriend, not fight-and-flight. *Psychological Review, 107,* 411–429.

Tuosignant, M., Brousseau, R., & Tremblay, L. (1987). Sex biases in mental health scales: Do women tend to report less serious symptoms and confide more than men? *Psychological Medicine, 17,* 203–215.

Vinokur, A., Price, R. H., & Caplan, R. D. (1996). Hard times and hurtful partners: How financial strain affects depression and relationship satisfaction of unemployed persons and their spouses. *Journal of Personality and Social Psychology, 71*, 166–179.

Westman, M. (2001). Stress and strain crossover. *Human Relations, 54*, 717–751.

Westman, M., & Etzion, D. (1995). Crossover of stress, strain and resources from one spouse to another. *Journal of Organizational Behavior, 16*, 169–181.

Westman, M., Etzion, D., & Danon, E. (2001). Job insecurity and crossover of burnout in married couples. *Journal of Organizational Behavior, 22*, 467–481.

Westman, M., Etzion, D., & Segev, K. (2000, June). *The crossover process of work–family conflict from one spouse to another*. Paper presented at the 7th International Society for the Study of Work and Organizational Values (ISS-WOV) Conference, Jerusalem, Israel.

Westman, M., & Shirom, A. (1995). Dimensions of coping behavior: A proposed conceptual framework. *Anxiety, Stress, and Coping, 8*, 87–100.

Westman, M., & Vinokur, A. (1998). Unraveling the relationship of distress levels within couples: Common stressors, emphatic reactions, or crossover via social interactions? *Human Relations, 51*, 137–156.

Wethington, E., & McLeod, J. D. (1987). The importance of life events for explaining sex differences in psychological distress. In R. C. Barnett, L. Biener, & G. K. Baruch (Eds.), *Gender and stress* (pp. 144–158). New York: The Free Press.

Zedeck, S. (1992). Introduction: Exploring the domain of work and family concerns. In S. Zedeck (Ed.), *Work, families, and organizations* (pp. 1–32). San Francisco: Jossey-Bass.

III

PREVENTION AND INTERVENTIONS

INTRODUCTION:
PREVENTION AND INTERVENTIONS

It is no exaggeration to say that interventions are the most understudied topic of research on gender, work stress, and health. Chapter 10 presents
a summary of research conducted by Catalyst on reduced workload arrangements, and chapter 11 continues this thread by examining the reasons individuals benefit from such arrangements. In chapter 12, sexual harassment is
discussed as a threat to health and well-being, and a novel framework is presented to guide organizational interventions and prevention efforts. Family-
friendly policies increasingly are needed in the workplace, and chapter 13
examines the efficacy of these programs.

10

REDUCED WORK ARRANGEMENTS FOR MANAGERS AND PROFESSIONALS: A POTENTIAL SOLUTION TO CONFLICTING DEMANDS

MARCIA BRUMIT KROPF

In the past, the common work schedule—a nine-to-five day, Monday-to-Friday week—reflected a focus on manufacturing work in prescribed places at prescribed times. This schedule worked well for a managerial workforce composed primarily of men in single-earner families. The demographics of the U.S. workforce have changed, with women now comprising 46.6% of the labor force and 50.3% of managerial and professional specialty positions (Bureau of Labor Statistics, 2001). At the same time, work schedules have changed, with business taking place beyond traditional work hours because of the transition to a knowledge- and service-based economy characterized by 24-hour, 365-day customer service and work interactions across different time zones (Catalyst, 1997).

One result of these changes is that voluntary, temporary part-time options for managers and professionals have become more visible since the 1980s. These options involve individually negotiated work schedules that are formally reduced to below the company standard. They can be on a weekly, monthly, annual, or project basis, and can include job-sharing or telecommuting. They affect salary, benefits, and professional advancement.

NEED, AVAILABILITY, AND ACCEPTANCE

This chapter will focus on findings from a series of major studies conducted by Catalyst, the not-for-profit organization working to advance women in business (Exhibit 10.1). These studies clarify the growing importance of voluntary reduced work arrangements, the difficulties accompanying their use, and strategies to ensure their success. These studies also shed light on why reduced work options provide necessary support for women at key points in their careers and how the use of these arrangements impacts women's career advancement.

EXHIBIT 10.1
Catalyst Research Methodologies

Making Work Flexible: Policy to Practice (1996) funded by Deloitte & Touche LLP.

- Confidential interviews with human resources representatives at 16 corporations and 15 professional firms with nationally recognized experience with workplace flexibility.
- A review of the policies, procedures, communication tools, and practices at the 31 organizations.
- Three roundtable discussions with human resources representatives and professionals and managers to review and critique the draft implementation framework.

A New Approach to Flexibility: Managing the Work/Time Equation (1997) funded by the Alfred P. Sloan Foundation.

- A review of the company's policies, procedures, and communication related to flexible arrangements.
- Twenty-eight focus groups with 214 participants—professionals who work part-time, supervisors, colleagues, and newly-hired professionals.
- Seventeen in-person interviews—senior managers, senior Human Resources representative, company experts, and supervisors.
- Eighty telephone interviews—professionals who work part-time, alumnae, clients, and company experts.
- A work schedule questionnaire sent to all 6,134 professional-level employees in the targeted segments of the workforce to assess work arrangements (2,124 responded—a 35% response rate).
- An in-depth survey sent to 1,695 volunteers from the earlier questionnaire (1,105 responded—a 65% response rate), designed to allow for comparison of responses between the part-time employees, their full-time colleagues, and supervisors of participating part-time employees.

Two Careers, One Marriage: Making It Work in the Workplace (1998) funded by Philip Morris Companies, Inc.

- In-depth telephone interviews with both members of 25 dual-career marriages.
- A 20-minute telephone survey of 802 randomly selected members of dual-career marriages conducted by Yankelovich Partners, Inc. Criteria for selection included:
  - Both members of couple were at least 25 years of age.
  - Both were employed full-time in the past 12 months.
  - One member worked in the private sector. One member could be self-employed.
- Total household income was greater than $35,000.

Flexible Work Arrangements III: A Ten Year Retrospective of Part-time Options for Managers and Professionals (2000) funded by McDonald's Corporation.

- In-depth telephone interviews with 24 of the participants in *Flexible Work Arrangements: Establishing Options for Managers and Professionals* (1989) and *Flexible Work Arrangements II: Succeeding with Part-time Options* (1993).

Exhibit 10.1 *(Continued)*

The MBA: Women Define Success (2000) conducted with the University of Michigan Business School and the Center for the Education of Women at the University of Michigan and funded by a consortium of 13 companies.

- Written survey with responses from 1,684 men and women graduates of 12 top-ranked business schools (41% response rate). The respondents are 53% women, 47% men, 25% people of color.
- Four focus groups with 31 undergraduate women posessing a GPA of 3.5 or above, not currently majoring in business, from top-tier schools.
- Five focus groups with 35 women graduate students enrolled in public policy, public health, or law school graduate programs.
- Four focus groups with MBA graduates of several participating schools.

Women in Law: Making the Case (2001) funded by the Columbia Law School with a special grant from The New York Community Trust—Wallace Reader's Digest Special Projects Fund; Harvard Law School; University of California–Berkeley (Boalt Hall) Law School; University of Michigan Law School; and Yale Law School.

- Written mail survey with responses from 1,439 graduates (a 24% response rate) from law schools at Columbia, Harvard, University of California (Berkeley), University of Michigan, and Yale from 1970 to 1999. The respondents are 64% women, 36% men, 17% people of color.
- Telephone interviews with 21 lawyers.
- Group discussions and focus groups with women associates at New York City firms, women students at Yale Law School, the American Bar Association's Commission on Women in the Profession, women general counsels, and members of a national legal search firm.

Women in Financial Services: Word on the Street (2001), an independent study, was undertaken by Catalyst under the terms of the settlement of the case of Martens, et al. vs. Smith Barney (S.D.N.Y., 96 Civ. 3779).

- Written mail survey with responses from 838 employees (a 38% response rate) in pipeline and senior leadership positions in seven major securities firms. The respondents are 58% women, 42% men, 11% people of color.
- Nine focus groups with women and men in pipeline and senior leadership positions in the securities industry in Chicago, New York, and San Francisco.

Need for Part-Time Arrangements

The change in the way work is done has created both a difficult situation for many employees facing inflexible responsibilities at home and at work, and a demand for employers to respond by creating more flexible work environments. Managerial and professional men and women in dual-career marriages, both with and without children, are asking to alter traditional work schedules (Catalyst, 1998). As demonstrated in Figure 10.1, employees also look for flexibility when looking for a new employer.

Several situations are driving the increasing interest in voluntary part-time arrangements. First, employees report working longer hours in 1997, as

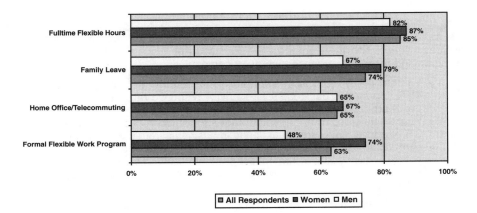

Fulltime Flexible Hours: 82%, 87%, 85%

Family Leave: 67%, 79%, 74%

Home Office/Telecommuting: 65%, 67%, 65%

Formal Flexible Work Program: 48%, 74%, 63%

0% 20% 40% 60% 80% 100%

☐ All Respondents ■ Women ☐ Men

Figure 10.1. Data from "Programs Employees Look for in a New Employer," in *Two Careers, One Marriage: Making It Work in the Workplace,* (pp. 32, 34), by Catalyst, 1998, New York: Catalyst. Copyright 1998 by Catalyst. Adapted with permission.

compared to 1977, and they say that they would like to reduce the work-week by 11 hours on average if they could (an increase of 17 percentage points since 1992) (Bond, Galinsky, & Swanberg, 1998).

Recently, Catalyst (2000b) found that MBA graduates working full-time in the private sector report working an average of 53.5 hours per week. Not surprisingly, the study also finds that the more hours worked, the less satisfied respondents are with work–life balance—particularly true for female respondents. Catalyst (2001a, 2001b) found that law school graduates report working an average of 52.5 hours per week and employees in financial service firms report working 55.8 hours per week. Professionals with long work hours struggle to carve out the time they need for their personal lives and families and, in specific circumstances, may need to create reduced arrangements that allow them to devote time to child rearing or elder care while continuing their careers.

Long work hours, however, are only part of the intense commitment demanded of managers and professionals. Perlow (1997) describes constant interruptions, a crisis mentality, and reward systems emphasizing individual heroics as common characteristics of today's workplace. Friedman & Greenhaus (2000) go beyond the issue of hours to describe the more subtle and pervasive problem of the psychological interference of work with family and family with work. Galinsky, Bond, and Kim (2001) identify the pressures and demands of work that lead to a feeling of being overworked: pressure to work very fast, pressure to work very hard, never having enough time to get everything done, having difficulty focusing on work, experiencing work interruptions, and having to work on too many tasks at the same time. They also find that women feel more overworked than do men, as they are more likely to be interrupted more frequently while working and have too many tasks to do at the same time.

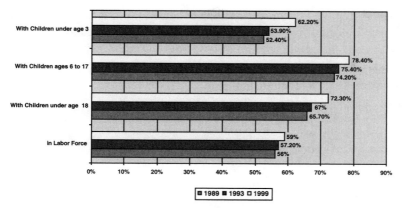

With Children under age 3 — 62.20% / 53.90% / 52.40%

With Children ages 6 to 17 — 78.40% / 75.40% / 74.20%

With Children under age 18 — 72.30% / 67% / 65.70%

In Labor Force — 59% / 57.20% / 56%

0% 10% 20% 30% 40% 50% 60% 70% 80% 90%

■ 1989 ■ 1993 □ 1999

Figure 10.2. Data from "Labor Force Participation, Women Age 25 and Older," in *Flexible Work Arrangements III: A Ten Year Retrospective* (p. 12), by Catalyst, 2000, New York: Catalyst. Copyright 2000 by Catalyst. Adapted with permission.

In addition, women make up almost half of the workforce. Increasingly, as Figure 10.2 illustrates, women with children living at home continue their careers. Women with caregiving responsibilities that conflict with their full-time work schedules are the primary users of voluntary, temporary reduced work arrangements (Catalyst, 1997, 2000b, 2001a, 2001b; Epstein, Seron, Oglensky, & Saute, 1999; Friedman & Greenhaus, 2000; Lee & MacDermid, 1999; Levy, Flynn, & Kellogg, 1998; Schneer & Reitman, 1997).

An in-depth study (Catalyst, 1997) of the use of part-time arrangements in four organizations found that a small but meaningful percentage (7%) of professionals actually use part-time arrangements at a given time. Because these arrangements are used to manage specific types of conflicting responsibilities that vary across a life cycle, it is also important to look at the use of these arrangements over the course of employees' careers. The study found that 21% of respondents will work part-time at some time in their careers (36% of the women and 11% of the men). These reduced arrangements are important then, not because large numbers of employees use them at one time, but because large numbers of employees need them and use them over time.

Availability of Part-Time Work Options

Employers are realizing the impact these arrangements have on recruiting and retaining valued talent. As a result, these reduced work arrangements have become increasingly available for managers and professionals (Lee & MacDermid, 1999; Levy et al., 1998; Society for Human Resource Management, 1997). In fact, in 1999, *Working Mother* magazine identified the offering of flexible schedules as the top trend for companies on the list of *100 Best Companies for Working Mothers*. All of the companies on the 1999 list offered flextime; the majority offered other types of flexible arrangements; 69 of the 100 were training managers to better supervise those with flexible arrangements.

Acceptance of Part-Time Arrangements

As the need for these arrangements has become more critical and the availability more widespread, part-time options have become more accepted as a viable choice for managers and professionals. Catalyst (2000a) describes the results of a longitudinal study of 24 women who pioneered part-time arrangements in the late 1980s. These women describe the changes they have witnessed:

> [My flexible work arrangement] had a huge impact. What's happened over the last 12 years has been incredible. We now have hundreds of people working on alternative arrangements. We're starting to see more telecommuting. It's gone so far beyond the traditional job-share and part-time arrangement. We're starting to see people who want to ease into retirement working part-time. We're starting to see men job-sharing for family reasons, or for education reasons.
>
> [The flexible work arrangement program] has grown, and women aren't as timid to ask for it. I haven't heard one employee say their boss flat out said "no." They might not have ended up with an arrangement that they were hoping for, but it was some kind of compromise. Whereas when I started my situation, there were "no's" handed out [all the time].

Lee & MacDermid (1999) also reported high levels of success with reduced work arrangements in a wide variety of industries. Friedman & Greenhaus (2000) found that women who work part-time feel more supported by their employers than those who work full-time.

A SOLUTION WITH MIXED RESULTS

Part-time arrangements can be an effective solution for managerial and professional employees facing conflicting sets of responsibilities and commitments. As the need for these options is better understood, they become more available and more accepted. To be an effective solution, however, part-time options must be available and then implemented well at several levels: the employing organization, the manager or supervisor, and the individual employee with the arrangement.

Implementation Difficulties at the Organizational Level

One issue managers and professionals face is that many employers continue to ignore this option. A 1998 Families and Work Institute study found that 43% of companies with 100 or more employees did not allow employees to move from full-time to part-time work and back again while remaining in the same position or at the same level (Galinsky & Bond, 1998).

Other employers, understanding the need for these arrangements, may respond by creating a policy or program, but that act does not create a more flexible work environment. Rather, it is just the beginning. Effective programs are characterized by strong leadership commitment and vision, an articulated business rationale, a focus on continuous learning and improvement, formal guidance and support for supervisors and employees, established performance expectations, internal systems that support flexibility, and a focus on work productivity. Even so, policies are often ambiguous, not clearly communicated, and lack critical information (Catalyst, 1993, 1996, 1997).

In fact, individuals may find themselves pioneering change by negotiating and using a reduced work arrangement. Rapoport & Bailyn (1996) have clarified the difficulties that persist when individuals change, but the system remains the same. They found that individualistic approaches often fail the individuals involved and may lead to negative career repercussions.

Implementation Difficulties at the Supervisor Level

Supervisors increasingly find themselves managing employees with widely varying schedules and arrangements. They struggle with the mixed messages received from senior leadership, promoting a flexible arrangement policy while continuing the systems that create a facetime culture. Supervisors are integral to the success of part-time arrangements and need to hone their ability to focus on work productivity rather than time in the office, plan schedules proactively, facilitate communication across teams and colleagues, communicate clear performance standards, and manage expectations (Catalyst, 1997, 2000a). As one manager in the 1997 study explained: "The truth is, [the part-time arrangement] forced us to be a little more deliberate about how we ordered priorities and what we did . . . . It has forced us to stop managing by spasm."

The study of the use of part-time schedules in four organizations (Catalyst, 1997) found that management of part-time arrangements was inconsistent in terms of commitment to such arrangements, ease and comfort in supervising these arrangements, and the ability of the supervisor to mediate false deadlines and false emergencies. In addition, changes in supervisors can require renegotiation or termination of arrangements. A full-time professional noted: "I've had three managers over the last $2^{1}/_{2}$ years, and it's been like windshield wipers—from one extreme to another, and back again."

Implementation Difficulties at the Individual Level

Individuals using alternative work arrangements deal with a number of implementation difficulties (Catalyst, 1997):

- Part-time arrangements are often seen as an accommodation for women with young children and not available to others.
- Colleagues often hold resentments, misconceptions, and stereotypes about those who work part-time as being uncommitted to their careers and employers.
- Assignments may be limited especially in terms of client service, supervisory responsibility, and high-profile opportunities.

The longitudinal study highlights the continuing existence of stereotypes and assumptions about part-time arrangements in general and the individuals who use them (Catalyst, 2000a). One woman told us: "There are certain assumptions made about part-time workers—that you're not committed, you don't have the potential that people have who work full-time." Another said: "Simply because you work a flexible schedule, even though you were extremely committed, some people may view you as less committed or less professional." Fortunately, part-time professionals who have returned to full-time arrangements report that these assumptions about their commitment disappear (Catalyst, 1998, 2000a).

A startling finding in the study of the use of part-time arrangements in four organizations was that only 39% of part-time professionals reported a decrease in their work responsibilities when they decreased their work hours. In fact, as noted in Figure 10.3, the majority of part-time professionals reported that their work responsibilities stayed the same or increased when they moved from full-time to a part-time arrangement (Catalyst, 1997). Almost half of their direct supervisors and full-time colleagues agreed.

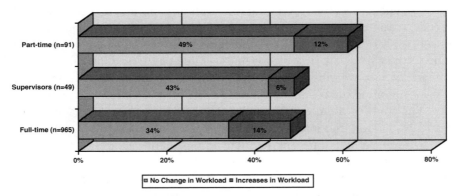

Figure 10.3. Data from "Changes in Workload When Moving to Part-time," in *A New Approach to Flexibility: Managing the Work/Time Equation* (p. 48), by Catalyst, 1997, New York: Catalyst. Copyright 1998 by Catalyst. Adapted with permission.

Undesirable Outcomes

The difficulties discussed thus far, especially inappropriately adjusted workloads, can result in blurred boundaries between work and home, failed arrangements and stress, negative impacts on career advancement, demotions and limited compensation, and misconceptions and resentment that feed negative stereotypes about these arrangements. Of the 1,056 participants in a survey of four organizations, 37% of part-time professionals reported an increase in work-related stress after moving to part-time; 36% of full-time professionals agreed that part-time professionals experience an increase in work-related stress (Catalyst, 1997). Catalyst found a significant correlation ($p < 0.5$) between stress and workload. In that study, part-time employees explained:

> I was willing to work until midnight at home and work weekends and all that just to make the arrangement work. My manager was saying "Hey, I'm giving you the flexibility, but the work still has to get done." And I took a pay cut.

SUCCESS STRATEGIES FOR SUPERVISORS AND EMPLOYEES

A decade of Catalyst research examining flexible work arrangements has delineated the problems with their implementation. This research has also highlighted many examples of successful part-time arrangements. Because voluntary, temporary part-time arrangements are a negotiated arrangement between an individual employee and a supervisor, the most critical activity involves explicit regular discussions about long-term career goals and plans, the specifics of the arrangement and how to make it work, as well as work schedules, plans, and commitments.

Being Informed About Flexible Work Options

Effective negotiation of the arrangement requires that both the supervisor and the individual have a clear understanding of the policy available, the benefits to the employer, and the strategies and practices needed to design and carry out a successful arrangement. Of the part-time professionals in a Catalyst study, 85% proposed the arrangements themselves and nearly half (47%) were the first in their group or department to establish an arrangement (Catalyst, 1997). The first step for many of them was to investigate their options, the experiences of others, and existing information on the topic.

> We started researching pairs who job-shared in management positions. Through word of mouth we were able to find five such pairs. We spoke with them for background, best practice ideas, etc. The proposal was

very detailed in nature, responding to many of the questions which we expected would be asked of us. (Catalyst 1997, p. 70)

Formalizing and Evaluating the Arrangement

Another characteristic of successful part-time arrangements recurring in Catalyst research is the importance of formal, explicit discussions between the employee and the supervisor, documented in writing. These discussions should include an agreement on how work responsibilities will be reduced, as well as the parameters of the arrangement and work expectations (Catalyst, 1993, 1996, 1997, 2000a). Such agreements ensure a shared understanding about the arrangement and an opportunity to discuss issues and concerns before they become problems. They can be used to clarify ways to modify and improve the arrangement. A pioneer of part-time arrangements explained: "You have to be careful that you're not biting off more than you can chew. You need to understand what the expectations are. You have to make sure all the stakeholders are getting what they need."

Allowing Arrangements to Evolve

Many of the part-time arrangements studied in Catalyst research evolve over time. The arrangement may begin with the birth of a child and quite limited work hours. Over time, as family responsibilities change and evolve, work hours and schedule, may change. Work opportunities also may motivate a change in the arrangement. Both the supervisor and the employee must be open to the concept that the most successful arrangements evolve in terms of hours and schedule.

Building Trusting Relationships

Employees with part-time arrangements also describe trusting relationships with supervisors, clients, and colleagues as critical to their success (Catalyst, 1997). They invest time in building those relationships that allow for open, comfortable discussions about schedules, workload, work expectations, and deadlines. Supervisors need to understand the importance of these relationships and work to build them as well.

CONCLUSION

Managers and professionals with successful part-time arrangements move into those arrangements very aware of the potential problems and the tradeoffs they are making. Recent research (Lee & MacDermid, 1999; Levy et al., 1998) has found that managers and professionals are willing to plateau their career advancement in order to attend to critical personal commitments or to create a valued lifestyle. In fact, 93% of the part-time employees in Catalyst's 1997 study reported that their ability to juggle work and family responsibilities improved when they went part-time (Catalyst, 1997). In addition, they reported increases in productivity, morale, and their commitment to their employer and job. Supervisors and colleagues also noted these improvements. A man working part-time shared this point of view: "My relationship with my son has improved tremendously and my productivity at work has improved. I feel a new sense of balance and want to be able to share my experience with others and help them have the same."

The critical benefit for employers is retention—retention of valuable talent, expertise, and experience—capitalizing on the investment in training and development and eliminating the cost of recruitment and orientation of replacement employees. In addition, supervisors benefit from the increases in productivity, morale, and proactive management described previously in this chapter. In the longitudinal study (Catalyst, 2000a), 12 of 24 women have returned to full-time work with their companies. All 24 credit the part-time option with their ability to remain in the workforce. Thirteen, more than half, earned promotions while they maintained their part-time arrangement.

Part-time solutions are critical options in the modern workplace, which is characterized by a workforce with a wide range of personal situations and by a dramatic expansion in terms of when and where work takes place. Managers and professionals working in this world have new ways of looking at their career goals. The 24 pioneers of part-time arrangements featured in Catalyst's longitudinal study (Catalyst, 2000a) describe making conscious decisions as they manage their family responsibilities and their careers. They talk about priorities that change over time and changing values depending upon circumstances.

> When I was part-time and the boys were younger, I found I had a better total mix of equal parts of family, career, volunteer work, and social relationships. Right now it's much heavier on the career. And that's not good or bad, it's just about choices and consequences.

They are satisfied with the choices they have made and shared a common view that working part-time was "the best of it all."

> I am in a position that if I wanted to get back full force into this career, I could. And it's because I've had these flexible arrangements. It would take some catching up, because I chose to take it slow. Another person with more pressure would have read up more and would have worked harder, and maybe wouldn't have done all the community things I did. But I did very much what I wanted to do.

Part-time options are necessary and beneficial for both employers and employees. There is considerable evidence that these are used by a large group of employees during the course of their work lives. However, much of the business community continues to view these arrangements as atypical and nontraditional, as exceptions and accommodations. It is critical to realize that these options are actually quite typical and will become even more so, making it mandatory to deal with remaining barriers to acceptance and implementation.

REFERENCES

Bond, J. T., Galinsky, E., & Swanberg, J. E. (1998). *The 1997 national study of the changing workforce.* New York: Families and Work Institute.

Bureau of Labor Statistics (2001). *Employment and earnings.* Washington, DC: Author.

Catalyst (1993). *Flexible work arrangements II: Succeeding with part-time options.* New York: Author.

Catalyst (1996). *Making work flexible: Policy to practice.* New York: Author.

Catalyst (1997). *A new approach to flexibility: Managing the work/time equation.* New York: Author.

Catalyst (1998). *Two careers, one marriage: Making it work in the workplace.* New York: Author.

Catalyst (2000a). *Flexible work arrangements III: A ten year retrospective of part-time options for managers and professionals.* New York: Author.

Catalyst (2000b). *The MBA: Women define success.* New York: Author.

Catalyst (2001a). *Women in financial services: Word on the street.* New York: Author.

Catalyst (2001b). *Women in law: Making the case.* New York: Author.

Epstein, C. F., Seron, C., Oglensky, B., & Saute, R. (1999). *The part-time paradox: Time norms, professional life, family and gender.* New York: Routledge.

Friedman, S. D., & Greenhaus, J. H. (2000). *Work and family—Allies or enemies? What happens when business professionals confront life choices.* New York: Oxford University Press.

Galinsky, E., & Bond, T. (1998). *The 1998 business work–life study: A sourcebook.* New York: Families and Work Institute.

Galinsky, E., Bond, J. T., & Kim, S. (2001). *Feeling overworked: When work becomes too much.* New York: Families & Work Institute.

Lee, M. D., & MacDermid, S. (1999). *Improvising new careers: Accommodation, elaboration & transformation.* West Lafayette, IN: The Center for Families at Purdue University.

Levy, E. S., Flynn, P. M., & Kellogg, D. M. (1998). *Customized work arrangements in the accounting profession: An uncertain future.* New York: Grant report issued by the Alfred P. Sloan Foundation.

Perlow, L. A. (1997). *Finding time: How corporations, individuals, and families can benefit from new work practices*. Ithaca, NY: ILR Press.

Rapoport, R., & Bailyn, L. (1996). *Relinking life and work: Toward a better future*. New York: Ford Foundation.

Schneer, J. A., & Reitman, F. (1997). The interrupted managerial career path: A longitudinal study of MBAs. *The Journal of Vocational Behavior, 51*, 411–434.

Society for Human Resource Management (1997). *Work and family survey*. Alexandria, VA: Author.

Working Mother Magazine (staff) (1999, October). 100 best companies for working mothers.

11

REDUCED-LOAD WORK ARRANGEMENTS: RESPONSE TO STRESS OR QUEST FOR INTEGRITY OF FUNCTIONING?

MARY DEAN LEE, SHELLEY M. MACDERMID, AND MICHELLE L. BUCK

In North America the growth of part-time work in general has been well documented (Blossfeld & Hakim, 1997; Vroman, 1999), and has not been limited to low-wage occupations. As far back as the late 1980s and early 1990s, increases have been noted in the percentage of employees working less than full time in professional fields such as law, medicine, and accounting (Lee, Engler, & Wright, 2002). The growth in part-time work in general has been interpreted as resulting from the changing demographics of the workforce. As the numbers of dual-earner and single parent families increase, workers need more options enabling them to balance their work and family commitments. In all industrialized countries, the majority of those working part-time are women. One explanation for this pattern is the fact that women continue to take primary responsibility for raising children (Fagan & O'Reilly, 1998). Furthermore, we know that in the United States, two thirds to three quarters of those who work part-time do so voluntarily, rather than because they could not get full-time work (Barnett & Gareis, 2000; Negrey, 1993). Nevertheless, research indicates that part-time work in general, whatever the reason and whether done by men or women, continues to carry heavy penalties in the form of lower wages, lack of health and pension benefits, and fewer opportunities for advancement (Wenger, 2001).

Part-time work among professionals, however, is a somewhat different phenomenon than part-time work in the labor force in general. For example,

We are deeply indebted to the more than 350 men and women who shared their time and insights with us. Other members of the research team were: Margaret L. Williams, Carol Schreiber, Leslie Borrelli, Sharon Leiba-O'Sullivan, Minda Bernstein, Stephen Smith, and Pamela Dohring. This research was made possible by financial support from the Alfred P. Sloan Foundation and the Social Sciences and Humanities Research Council of Canada.

part-time professionals are in high-status occupations, generally well remunerated, and typically work more than half-time. Their work arrangements are often called "reduced load" or "customized" (Lee et al., 2002; Levy, Flynn, & Kellogg, 1997), and are measured in terms of a percentage of full-time (e.g., 60% or 80%). Part-time professionals also tend to be paid a salary corresponding to the workload percentage, and they continue to receive the same or proportionate benefits (Lee et al., 1999). Recent studies also suggest that although part-time professionals definitely pay a financial price for working less, their careers are not necessarily stalled, and they may continue to advance even while remaining part-time (Buck, Lee, MacDermid, & Smith, 2000; Catalyst, 2000; MacDermid, Lee, Buck, & Williams, 2001; Raabe, 1998).

The purpose of this chapter is to look more closely at part-time work among professionals, to determine whether this phenomenon is more accurately interpreted as a response to stress, or simply experimentation with different ways of working given the changing demographics in the workforce. Part-time work among professionals has emerged only recently as a distinct phenomenon, but research on reduced-load work in a variety of professions recently has been reported: law (Epstein, Seron, Oglensky, & Saute, 1999); accounting (Clark, 1998; Levy et al., 1997); engineering and computer science (Meiksins & Whalley, 1996); medicine (Barnett & Gareis, 2000); management (Lee, MacDermid, & Buck, 2000; see also chapter 10). However, none of these studies has focused specifically on alternative interpretations or explanations for the dramatic increase in part-time work among professionals.

This chapter examines individual motivation and outcomes of reduced-load work arrangements in 82 cases of professionals and managers working part-time. The data are analyzed from the perspective of two alternate models. The first interprets part-time work as a coping strategy designed to reduce stress. The second interprets part-time work as an effort to increase the fit between the individual's desired and actual patterns of managing multiple commitments under changing conditions in the environment. The primary research question is whether reduced-load work among professionals is better understood as an exercise in stress reduction or as an ongoing process of adaptation to change.

There have been many different approaches to studying work stress and health that may help our understanding of why more professionals are working part-time. (Schabracq, Cooper, & Winnubst, 1996). One of the more influential models in explaining work stress has been the *job demand–job control* model (Karasek, 1979; Karasek & Theorell, 1990), which predicts that stress-related health problems increase as job demands increase and job control (decision latitude) decreases. When applied to the study of reduced-load work arrangements, this model would suggest that reduced load might lead to fewer stress-related health problems or better psychological well-being, as a result of lowered job demands and/or greater job control. Kelloway and Gottlieb (1998) actually tested the efficacy of the demand–control model in explaining the impact of alternative work arrangements on women's stress and family role competence. They found that alternative work arrangements involving reduced hours of employment (e.g., part-time or job sharing) promoted well-being by reducing perceived job demands; alternative work arrangements involving scheduling flexibility (e.g., flex-time or telecommuting) promoted well-being by increasing perceived control over time.

Another theoretical model for explaining relationships between health outcomes and balancing work and family demands is the *human ecology* framework proposed by Schabracq et al. (1996), which builds on systems theory in studying families (Bronfenbrenner, 1979) as well as the person–environment fit model of work stress (e.g., Caplan, 1987). According to the human ecology framework, human beings exist in environments that they select and shape according to preferences, and they develop regular, repetitive ways of minimizing undesired surprises or intrusions into their territory. At the same time, they are attuning themselves to the characteristics of the environment so that they function more smoothly within it. In this process, people reduce the options available to them and simplify their lives to deal almost automatically with routine interactions and problems. This frees them up to deal with nonroutine challenges and new skill development on an ad hoc basis, when necessary.

As the environment changes, humans engage in a continuous process of adaptation to establish a new equilibrium. This state of equilibrium is called *integrity of individual functioning*, which is achieved when the environment is adapted to meet the specific configuration of the individual's abilities, skills, and needs. From a human ecology perspective, reduced-load work arrangements would be viewed not as a coping strategy for dealing with stress, as in the demand–control model, but rather as a process of adaptation driven by individuals seeking integrity of functioning. Negotiation of work arrangement alternatives would be considered an example of individuals trying to increase the person–environment "fit" under conditions of changing family circumstances.

As more men and women struggle to balance work and family, it is important that we understand what kinds of approaches or coping strategies are more likely to be beneficial and under what circumstances. Reduced-load work is clearly one approach being explored by higher-level employees in organizations. The qualitative study reported here explored in depth the motivation and outcomes associated with reduced-load work arrangements. Because the study was exploratory—investigating a relatively new phenomenon—it was conceived as theory generating as opposed to hypothesis testing. Therefore, no specific theoretical model was chosen a priori to generate predictions about results. However, we examine the findings in a post hoc manner to reflect on the utility of the demand–control model and the human ecology framework.

We summarize general findings related to the impetus and rationale for seeking reduced-load work and the positive outcomes or benefits associated with reduced-load work. We then critically examine how well these descriptive findings "map" onto the two theoretical perspectives. We also analyze data from a subset of our sample, those benefiting most and least from the reduced-load work, to assess how well the two theoretical frameworks predict differences in the two groups.

STUDYING REDUCED-LOAD WORK ARRANGEMENTS

Results reported in this chapter come from an exploratory study of 82 reduced-load work arrangements involving 46 managers and 36 professionals, all of whom were currently or had recently worked on a reduced-load basis for at least 6 months. Managers were distinguished from professionals by having responsibility for three or more direct reports. Reduced-load work was defined as voluntarily working .90 Full-time Equivalent or less, with an accompanying reduction in compensation.

The cases studied came from 42 employers throughout North America, in a variety of industries including manufacturing, financial services, natural resources, telecommunications, and professional and managerial services. We interviewed 86 managers and professionals working in 82 part-time work arrangements (4 were job shares). Most of these individuals were women ($n = 77$), married ($n = 78$), and parents ($n = 80$) of relatively young children (average age of youngest child = 4.7 years). On average, the reduced-load arrangements had been in existence 4.2 years and involved .72 FTE. The average number of hours worked each week was 32, about 17 hours less than had been worked on a full-time basis. Prorated to a full-time equivalent, salaries ranged from $31,111 to $175,000, with an average of $79,441 U.S. at the time of data collection (1996–1998). Sample job titles included Principal Research Scientist, Vice President–Finance, Sales Manager, Manager–Export Operations, Software Engineer, Actuary Senior Manager, and Marketing Director.

Multiple sources of data and methods of collection were used. We conducted face-to-face interviews with each manager or professional, his or her spouse or partner, a senior manager, a peer co-worker, and a human resources representative. Interviews with the target respondent lasted about 1.5 hours; other interviews lasted about 45 minutes. In all, 376 interviews were conducted, each transcribed *verbatim* for analysis. Each complete case generated about 100 pages of single-spaced transcripts.

Interviews were semistructured and covered the following topics: (a) how and why the reduced-load work arrangement came about; (b) how the job was restructured or created to accommodate the reduced-load schedule; (c) perceptions of the challenges and difficulties involved in restructuring the job; (d) costs and benefits of reduced-load work arrangements from multiple perspectives; and (e) factors important in making the reduced-load work arrangements successful or unsuccessful.

We analyzed the data using a variety of qualitative methods, including a form of *axial coding*, where interviewers reviewed each transcript for information relevant to several preselected issues (Miles & Huberman, 1994). These included the outcomes, costs and benefits of the reduced-load arrangement, as well as the factors that facilitated and hindered its success. The results of the axial coding were compiled in *analytic memos* written for each case by the researcher who conducted the interviews. Material extracted from the transcripts was organized according to respondent (e.g., spouse, coworker, boss, etc.).

The analytic memos provided long lists of examples and quotes related to each of the key issues, which were then aggregated across cases. As this occurred, clusters of similar ideas or themes became evident within the compiled lists, and it became possible to see how prevalent each theme was across all the cases in the data set. The final section of the analytic memo mentioned subtexts, notable consistencies or inconsistencies across stakeholders within each case, and data that seemed puzzling, followed by the interviewer's ratings of overall outcomes of the reduced-load work arrangement. The ratings summarized the costs, benefits, and overall success of the case, taking into account the perspectives of all stakeholders. The ratings did not reflect the interviewer's personal opinion; rather, they were intended to summarize respondents' perceptions of costs and benefits. Using a scale from 1 to 7 (1 = low), interviewers first rated separately the costs and benefits of the reduced-load work arrangement from three perspectives—the target individual, the family, and the organization—generating a total of 6 ratings. By subtracting costs from benefits in each domain, three "net benefit" scores were created for the individual, the family, and the organizational domains: individual net benefits (INB), family net benefits (FNB), and organizational net benefits (ONB).

A final global success rating was assigned to each case by the interviewer, after writing the analytic memo, reviewing all field notes, and assigning preliminary net benefit ratings as described previously. This overall rating was designed to be a summary measure, allowing us to make comparisons across cases on the overall success of the reduced-load work arrangement, using multiple perspectives. The interviewers considered the following criteria simultaneously, taking into account the perspectives of all stakeholders: (a) the extent to which individual professionals or managers were happy with their work arrangements, including from a long term career perspective; (b) the extent to which the senior manager and coworkers reported positive outcomes; and (c) the extent to which the spouse or partner and target individual reported positive effects on children, family life, and/or the couple relationship. A rating of "1" indicated consistently negative outcomes reported across stakeholders and a "9" indicated consistently positive outcomes. Two researchers rated each case, and any differences were discussed and resolved. After the ratings were complete, three groups were created: high (scores of 7–9), moderate (5–6), and low (1–4) success. Sixty-two (62%) percent of the cases fell in the high success group, 31% in the moderate success group, and 7% in the low success group.

For purposes of examining more in-depth cases where individuals appeared to benefit most and least from the reduced-load work arrangements, the INB rating was used as a crude indicator of positive or negative consequences of the reduced-load arrangement from a personal perspective. Two groups (high INB and low INB) were created to examine in more depth what circumstances or what factors differentiated individuals who had gained the most and the least. The range of scores on INB was –5 to +6, and the mean was 2.75. The low INB group consisted of all who had negative (–1 to –5) INB scores ($n = 8$), or all who were rated as experiencing greater costs than benefits from the reduced-load arrangements. The high INB group consisted of all whose INB score was the maximum, 6 ($n = 12$). These two groups were then examined for demographic or status differences (age, family status, managerial versus professional, salary, hours worked, percentage of reduced load). No significant differences were found. It was noted that men were overrepresented in the high INB group, in that there were 11% in the sample as a whole, but 25% in this subgroup.

Two additional measures were constructed to estimate level of job demands. The first consisted of computing the average percentage of full-time being worked per week. This figure was used to represent the *decrease in job demands*. The lower the percentage of full-time being worked, the greater the decrease in job demands. The sample mean percentage of full-time being worked was 72%, and the range was 40% to 90%.

The second measure of job demands constructed was a categorical variable, called *real load reduction*, which involved rating each case in terms of whether or not there was actually an adjustment made in the amount of work the individual was responsible for when the reduced-load work arrangement was first negotiated. The interviewers' assessments were based on information gathered from the multiple stakeholders in each case, including the boss and a co-worker. In 11% ($n = 9$) of the total sample of cases ($n = 82$), there was within-case agreement that the reduced-load work arrangement had not actually involved a reduction in workload. These cases were rated "0" and all others were rated "1." The total sample mean for real load reduction was .88.

FINDINGS

First, we analyze emergent themes related to the impetus and motivation behind reduced-load arrangements across all 82 cases in the sample. The findings are interpreted as being more or less consistent with the demand control model of stress and the human ecology framework.

Next, we provide a brief summary of findings related to the overall success of the reduced-load arrangements studied, and we highlight recurrent themes related to positive and negative outcomes from a personal and family perspective. These themes are also critically assessed for consistency with the two theoretical frameworks.

Finally, the high and low INB groups are compared to look for differences that might be more adequately explained by the demand–control model as opposed to the human ecology approach to explaining health outcomes. More specifically, we compare these groups on: (a) measures of job demand (decrease in job demands and real load reduction); (b) prevalence of and perceived importance of "control" versus other factors in respondent explanations of effects of reduced-load work arrangements; (c) context of talk about "control" and related terms; and (d) outcomes attributed to gains in control versus other processes.

Impetus–Motivation

In the interviews with study participants, a good deal of time was spent probing the circumstances around the initial negotiation of the reduced-load work arrangements. The average length of time these individuals had been working less than full-time was 4.2 years, and many of them had been in more than one part-time position. In addition, even those who had been in the same reduced-load job from the beginning often described a continuous process of fine-tuning and adjustment of the logistics of the arrangement, rather than a fixed contract. In the stories we heard about the initiation of reduced-load work, there were two recurring issues in themes having to do with impetus or motivation. One had to do with timing—*when* the individual began thinking about or planning to seek reduced load. The other had to do with the rationale—the explanation for *why* they wanted to work less.

Timing. As for the timing of the request to work less, in 18% percent of the cases where children were involved (76 of 82), the individuals realized *before* having their first child that they would not want to continue working in the same way after becoming parents. In 62% of the cases, the desire to work less came within 2 years after the birth of a child. In some cases these individuals attempted to return to full-time status after maternity leave and experienced childcare problems, or realized that they could not maintain their high level of involvement in their careers and also have the kind of contact they wanted with their children. More commonly, these individuals returned to work on a part-time basis after maternity leave and expected to phase back to full-time within 3 to 6 months. However, they found that the reduced-load work suited them and then sought to create or find a more permanent reduced-load position. Another common scenario was that these individuals came back to work full-time after the birth of their first children, realized it was a "stretch" and decided that when they had a second child they would try to work part-time. The timing of pursuing reduced load then, was largely related to birth of a child. However, it must be noted that in 10% of the cases, where reduced load was not connected to children, there did not seem to be any consistent pattern of timing in that these individuals were at very different stages of their careers (early, mid, late) and lives.

Rationale. As for explanations given for working less, most individuals had multiple reasons for pursuing a reduced-load arrangement. Of those with children (82 of 87 cases), 76 of them included wanting to spend more time with children as one of the important reasons for working reduced load. Most of these target individuals also talked about wanting more time to relax, to enjoy time with their kids and the whole family, and a chance to slow down the hectic pace of life. Reasons given less frequently included specific personal health or marital problems, or wanting to free up time for other interests or priorities such as hobbies, sports and recreation activities, or volunteer work. In the majority of cases (85%), the target individuals did not seek to work less after reaching a crisis, whether related to their children or themselves. Rather, the alternative work arrangement was pursued in the context of changing family or personal circumstances and a gradual realization of a need for change in the work situation.

The second common rationale for reduced load related more to the target individuals' desire for more balance in their lives, or more freedom to pursue greater personal fulfillment through their own particular interests and values. The motivation for working less was based not simply on the children's needs or the family's needs, but rather on an expression of personal needs and self-interest. For example, a man who was a Senior Principal in Information Technology in a large accounting firm put it this way:

> I spent my entire life in here in my 20s and 30s . . . It was actually during that kind of phase that I said, "there's got to be something else," like a midlife crisis, I would have been [in my] late thirties at the time, "I've got to do something else other than work." That was when I got married and . . . we decided we wanted a home and a family and that we both had to stop working those weird hours. So I went to my boss and said, "I want to slow down . . . I want to change the focus of my life."

A woman who was a Senior Function Manager with 17 direct reports in a telecommunications firm talked about what she had achieved with a reduced load in a different way:

> Before it used to feel like I worked five days a week and I had a two-day weekend. Now it feels like I have a life. Even though I am in here every single day. I just can't believe the emotional difference it makes. It is, I have an integrated life that all works. And I work here, I work there, I play here, I play there, and it is just a patchwork quilt that all fits together and makes sense.

The desire for personal fulfillment was also the main recurrent theme in reasons given for the reduced load by those individuals who did not have children or whose children were grown. In both kinds of cases the rationale was self-fulfillment, not self-sacrifice for the sake of the family.

In summary, the impetus and motivation behind these cases of reduced-load work appears to be consistent with a human ecology interpretation. Respondents describe themselves as existing in a continuously changing social context both at work and at home, and they demonstrate strategic anticipation, rather than a more passive or post hoc reaction to untenable work situations. Their negotiation of reduced-load work can be interpreted as their attempt to adjust and adapt their environment to achieve integrity of functioning.

> I have come to realize as an adult that no one is ever going to be happy with what you are doing all the time. And it has got to be right for you. Obviously you are not in isolation, so you have got to make sure that your job is okay and that your manager is okay with it and your husband and your kids are okay with it, but in the end, you are on your own here. So it has got to be what I am happy with.

This quote illustrates the individual's awareness of change and awareness of self in a broader context. Alternative work arrangements appear to be a mechanism for maintaining health and psychological well-being, because they allow for customized role embracement and therefore preservation of integrity of functioning. That is, these individuals are able to continue in their careers while also coming to terms with family commitments after experiencing the reality of becoming parents.

The demand–control model of stress (Karasek & Theorell, 1990) appears to fit these data on impetus and motivation less well, because in the majority of cases, reduced load was not sought under crisis conditions. If the predominant driving force behind seeking reduced load was relief from stress, we might have expected to see the following kind of explanation as the norm:

> I just found I wasn't doing the job 100%. I wasn't doing home 100%. I wasn't doing anything at 100%. And I just sat back and said, "This is crazy!" My child, instead of screaming when I go away and [being]

happy when I come back, was actually screaming when I came home. So I said, "Wait a second, I'm going to get off this roller coaster and just work three days a week."

Among the 82 cases, only 5 expressed similar sentiments in explaining why they had sought reduced-load work. The predominant context for negotiating the alternative work arrangement was not one of seeking relief, or fleeing an overload situation at work. In fact, the impetus typically emanated from a desire to move *toward* something else, rather than *away* from the heavy demands of the job. Furthermore, the "something else" inspiring individuals to work less was not a desire for increased control at work, which we expected to find, but rather a desire for greater involvement with family, better work–life integration, or personal fulfillment through other activities and roles in the nonwork domain.

A second reason why the demand–control model may not be so useful is that in this study, all participants were seasoned professionals or managers with an average of 10 years' experience with their employers. These individuals already had a great deal of job control, in the sense of decision latitude, *before* seeking to work less. The significance of the reduced-load arrangement was the lowering of job demands, not necessarily the increase of job control. The lowering of job demands gave individuals more time and therefore flexibility to find the right balance of career and family in the context of their children's needs, the logistics and finances of their childcare arrangements and options, their spouses' work constraints, and their own particular needs for time to themselves, or involvement in their community.

Success

Highlights of General Findings. A complete report of the study findings can be obtained from either of the first two authors of this chapter (Lee et al., 1999). Other published papers focus on various aspects of the study (Buck et al., 2000; Lee et al., 2000; MacDermid et al., 2001). However, a few highlights of general findings from the whole sample of 82 cases are summarized here. Overall we found a high level of success in the reduced-load arrangements observed, based on interviewers' global success ratings. The majority of the cases, 62%, fell in the high success group (with ratings of 7–9), 31% in the moderate group (with ratings of 5–6), and 7% in the low group (with ratings of 1–4). On average, the subordinates of the managers on reduced load rated their managers' effectiveness at 7.2 on a scale from 1 to 9. Both the managers and professionals had gained an average of 18 hours per week by working reduced load, and 91% were happier and more satisfied with the balance between home and work. Of respondents, 90% reported that the extra time allowed them to build better relationships with their children.

For most of the managers and professionals working reduced load, and their colleagues and families, this way of working was not a temporary "blip" in their career, but rather a longer-term adaptation. The average length of time on reduced load was 4 years, and only 10% of the sample planned to return to full-time within the next 3 years. The costs of working reduced load were considered temporary and "worth it." Two thirds of respondents reported believing that their career progress had been slowed, not stopped, and their bosses agreed. In two thirds of the cases the bosses believed that the target individuals could immediately resume their former progress if they were to return to full-time work. Of our respondents, 35% had actually been promoted while on reduced load.

Finally, respondents attributed the success of their reduced-load arrangements to a variety of factors, including personal characteristics or strategies as well as contextual factors. There was a consensus that success did not depend on the presence of just one or two variables, but rather on a convergence of multiple ingredients. It was clear from interviews with bosses and coworkers that these individuals were highly skilled and had strong track records. They were also described as working in a very organized and highly focused manner and as being very flexible in responding to work demands. Competent and supportive peers or direct reports also ranked high among factors listed as critical. A supportive organizational culture, or the existence of companywide work–life policies and programs were also seen as helpful, but not essential for success. Thus, respondents tended to provide examples of concurrent forces and synergy operating when the reduced-load arrangement was truly successful.

Positive and Negative Outcomes of Reduced-Load Work. Respondents tended to talk about a variety of outcomes and consequences from working reduced load; most were positive, but some were negative. We will highlight here recurrent themes from a personal and family perspective.

As mentioned previously, enhanced personal well-being was reported in 91% of all cases. At a psychological level this involved a feeling of greater happiness and/or greater balance between work and home. The target individuals described themselves as more energetic, more creative, more focused, and more fresh. Some described specific improvements in quality of life, such as "having the time, energy, and mindset to enjoy my kids when I'm with them." Others emphasized the advantages of gaining an extra day in their schedule. They liked being able to get a lot of errands or chores out of the way on their day off, so that the weekend was free for more relaxation and fun with the whole family. They talked about being pleased to be able to live more in accordance with their personal priorities and to feel successful both at home and at work.

On a more physical level, enhanced personal well-being meant relief from the hectic pace of life, a decrease in stress, less fatigue, and fewer health problems such as headaches, eye strain, neck pain, high blood pressure, and hair loss. In half of the cases, individuals described specific improvements in overall health or physical well-being that they felt had been achieved because of the reduced-load work arrangement.

The third dominant theme in positive outcomes, from strictly a personal point of view, was enhanced satisfaction with life due to time gained for self. The most common investment of additional time was in self-development activities, such as taking jazz piano lessons, attending fitness classes, playing tennis, or pursuing continuing education. In other cases these activities were more clearly leisure oriented: shopping, sleeping in, reading, or gardening. Another set of activities involved connecting with social networks—socializing with friends, neighbors, family, and children's friends and their families. Finally, there were also many cases where these individuals chose to use their extra time to volunteer in community activities such as coaching children's sports teams or teaching Bible School.

As for negative outcomes, the biggest problem reported (in about a third of the cases) was that these individuals felt conflicted at times—they were still quite busy and struggling to get time for themselves. They reported that it was a constant challenge to contain their workload and resist the pressure either to return to full-time, or to do a full-time job in fewer hours.

From a *family* perspective the most dominant theme found in positive outcomes of reduced-load work arrangements was being more involved with children, participating in more activities with them, or having improved relationships with them. This was found in virtually all cases where children were one of the motivating factors for respondents to work less. They talked about getting involved with their children's schools or neighborhood activities. They described being able to interact with kids in a different, more playful way, and in a less structured and constrained time frame. They felt more in touch with their kids' interests and needs, and they believed they were able to respond more quickly to problems or issues as they arose.

The second most common recurrent theme in positive family outcomes was reports of direct improvement in children's well-being as a result of the reduced-load work arrangement. In some cases this had to do with the individual providing more of the childcare directly, or the parents sharing more of the care. In other cases the explanation was that the children were just happier having their parents around more, or that children were getting more attention in regard to homework and after-school activities. Finally, improvement in children's well-being was sometimes attributed to children benefiting from parental role modelling of desirable behavior and attitudes.

The only strongly recurrent negative theme in family outcomes was disappointment that the reduced load had not necessarily improved the marital relationship. The extra time gained did not tend to get devoted to things for husband and wife to do together. However, this theme was present in only 25% of the cases.

The predominant themes in respondents' observations about the pros and cons of reduced-load work provide some support for both a human ecology perspective and a demand–control model of stress. Comments about reduced load allowing greater balance and realignment of priorities is consistent with the conceptualization of individuals seeking to achieve an equilibrium in a broader context. The positive redirection of time and energy into other pursuits, including but not restricted to children and family, suggests further that the reduced-load work represents adjusting levels of involvement in work, family and other roles as part of the pursuit of integrity of functioning.

On the other hand, participants also clearly indicated relief from stress and strain and a decrease in health symptoms, which is consistent with the concept of reduced load as a coping strategy for reducing stress. It appears that the reduced load decreases demands in the workplace, therefore decreasing the level of strain, as in the demand–control model. However, the themes involving relief from something "bad" were not as strong as themes about positive things achieved or experienced. For those participants who simply used the time gained from reduced load to do more of the family work (errands, chores, childcare), there was no net decrease in demands, there was just a shift in the origin or locus of the demands. However, if family work is *chosen* over paid work, and if the decrease in work demands gives these individuals more control over how and when to accomplish the family work, then the ultimate reported increase in happiness and decrease in strain is still consistent with this model.

Differences Between High and Low Individual Net Benefit Groups

Demands. On the first measure of work demands, decrease in job demands, there was no significant difference between the means of the high and low INB groups; the high individual net benefit group was working on average 75% of full-time, whereas the low individual net benefit group was working 71% of full-time. The expectation according to the demand–control model would have been that the high INB group would have a greater decrease in job demands, manifested in working a lower percentage of full-time. However, on the other measure of work demands, real load reduction, the results were as predicted, even though they were not statistically significant. In the high INB group, everyone (100%) had experienced having their jobs truly restructured and reduced, resulting in a mean score of 1.00 on real load reduction. The low INB group mean score on real load reduction was .72. While this finding was not statistically significant, it was in the expected direction and provides some support for the notion that some benefit more than others from reduced-load work arrangements, because they actually experience a real decrease in work demands.

Control. To examine the role of control in the effects of these reduced-load work arrangements, we performed a content analysis of the interview transcripts looking for: (a) the prevalence of the word or theme "control"; (b) the contexts in which control was mentioned; and (c) outcomes attributed to perceived control gains (or lack of perceived control) or other processes.

There was a marked difference in the prevalence of the word "control" in the high and low INB groups. In the high INB group the term "control" was only found repeatedly in 3 of the 12 cases. In the low INB group control came up explicitly as an important issue in 5 of the 8 cases. In another two, although the word itself was not used, control was an implicit theme throughout the case. Of these 7 cases with strong explicit or implicit control themes, 5 of them involved lack or loss of control related to their jobs, but not necessarily related to the reduced-load arrangement. For example, one individual talked about the lack of control in her job caused by the servicing clients aspect of the job:

> You keep them happy and you don't say no . . . the job has to get done, you have to find time to do it. If it means that you're not going to have a day off for the next 2 weeks, that's just too bad.

Although the term "control" was not prevalent in the high INB cases, other terms found frequently included "flexibility," "freedom," and "choice." Although the meanings of these terms are quite different, they all imply an increase in individual discretion, which is inherent in the concept of control.

Among the high individual net benefits cases, the context of talk about control had to do with being able to draw boundaries, or set some limits on work. For example, one individual talked about the importance of being able to choose not to bring work home and to not check e-mail on days off. The second most common context of talk about control in a more implicit sense dealt with having discretion to determine when and where to work, and when to take time off for other commitments or pursuits. These individuals felt that through reduced-load work arrangements they had gained greater flexibility, and more options in their lives as a whole. Control also came up in these cases in discussions of what kinds of jobs give more or less control to the individual. Some expressed the view that higher level jobs, jobs with lots of travel, and jobs where there are more interdependent relationships with others, give the individual less control. Finally, control in the work context came up in connection with whether individuals felt that they either could return to full-time status whenever they wanted, or whether they felt they could afford to resign if their reduced-load work arrangement was in jeopardy for any reason. Individuals' perceptions that they were in control of their own destinies seemed to be an important element in the reduced-load arrangement.

Control also came up among the high INB employees in the context of family and personal life. These individuals talked about the fact that reduced-load work had resulted in family life being "not out of control," or being able to be "more in control" when dealing with children. They talked about the lower workload allowing more relaxation and things to be more organized at home, which "controlled stress."

Among the low INB individuals, the most common context of talk about control involved perceived lack of control over workload. In 6 of the 8 cases, these individuals discussed the specific ways and sometimes the reasons why they had not gained control from the reduced-load arrangement.

> If the client has a problem, it has to be fixed no matter how long it takes.
>
> It's called service . . . Most of us can't walk away from a client situation and leave the client unserviced. I think in any professional service organization that you're going to run into that. The client still has to be serviced whether or not your kid's happy.

It should be noted that even though responsibility for external clients seemed to be connected to feelings of lack of control in the low INB group, in the overall sample there was no consistent evidence that responsibility for external clients was a job factor that hindered successful reduced-load arrangements. In fact, of the nine cases where direct external client accountability was noted, five were rated highly successful (7–9) on Global Success. However, the remaining four cases were all rated as not very successful (1–4). So it appears that this type of job may offer special challenges, which if met are not a problem, but if not can lead to rather disastrous consequences for the individual.

In the other two cases in the low INB group, the control issues played out quite differently. In one situation, the individual had gained enormous control over her workload and talked about how important that was. Yet she was still in the low INB group, because of her account of the personal and career consequences of working reduced load. She did not mention any specific positive outcomes or gains that had accrued directly to her as a result of working on a reduced-load basis. She also discussed the control gained more in relation to the family context, rather than the work context. She liked relying less on childcare and being more involved and in control of what was happening in the family scene:

> I feel that I have a bit more control in that there's no longer a Nanny, an outside party, that I have to coordinate with and be dependent upon.

In the other case, the individual had moved from not working at all to working part-time. She talked about her mental health improving because of increased involvement at work, which she was able to control well, which she felt was essential. However, she also discussed how she felt she had little or no control in the family context, because of the long work hours of her husband. Working part-time added to her overall workload, but she had a good deal of control over that work; meanwhile, she had little control over her workload in the home and saw no way to decrease the demands there.

As for outcomes attributed to control gained from the reduced-load arrangement, the high INB group did not describe the positive consequences in these terms. Individuals in the low net benefits group did tend to explain both positive and negative outcomes directly in control terms. Of the 8 individuals in the low net benefits group, 5 talked about lack of control of their workload or work situation being responsible for things such as health problems (headaches, wrist aches, high blood pressure, weight gain, miscarriages, poor fitness because of no time to work out, anxiety, stress); family life being chaotic, hectic, or pressed; or children's problems (frequent illnesses, psychological distress, and clinginess). Positive outcomes attributed to a gain in control included being able to draw some boundaries around work and being more in control of children's activities because of lower reliance on others for childcare.

Integrity of Functioning. In the high INB group, terms other than control came up consistently in explanations of how reduced load was helpful. These terms included flexibility, freedom, and choice. Flexibility was gained in that these individuals now had an extra day, or other additional time to schedule events and activities outside of work. This group talked about being able to spend more time with their kids, volunteering in the school and community, and pursuing leisure activities for themselves. More time gave them greater freedom to orchestrate their lives as needed, to work when and where it suited them, to take an afternoon off to go on a child's school field trip, for example. They talked about the importance of having choices such as whether to work full-time or part-time, what parts of a job to let go, putting family before work, and whether to work at night and on weekends. The recurrent themes of flexibility, freedom, and choice were talked about not as internal states, but as intermediary outcomes of reduced load which allowed them to do other things. Although these terms could be interpreted as manifestations of increased control, the focus in the narratives was not on the perceived discretion per se but rather what they did with it.

> I like the flexibility and freedom to keep doing what I'm doing and not get burned out.
> I love, I really do enjoy being in a meeting here, in a suit, with some high powered executives, and then going off to put on my jeans and go and work in a classroom environment with a bunch of rowdy kids.

Additional recurrent terms or phrases found in the high individual net benefits group which suggest that a process other than control accounts for positive outcomes were: integration, getting it right, aligning priorities, and making tradeoffs. These kinds of terms were used in a way that suggested these individuals thought of the reduced-load arrangement as part of their own attempt to recalibrate their lives, make adjustments, and create more balance. They viewed themselves as actors in an environment that they could influence as well as adapt to, in order to increase their own "fit" within it. They painted a picture of an ongoing process of negotiation and adaptation to achieve and maintain integrity of functioning.

> I feel I am able to actualize two important parts of . . . important goals for myself. And that is probably the most positive piece of the whole thing.
>
> I have so many other things I like to do outside of work . . . things I just wasn't getting to do . . . and I was just not . . . happy with . . . working all the time.

CONCLUSION

The findings reported in this chapter have focused on individual motivation and the outcomes of reduced-load work arrangements in general in this sample, and differences found between two groups benefiting most and least from these arrangements. It is important to keep in mind the limitations of this study as we reflect on its implications. The sample of professionals and managers studied was not representative, and so we cannot generalize the findings. However, the data triangulation method utilized to capture multiple stakeholder perspectives adds validity to the results. The second part of the results examined involved a small subsample of 20 out of the 82 cases, which means caution should be exercised in interpreting patterns found.

Demand–Control Model

From a motivation perspective, it seems clear that although stress reduction or relief from health symptoms was sometimes a factor, it was not the primary driver for those seeking reduced-load work arrangements. Instead, "seeking integrity of functioning" better describes these individuals' efforts to spend more time with their children, increase the quality of family time on the weekend, or simply create greater balance between career and family. Although relief from stress and specific health-related problems was one commonly reported and important outcome, other equally important outcomes were described that are not accounted for by the demand–control model of stress. There appears, therefore, to be more going on in reduced-load work than just stress reduction.

As for work demand levels explaining the differences in the high and low INB groups, there were no significant differences between the groups on the two objective measures of work demand. However, the pattern of results with real load reduction calls for further investigation of this variable. The term "control" was also not a predominant theme in the high INB cases. However, *lack* of control was an important factor in the negative outcomes in the low individual net benefit group, suggesting that perceived control over workload may be a necessary, but insufficient, condition for achieving positive gains from reduced workload. Respondents' ways of describing how reduced-load work arrangements led to benefits achieved (or not), suggest that for those benefiting the least from reduced load, the traditional demand–control stress model may be helpful. It doesn't explain the positive outcomes for the high INB group, however.

One limitation in the traditional demand–control model of stress is that it looks only at demand and control factors in the work context. When looking at the effects of reduced-load work arrangements, research suggests that it is important to think of individuals in the overall context of their lives, which includes work, family, and personal life. Individuals also have different levels of demand and control, not only in their careers, but also in their families and personal lives. For example, if a person's career demands decrease as a result of reduced load, but the family workload goes up, then there is perhaps no net gain, unless of course there is greater personal enjoyment or fulfillment from the family work. An individual may have more control in the workplace than at home because of nonexistent partner support (whether on ideological grounds or due to work commitments) or as a result of greater uncertainty or unpredictability from sources such as children or hired help. Certainly demand levels and control must be examined in the family or personal life context as well as at work, if we are looking to develop robust predictions about when individuals are most likely to benefit from reduced-load work arrangements.

Another issue which emerges from these findings when using a demand–control theoretical perspective is the question of why the simple decrease in work demands does not differentiate the high and low INB groups. Exploratory analysis of data from the high success respondents in the total sample of the study also shows that level of demands, as measured by the percentage of full-time worked, is not a good predictor of individuals' satisfaction with their work arrangements. While our findings are consistent with other research on the relationship between hours worked and health outcomes (Barnett & Gareis, 2000), our results also indicate that the reduction in load appears to be critical in individuals' getting the extra time they want or need for family or other pursuits. Further research needs to explore what processes beyond actual degree of work-load reduction account for gains in personal fulfillment.

Human Ecology Model

The human ecology model certainly seems to better "map" respondents' descriptions of their experiences with reduced-load work arrangements in this study. Explanations of the timing and rationale behind the reduced load were more consistent with an ongoing process of adjustment and adaptation. Description of the positive consequences of reduced load dealt more with the benefits these individuals derived from their extra time rather than the difficulties from which they had escaped. When the high INB group talked about the gains they had achieved through reduced load, they used terms such as flexibility, freedom, and choice, rather than control. Their descriptions of what the reduced load had allowed them to do fit more with the human ecology framework, which cast them as actors in a dynamic environment. However, as control was definitely an issue for those in the low INB group, it is possible that when people perceive themselves as having control, they use other terms to describe it; whereas, when there is a lack of perceived control, people articulate it exactly in those terms. This inconsistency in the prevalence of control as a theme warrants further investigation to clarify how individuals make sense of their experiences.

However, the human ecology model needs to go further in developing some of its constructs, such as integrity of functioning, to enable predictions about antecedents and consequences of successful reduced-load work arrangements. For example, if we think about how the human ecology framework might predict differences in the high and low INB groups, what we might look for is differences in clarity of priorities. That is, one could reason that integrity of functioning is likely to be difficult to achieve unless people know what they want. Future research could examine whether clarity of priorities truly helps explain why some benefit more than others from reduced-load work arrangements.

From the examination of reduced-load work from a stress perspective, the human ecology framework appears to offer more promise than the demand–control model in expanding our understanding of alternative work arrangements. Barnett's (1998) proposition that there are proximal and distal conditions which affect work–family outcomes could provide more specificity to the human ecology framework and suggest additional ways to measure integrity of functioning. It also seems clear that there are critical processes other than control when individuals succeed in achieving integrity of functioning. Further probing of the meaning and role of these other processes—freedom, flexibility, choice—could make an important contribution to our understanding of how people arrive at a state of integrity of functioning.

Consideration of the implications of the findings presented here must be very tentative given the limitations of the study. However, the greater usefulness of the human ecology framework in interpreting the results suggests that there is no neat formula for assuring a beneficial reduced-load work arrangement. Rather, a great deal of onus is likely to be on the individual to create, negotiate, and continuously fine-tune the work arrangement to suit shifting priorities. In addition, what works for one person will not necessarily work for another, because of all the different factors that play a role in success. A systems framework for understanding circumstances conducive to successful reduced-load work arrangements highlights the importance of the supportiveness of the work environment. Broader findings from the study indicate that professional part-time work arrangements exist in a variety of jobs and industries, and that they can be highly beneficial for both the individual and the organization.

Of course, further research is necessary to ascertain what kinds of processes are critical to shaping mutually beneficial reduced-load work arrangements. Clarity of values or priorities is a construct that could be measured and examined as a critical factor in successful alternative work arrangements according to the human ecology model. Furthermore, extrapolation of the demand–control model to the family domain has the potential to shed light on the nature of family work and the great variability in parental satisfaction in this area. There is a great deal more to be done before we can clarify under what conditions reduced-load work arrangements are likely to lead to beneficial outcomes for those seeking greater work–family balance. This kind of research is very important given the likely emergence of new ways of working in the near future and the increasing number of people in the global workforce looking to successfully combine a high level of commitment to career and family.

REFERENCES

Barnett, R. C. (1998). Toward a review and reconceptualization of the work/family literature. *Genetic, Social, and General Psychology Monographs, 124,* 125–182.

Barnett, R. C., & Gareis, K. C. (2000). Reduced-hours employment. *Work and Occupations, 27,* 168–187.

Blossfeld, Hans-Peter, & Hakim, C. (1997). *Between equalization and marginalization: Women working part-time in Europe and the United States of America.* Oxford, UK: Oxford University Press.

Bronfenbrenner, U. (1979). *The ecology of human development.* Cambridge, MA: Harvard University Press.

Buck, M. L., Lee, M. D., MacDermid, S. M., & Smith, S. (2000). Reduced load work and the experience of time among professionals and managers: Implications for personal and organizational life. In C. L. Cooper, & D. Rousseau (Eds.), *Trends in organizational behavior,* Vol. 7 (pp. 13–36). New York: John Wiley.

Caplan, R. D. (1987). Person–environment fit theory and organizations: Commensurate dimensions, time perspectives, and mechanisms. *Journal of Vocational Behavior, 31,* 246–267.

Catalyst (2000). *Ten years later pioneers of flexible work schedules satisfied with career outcome.* [Press Release]. New York: Author.

Clark, V. S. (1998). *Making sense of part-time professional work arrangements*. Doctoral dissertation. Vancouver, Canada: The University of British Columbia.

Epstein, C. F., Seron, C., Oglensky, B., & Saute, R. (1999). *The part-time paradox*. New York: Routledge.

Fagan, C., & O'Reilly, J. (1998). Conceptualising part-time work. In J. O'Reilly, & C. Fagan (Eds.), *Part-time prospects* (pp. 1–32). New York: Routledge.

Karasek, R. A. (1979). Job demands, job decision latitude and mental strain: Implications for job redesign. *Administrative Science Quarterly, 24*, 285–307.

Karasek, R. A., & Theorell, T. (1990). *Healthy work: Stress, productivity and the reconstruction of working life*. New York: Basic Books.

Kelloway, E. K., & Gottlieb, B. H. (1998). The effect of alternative work arrangements on women's well-being: A demand–control model. *Women's Health: Research on Gender, Behavior, and Policy, 4*, 1–18.

Lee, M. D., Engler, L., & Wright, L. (2002). Exploring the boundaries in professional careers: Reduced load work arrangements in law, medicine, and accounting. In R. J. Burke, & D. L. Nelson (Eds.), *Advancing women's careers* (pp. 174–205). Malden, MA: Blackwell.

Lee, M. D., MacDermid, S. M., & Buck, M. L. (2000). Organizational paradigms of reduced-load work: Accommodation, elaboration, transformation. *Academy of Management Journal, 43*, 1–16.

Lee, M. D., MacDermid, S. M., Williams, M., Buck, M. L., Schreiber, C., Borrelli, L., et al. (1999). *Reconceptualizing professional and managerial careers*. Technical Report prepared for the Alfred P. Sloan Foundation, New York.

Levy, E. S., Flynn, P. M., & Kellogg, D. M. (1997). *Customized work arrangements in the accounting profession: An uncertain future*. Executive Summary of Final Report to the Alfred P. Sloan Foundation, New York.

MacDermid, S. M., Lee, M. D., Buck, M. L., & Williams, M. L. (2001). Alternate work arrangements among professionals and managers: Rethinking career development and success. *Journal of Management Development, 20*, 305–317.

Meiksins, P., & Whalley, P. (1996). *Technical working and reduced work*. Paper presented at the Annual Meeting of the American Sociological Association, Washington, DC.

Miles, M. B., & Huberman, A. M. (1994). *Qualitative data analysis: An expanded sourcebook*. Thousand Oaks, CA: Sage.

Negrey, C. (1993). *Gender, time, and reduced work*. Albany, NY: State University of New York Press.

Raabe, P. (1998). Part-time managers in the federal government. In D. Vannoy, & P. Dubeck (Eds.), *Challenges for work and family in the 21ˢᵗ century* (pp. 81–92). New York: de Gruyter.

Schabracq, M., Cooper, C. L., & Winnubst, J. A. M. (1996). Work and health psychology: Toward a theoretical framework. In M. Schabracq, C. L. Cooper, &

J. A. M. Winnubst (Eds.), *Work and health psychology* (pp. 3–29). New York: John Wiley.

Vroman, W. (1999). *Changes in the work habits of American women and men, 1950 to 1997*. Washington, DC: The Urban Institute.

Wenger, J. (2001). *The continuing problems with part-time jobs.* (Economic Policy Institute Issue Brief #155). Washington, DC: The Economic Policy Institute.

12

AN AFFIRMATIVE DEFENSE: THE PREVENTIVE MANAGEMENT OF SEXUAL HARASSMENT

MYRTLE P. BELL, CYNDY S. CYCYOTA, AND JAMES CAMPBELL QUICK

It is estimated that nearly 50% of women will be sexually harassed in the course of their work or academic lives (Fitzgerald, 1993; Gruber, 1990). Of the nearly 24,000 participants sampled in the U. S. Merit Systems Protection Board (USMSPB) longitudinal studies, 42% of the women and 15% of the men were harassed (USMSPB, 1981, 1988). These rates of harassment are consistent with those reported in various occupations and settings, including airline workers (Littler-Bishop, Seidler-Feller, & Opaluch, 1982), auto workers (Gruber & Bjorn, 1982), lawyers (Burleigh & Goldberg, 1989), university staff and professors (Richman et al., 1999), and clergywomen. Though only a fraction of those who are harassed ever file complaints, more than 15,000 cases still are filed with the Equal Employment Opportunity Commission (EEOC) each year (Buhler, 1999; Charney & Russell, 1994; DuBois, Faley, Kustis, & Knapp, 1999; Gutek, 1997; USMSPB, 1981, 1988;). Given the large number of complaints filed, and large estimates of those who are harassed but never file complaints, it is quite possible that sexual harassment affects the majority of women workers (Sbraga & O'Donohue, 2000). Indeed, despite the more than 20 years that have passed since the EEOC's publication of guidelines on sexual harassment in 1980, sexual harassment remains a chronic and severe problem for working women, who now comprise nearly half the U. S. workforce.

In this chapter, we argue that sexual harassment is a chronic problem in the workplace and, as such, may be treated in a manner similar to chronic health problems by identifying its precursors and developing strategies to prevent it. We begin with a limited review of sexual harassment research, emphasizing the negative consequences of sexual harassment, and discussing the relationship between affirmative defense and preventive management tenets. We next develop and discuss our framework for the preventive management of sexual harassment, providing surveillance indicators and prevention strategies. Finally, we provide suggestions for research and implications for management, given our arguments that sexual harassment can be prevented or reduced through the preventive management approach. Although men are also harassment targets, we focus our discussion on harassment of women, as do other researchers (e.g., Gelfand, Fitzgerald, & Drasgow, 1995; Schneider, Swan, & Fitzgerald, 1997). The measures we propose are designed to prevent harassment of both women and men.

SEXUAL HARASSMENT: A CHRONIC PSYCHOSOCIAL PROBLEM

Sexual harassment is associated with negative outcomes for both individual employees and for the workplace in general. For individuals, long-term negative psychological, physical, and motivation-related outcomes have been linked to sexual harassment (Fitzgerald, Drasgow, Hulin, Gelfand, & Magley, 1997; Munson, Hulin, & Drasgow, 2000). Specifically, sexual harassment has been associated with lowered job satisfaction (Morrow, McElroy, & Phillips, 1994; O'Farrell & Harlan, 1982), increased turnover intentions (Shaffer, Joplin, Bell, Lau, & Oguz, 2000), stress (Crull, 1982; Shaffer et al., 2000), increased health care costs (Fitzgerald et al., 1997) and various other undesirable outcomes. Research also suggests that sexual harassment may have secondary impacts on the workers who are not themselves direct targets of the harassing behavior, but who are witnesses to it (Piotrkowski, 1997). Finally, sexual harassment may extend beyond the organization in which it occurs to affect relations with customers, suppliers, or clients (Fine, Shepard, & Josephs, 1999).

Given the far-reaching negative effects of sexual harassment, we must investigate what is being done to determine the antecedents of sexual harassment and what may be done to *prevent*, rather than react to it. A recent decision by the Ontario (Canada) Labour Relations Board found that sexual harassment was covered by the Occupational Health and Safety Act of the Province of Ontario (Au v. Lyndhurst Hospital: Decision 1517-94-OH, 1997). This indicates some level of governmental recognition of the negative health-related ramifications of sexual harassment, of employer responsibility for ensuring workers' safety from it, and the acknowledgment that sexual harassment is a workplace safety and health hazard. Further, although sexual harassment has not yet been formally recognized as a workplace hazard in the United States, the Occupational Safety and Health Administration (OSHA) imposes a "general duty" on employers to provide a safe, healthy working environment. Even without OSHA's formal determination that sexual harassment is a workplace hazard, the courts have repeatedly ruled that organizations may be found liable for sexual harassment by their employees, managers, or even their customers who harass their employees (Fine et al., 1999).

Affirmative Defense and Preventive Management

Recent Supreme Court (1998) rulings provide strong impetus for employers to actively work to prevent sexual harassment. Specifically, in *Burlington Industries v. Ellerth* (1998) and *Faragher v. City of Boca Raton* (1998), the Supreme Court declared that employers may avoid or limit liability for some sexual harassment by demonstrating that "reasonable care" was exercised to prevent and promptly correct any harassing behaviors, and that the complaining employee unreasonably failed to take advantage of preventive or corrective opportunities provided by the employer or to otherwise avoid the harassment. To qualify for this "affirmative defense," employers should have exercised reasonable care to prevent and promptly correct harassment, including having an antiharassment policy, communicating and training employees about what constitutes harassment and the penalties for doing so, conducting prompt investigations of charges of harassment, and, where warranted, taking corrective action to remedy the situation. Though EEOC guidelines on sexual harassment have long encouraged employers to have antiharassment policies, the guidelines provided in these Supreme Court rulings are the first time employers have been provided with *specific means* to avoid or limit liability in cases in which they had no actual knowledge of harassment, but were later sued.

These guidelines also require some level of responsibility of the harassment target to report harassment (thereby providing the organization with the opportunity to correct the problem) prior to bringing suit. If a harassment target "unreasonably" fails to follow the complaint procedures set forth by the organization, then files suit, the organization may not be found liable. Affirmative defense thus encourages employers to work to *prevent* sexual harassment in a more comprehensive and purposeful manner than the methods of prevention suggested in previous sexual harassment literature.

A strong, well-known policy against sexual harassment has long been suggested by considerable literature as one of the most important means of preventing it (e.g., Dekker & Barling, 1998; Gruber & Smith, 1995; Knapp, Faley, Ekeberg, & DuBois, 1997). However, empirical research demonstrating the efficacy of sexual harassment policies in preventing or reducing the occurrence of sexual harassment is virtually nonexistent (Grundmann, O'Donohue, & Peterson, 1997; Lengnick-Hall, 1995). While a strong, well-publicized sexual harassment policy should indeed be helpful in prevention (it is included as one of the steps in the affirmative defense strategy), we argue that it is certainly not enough. Rather, we believe that a much more comprehensive approach, such as preventive management, is required. The preventive management approach is grounded in the well-established traditions of public health and preventive medicine as applied to the prevention of chronic health problems, and in the emerging organizational behavior literature on dysfunctional behavior in organizations (Griffin, O'Leary-Kelly,

& Collins, 1998; Last & Wallace, 1992). By applying a grounded approach to the management of sexual harassment, we address one of the major concerns about sexual harassment research (Lengnick-Hall, 1995).

Preventive Management and Chronic Problems at Work

An illustration of the power of the preventive management approach is the dramatic decline in suicide rates in the U.S. Air Force in the late 1990s. Between 1994, when a very proactive prevention program was put into place, and 1999, suicides in the Air Force declined from 16 per 100,000 to an estimated 2.2 per 100,000 estimated for year end 1999 ("Air Force," 1999). That is, with the implementation of preventive management efforts, suicides declined by more than 80% in a 5-year period.

A more well-known chronic problem to which the preventive health model can be successfully applied is cardiovascular disease, which continues to be the leading cause of death for men and women in all developed countries (Quick, Quick, Nelson, & Hurrell, 1997). Chronic health problems such as cardiovascular disease are different from infectious and contagious ones; chronic health problems are systemic in nature and do not arise suddenly. Instead, chronic health problems often have multiple causes and develop gradually through a progression of stages or *natural life history*.

There are typically three stages in the life history of a chronic problem, identified as the *stage of susceptibility* (primary), the *early illness stage* (secondary), and finally, the *advanced or disabling disease stage* (tertiary). At the stage of susceptibility to cardiovascular disease, the individual is healthy, yet exposed to certain health risks or precursors to illness, such as a lack of physical exercise or cigarette smoking. If these risks lead to the development of arteriosclerotic plaques in the coronary arteries, the individual is at the stage of early or preclinical disease (secondary) in which few, if any, symptoms are present. As the disease advances, it becomes symptomatic of clinical disease. In the tertiary phase, angina pectoris and heart attacks are advanced manifestations of coronary artery disease. The natural life history of a chronic disease is not inevitable. There is growing evidence for natural protective mechanisms and defenses enabling individuals to remain healthy even when exposed to health risks.

Sexual harassment as a chronic problem fits Griffin et al.'s (1998) definition of dysfunctional behavior in organizations: motivated employee behavior that has negative consequences for one or more individuals in an organization as well as for the organization itself. O'Leary-Kelly, Paetzold, and Griffin (2000) have argued that sexual harassment is motivated, purposeful behavior. As chronic, motivated behavior, we suggest sexual harassment may be managed using the public health notions of prevention in an organizational context. These notions have also been applied to the management of organizational stress (e.g., Quick, Quick, & Nelson, 1998).

The two distinguishing features of the prevention framework offered in this paper are: (a) a data-based emphasis on tracking the natural life history of sexual harassment back to its roots, using the public health concept of surveillance; and (b) the application of preventive and treatment intervention at each stage in the life history of a chronic problem. These two features are depicted in Figure 12.1. The central stem of the model presents the life history of sexual harassment as a chronic problem and examples of dysfunctional behaviors in the workplace. In Stage 1, fertile ground for sexual harassment problems exists when precursors are present in a workplace. In Stage 2, these precursors have given rise to low-to-medium levels of harassment and there is an identifiable problem, though not as extreme as in the next stage. By Stage 3, there has been an escalation of the problem to a very serious level, which may include sexual coercion, rape, or even murder.

Sexual harassment indicators are depicted on the left side of the life history stem for the model. These are data-based means of gathering information about precursor–risk factors for sexual harassment, early warning signs of sexual harassment problems, and the most serious forms of sexual harassment and abuse. On the right side of the life history stem for the model are preventive interventions that aim to slow, stop, or reverse the progression of sexual harassment problems in a workplace. *Primary prevention* is designed to protect health at the stage of susceptibility by eliminating or reducing the precursors for sexual harassment; it is prevention before the

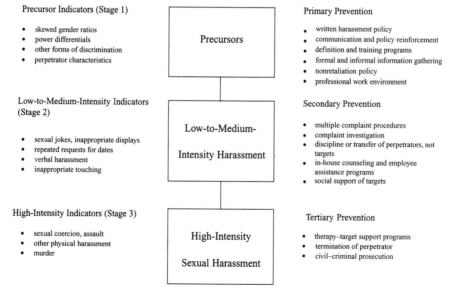

HARASSMENT INDICATORS   HARASSMENT BEHAVIOR   PREVENTIVE STRATEGIES

Precursor Indicators (Stage 1)

- skewed gender ratios
- power differentials
- other forms of discrimination
- perpetrator characteristics

Precursors

Primary Prevention

- written harassment policy
- communication and policy reinforcement
- definition and training programs
- formal and informal information gathering
- nonretaliation policy
- professional work environment

Low-to-Medium-Intensity Indicators (Stage 2)

- sexual jokes, inappropriate displays
- repeated requests for dates
- verbal harassment
- inappropriate touching

Low-to-Medium-Intensity Harassment

Secondary Prevention

- multiple complaint procedures
- complaint investigation
- discipline or transfer of perpetrators, not targets
- in-house counseling and employee assistance programs
- social support of targets

High-Intensity Indicators (Stage 3)

- sexual coercion, assault
- other physical harassment
- murder

High-Intensity Sexual Harassment

Tertiary Prevention

- therapy–target support programs
- termination of perpetrator
- civil–criminal prosecution

Figure 12.1. A framework of preventive strategies and indicators for sexual harassment.

onset of a problem (Winett, 1995). *Secondary prevention* strategies are designed for low-to-medium intensity sexual harassment problems and are designed as early intervention to correct the problem by modifying people's behavior (Last, 1988). *Tertiary prevention–treatment* strategies are therapeutic in nature, aimed at the treatment of symptoms or advanced disease, to alleviate discomfort, and to restore function (Last, 1988). In the case of sexual harassment, tertiary prevention strategies center around caregiving for the direct targets and bystander victims of high-intensity sexual harassment.

Prior to our more detailed discussion of our framework, we would like to clarify our terminology. Because our model is drawn from public health and preventive medicine, the terminology of primary, secondary, and tertiary may appear counterintuitive to those unfamiliar with them. In this arena, primary refers to the first, or lowest levels of harassment prevention. Secondary refers to more strenuous prevention strategies. Tertiary refers to the most strenuous methods of prevention and treatment strategies.

HARASSMENT INDICATORS

Gelfand et al.'s (1995) finding of three related, but conceptually distinct, dimensions of sexual harassment (gender harassment, unwanted sexual attention, and sexual coercion) is relevant to our arguments. *Gender harassment* includes behaviors (verbal and nonverbal) designed to convey "insulting, hostile, and degrading attitudes about women" (Gelfand et al., 1995, p. 168). Threatening or hostile acts, verbal slurs or jokes, and distribution of pornography or obscene materials at work are gender-harassing behaviors and are consistent with "hostile environment sexual harassment," recognized by the U.S. Courts. *Unwanted sexual attention* includes repeated requests for dates, letters or calls; physical contact such as touching or cornering; or sexual assault. Gender harassment and unwanted sexual attention constitute hostile environment sexual harassment. Gelfand et al.'s third dimension, *sexual coercion*, occurs when some job-related outcome is contingent upon sexual cooperation. This behavior may include bribes or threats to induce cooperation. Sexual coercion is equivalent to "quid pro quo" sexual harassment as described by the EEOC guidelines (EEOC, 1980). Though these three forms of sexual harassment are conceptually distinct, Gelfand et al. (1995) suggest that in organizations in which one is present, it is likely that others will also exist. Similarly, though discussed and depicted as independent in our model, the precursors, low-to-medium-intensity acts, and high-intensity acts could concurrently exist in one organization.

Though they are not exhaustive of potential surveillance indicators, the indicators discussed in the remainder of this chapter provide insight as to the situations in which sexual harassment may be likely to occur (or to be occurring). Given the knowledge of situations in which sexual harassment is likely to occur and the persons likely to perpetrate harassment, organizations may then act to prevent its occurrence by changing the mechanisms that make the environment ripe for sexual harassment. Ideally, through proper preventive management, precursors would be identified early and actions would be taken to prevent digression to sexual harassment. Because research indicates that sexual harassment is a function of environmental and organizational contexts (Knapp et al., 1997; Pryor, Giedd, & Williams, 1995), our model includes both individual and organizational indicators and prevention mechanisms.

Precursor Indicators

Precursors of harassment are those in which sexual harassment is at high risk to occur. The existence of these situations in an organization should indicate to management the potential for sexual harassment to ensue. As shown in Figure 1, some precursors to harassment are skewed sex ratios (Gutek, 1985; Gutek, Cohen, & Konrad, 1990), high power differentials between men and women workers (Gruber & Bjorn, 1982), the existence of other forms of discrimination (Yoder & Aniakudo, 1996), and employees who have a previous history of harassment behavior. Previous research indeed has found these precursors to be associated with sexual harassment.

Skewed Sex Ratios and Power Differentials. Skewed sex ratios are associated with sexual harassment when women are employed in male-dominated fields as well as when they are employed in female-dominated jobs, but are managed or supervised by men. In the former instance, women employed in traditionally male groups are more likely to experience hostile environment sexual harassment by coworkers and peers when entering these male-dominated work environments (Gruber & Bjorn, 1982; Gutek et al., 1990; Mansfield et al., 1991; O'Farrell & Harlan, 1982). These women may be subjected to gender harassment, sexual joking and horseplay, and other types of hostile behaviors by their male coworkers. Where women are managed or supervised by men, with high power differentials between the two, sexual coercion is more likely to occur.

Other Discrimination. Where other forms of discrimination exist, sexual harassment is also likely to exist (e.g., Mansfield et al., 1991). In their study of African American women firefighters, Yoder and Aniakudo (1996) found that race discrimination was associated with sexual harassment. Racism is a psychosocial organizational problem with negative consequences (Clark, Anderson, Clark, & Williams, 1999) similar to those of sexual harassment. Organizations that are aware of problems with discrimination on the basis of race, age, religion, or sexual orientation, may also be experiencing (unreported) sexual harassment and should take proactive measures to investigate and remedy the situation.

Perpetrator Characteristics. Finally, according to some research, in order to understand and prevent harassment, demographic characteristics, personality traits, and life experiences of perpetrators must be elucidated (Charney & Russell, 1994). Perpetrators rarely self-identify, thus other measures must be applied to identify persons with the likelihood to harass (Charney & Russell, 1994). Lengnick-Hall (1995) suggested that there are three distinct types of harassers: the hard core, the opportunist, and the insensitive. The *hard core* harasser may be prone to harassment or other dysfunctional behaviors, and is likely to seek out situations that provide the opportunity to perform such behaviors. When organizations are aware of an employee's previous harassing behavior, they must be vigilant about ensuring that it does not recur. Compared with hard core harassers, *opportunists* do not seek out situations in which they are able to harass, but when presented with them (such as in a supervisory role), they will take advantage of the situation. Finally, *insensitive* harassers are simply unaware that their behavior is offensive. Preventive management can be useful for each type of harasser, through training or changing the situation (such as removing them from power).

Low-to-Medium-Intensity Harassment Indicators

Low-to-medium-intensity acts of sexual harassment are those that could be construed as the first steps in harassment, beyond the precursor status, having digressed from situations where harassment was likely or imminent to those in which harassment is actually occurring. We note that the terminology "low to medium" is not intended to demean the seriousness or negative consequences associated with this type of harassment. Low-to-medium-intensity acts include persistent sexual joking or commentary, inappropriate displays of pictures or objects, repeated requests for dates, and verbal harassment. Physical contact, such as inappropriate touching, hugging, jostling, and groping are also included as low-to-medium-intensity acts. These behaviors are classified as "hostile environment" harassment and, as discussed previously, often occur in organizations or departments having skewed sex ratios.

High-Intensity Harassment Indicators

High-intensity sexual harassment is the most obvious and visible category and includes quid pro quo harassment (sexual coercion), sexual assault, other types of physical harassment, and at times, murder. Sexual coercion occurs when some job-related reward or punishment is contingent on whether the target complies with the harassing behavior. When women are in female-dominated jobs, working with other women, but supervised by men, their low status, authority, power, and earnings provide the opportunity for quid pro quo sexual harassment (Gruber, 1997), in which the supervisor requires sexual favors in exchange for some job-related benefit. Sexual coercion is the least common form of sexual harassment (O'Hare & O'Donohue, 1998), yet is extremely damaging. Perhaps the most well-known case of high-intensity sexual harassment is that of Michele Vinson, perpetrated by her boss at Meritor Saving Bank. Vinson was sexually coerced and assaulted repeatedly by her boss over a lengthy period (*Meritor v. Vinson*, 1986). Extrapolation from the Merit Systems Protection Board studies (USMSPB, 1981, 1988) suggests that 12,000 female federal workers may have been victims of rape or attempted rape in the 2-year period covered in the study (Fitzgerald, 1993).

High-intensity sexual harassment may also result in murder of the harassment target. One such case occurred in the mid-1990s, when an employee of Bank One began harassing Tracey Stevens, also a bank employee. Stevens complained about the harassment, which included leaving a single red rose on her desk daily. The harasser was disciplined and ultimately fired. Months later, the still-angry harasser broke into Stevens' home and killed her, her husband, and infant daughter (Cadwallader, 1996).

Having identified surveillance indicators for sexual harassment, we next discuss measures that organizations may incorporate to prevent the occurrence of sexual harassment and to reduce the intensity, frequency, and duration of its adverse effects.

PREVENTION STRATEGIES FOR SEXUAL HARASSMENT

As depicted in Figure 12.1, preventive management strategies may fall into one of three categories. Primary prevention aims to remove or neutralize the precursors of sexual harassment. Secondary prevention strategies are designed to reverse and minimize the damage of low-to-medium-intensity sexual harassment. Tertiary prevention strategies are designed to treat the victims and manage the perpetrators of high-intensity sexual harassment.

Primary Prevention

Policies and Communication.   Much research argues that a written non-harassment policy is the starting point in the prevention of sexual harassment in the workplace (e.g., Piotrkowski, 1998; Rowe, 1996). Policies must be communicated to all levels of an organization (Kulik, Perry, & Schumidtke, 1997) and openly supported by all levels of management. In

Faragher v. City of Boca Raton (1998), although Boca Raton had a sexual harassment policy, the City was still liable for the harassment because the policy had not been disseminated to employees.

Sexual harassment policies should be posted (*Jones v. USA Petroleum,* 1998), as are other important (e.g., safety, equal employment opportunity) policies. Having a formal, widely communicated harassment policy (including consequences for such behavior) may deter potential harassers (O'Hare & O'Donohue, 1998). Further, formal harassment policies have been associated with more assertive reactions to or reporting of harassment (Gruber & Smith, 1995).

Definition and Training. Policies can have little preventive effect if organization members do not share an understanding of what sexual harassment actually is. Organizations should design training programs that define sexual harassment, describe harassing behaviors, outline the procedures to be used in making a complaint, explain the process for handling these claims, and identify the potential punishment for harassment (O'Hare & O'Donohue, 1998). Training should also educate potential targets of their rights and their responsibilities to report harassment, especially given the affirmative defense strategy.

New hires should receive sexual harassment training as an important part of their orientation (Buhler, 1999). The inclusion of sexual harassment training would set the stage for zero tolerance and make clear the organization's position. Existing employees should also be trained regularly, reinforcing the organization's position and providing updates that reflect recent court decisions (Buhler, 1999).

Kulik et al. (1997) outline training programs that utilize role-playing techniques to define harassment under the "reasonable woman" standard. This standard requires that observers view harassment incidents through the eyes of a reasonable woman experiencing harassment. Researchers suggest that observers who adopt the perspective of the target see harassment behavior as more serious than those who take the perspective of the perpetrator (Pryor & Day, 1988). Training programs should be developed and presented to all organizational members including potential targets, observers, and perpetrators (Grundmann et al., 1997; Kulik, et al., 1997; O'Hare & O'Donohue, 1998). Education and training on harassment are particularly important as more women label behaviors such as sexual remarks or discussion of one's personal or sex life as harassment more frequently than do men (Fitzgerald & Ormerod, 1991).

Formal and Informal Information Gathering. An important element of primary prevention involves both informal and formal communication and information gathering. Many targets may be reluctant to report harassment incidents, choosing instead to ignore them and hope the harasser will "go away" (Fitzgerald, Swan, & Fischer, 1995). It may be advisable, then, to include other means of detecting sexual harassment that is not formally reported by targets, such as observers who bring harassment to the attention of the employer. Observers who believe their organization will take appropriate action are more likely to report sexual harassment (DuBois et al., 1999).

The workplace grapevine may provide valuable information about potentially harassing behaviors. Such informal information should be noted and, respecting its source and the rights of all parties, followed up with more formal information gathering, such as anonymous attitude surveys. Anonymous surveys may provide important information that may not otherwise be obtained in face-to-face or formal complaint channels. Researchers suggest that the effectiveness of sexual harassment policies can be judged by surveys of employees (Fitzgerald & Shullman, 1993; Rowe, 1996). Along with measures of such things as job and pay satisfaction, and trust and confidence in management, attitude surveys should include measures assessing gender attitudes, knowledge of the sexual harassment policy, the existence of sexual harassment in the organization, and overall workplace norms. Detection of negative attitudes toward women or stereotypical perceptions of women's roles (which have been associated with harassing behaviors; Gruber, 1997; Gutek, 1985; Ragins & Scandura, 1995) may be aided by anonymous surveys.

Non-retaliation Policy. It is also important for employers to recognize that harassment targets may be reluctant to report harassment out of fear of retaliation from the perpetrator (Dandeker, 1990; Gutek & Koss, 1993; Riger, 1991). As an example, one of the authors learned of a workplace rape that occurred in California during the mid-1990s that was not officially reported because of the victim's fear of retaliation. Though she called the organization's (confidential) Employee Assistance Program for help, the victim was unwilling to file a complaint because she was not confident that the organization and senior management would be supportive and was fearful of reprisals in an already violent workplace.

Fitzgerald and Shullman (1993) suggest that retaliation in sexual harassment cases may be more emotionally charged than in other types of organizational whistle-blowing and that employers need to recognize this. It is the responsibility of the employer to make clear and widely communicate that adverse treatment of employees who report harassment or provide information related to harassment complaints will not be tolerated. Management should ensure that retaliation does not occur after a complaint by monitoring employment decisions about the target or witnesses. Under affirmative defense, if harassment targets who did not complain had *legitimate* fears of retaliation, employers are not free from liability. To be free from liability, the employer must be able to show that the target's fears of retaliation were "unreasonable," for example, by having multiple complaint channels or a widely disseminated nonretaliation policy.

Professional Work Environment. The last of our primary prevention strategies is a professional and mutually respectful work environment (Lengnick-Hall, 1995). Researchers have identified practices in work settings that facilitate or deter sexual harassment (Gutek, 1985). One specific practice that acts as an inhibitor to sexual harassment is a professional work environment (Grundmann, et al.,1997; O'Hare & O'Donohue, 1998). Managers and supervisors should clearly identify, model, and enforce professional behavior (O'Hare & O'Donohue, 1998). Deadrick, McAfee, & Champagne (1996) suggest that "preventing harassment involves developing employee responsibility for maintaining a harassment free environment, thus developing an environment of mutual respect where individuals take it upon themselves to monitor and eliminate harassment from the workplace" (p. 66). Such development requires that employees at all levels recognize that workplace problems (including harassment and other forms of discrimination) stem from a lack of mutual respect among workers and are harmful to everyone, regardless of whether they are directly targeted.

Secondary Prevention

Although a harassment-free environment is the goal for organizations, few have reached that point. When such behavior occurs, organizations must have multiple complaint procedures that may be used by targets, investigatory and discipline procedures, and social support and counseling for targets.

Multiple Complaint Procedures. As discussed previously, the inclusion of multiple complaint procedures can be helpful for targets who are reluctant to report sexual harassment incidents (Riger, 1991). Mechanisms for making complaints should include informal procedures and additional reporting channels that do not include a direct supervisor, who may be the perpetrator. Some studies indicate that reporting of sexual harassment increases when informal policies are offered along with formal policies (Biaggio, Watts, & Brownell, 1990; Rowe, 1996). This may be a result of targets being more likely to perceive that their organizations will support them as the number of formal and informal policies for the complaints increases (DuBois et al., 1999).

Investigatory and Disciplinary Procedures. Investigations of sexual harassment allegations should be prompt, thorough, and impartial. Where warranted, the perpetrator of harassment should be subject to discipline procedures as outlined by the organization's sexual harassment policies. These disciplinary actions may include transfer of the perpetrator, required participation in sexual harassment counseling, or other options that limit the potential for recurrence of harassment. Corrective actions should be appropriate to the seriousness of the sexual harassment incident (DuBois et al., 1999).

Social Support and Counseling. In-house counseling and employee assistance programs may be needed to help targets recover psychologically from harassment, which may have far-reaching consequences, including loss of self-esteem and guilt. Some organizational members may need explicit training to empathize with targets (Bresler & Thacker, 1993). Charney and Russell (1994) suggest that the key therapeutic tasks for harassment counselors are empathy, validation, and empowerment. These tasks may need to be performed by clinically trained professionals or offered through Employee Assistance Programs.

Tertiary Prevention Strategies

When primary and secondary prevention are not enough, tertiary prevention strategies are an essential last resort for sexual harassment problems. Tertiary prevention strategies fall into two categories: tertiary prevention strategies for victim(s) and tertiary prevention strategies for perpetrators.

Tertiary Prevention for Victims. High-intensity sexual harassment may yield one or more primary victims, as well as any number of bystander victims. Targets of sexual harassment may require physical, psychological, or spiritual caregiving by physicians, psychologists, or members of the clergy or chaplaincy. When someone is seriously threatened or harmed in the course of sexual harassment at work, the organization should provide medical and psychological services. The provision of emotional support and professional caregiving is an essential immediate response mechanism that every organization should have available.

Bystander victims, witnesses, colleagues, and others affected in the work environment may also need professional support and caregiving. High-intensity sexual harassment may threaten many employees' sense of security about the work environment to the point that professional and managerial support may be required to repair the damage. Planning for medical, psychological, and spiritual assistance for the victims is one essential form of tertiary prevention.

Tertiary Prevention for Perpetrator(s). No organization should tolerate high-intensity sexual harassment and perpetrators leave an organization few viable options. Security forces must act swiftly (see Rowe, 1996, for recommendations on addressing dangerous harassment cases). The perpetrator(s) must be terminated and subject to criminal or civil prosecution. For the organization to show full commitment to a comprehensive sexual harassment policy, and to mount an affirmative defense, it must fully pursue perpetrators of harassment. While the vast majority of high-intensity sexual harassment cases may simply require law enforcement and judicial action, organizations should be attuned to the potential for psychological evaluations or mandatory treatment for perpetrator(s), because passing the problem along to the larger society has its own social costs. Organizations may benefit from developing collaborative strategies with law enforcement and judicial authorities for the most effective management of perpetrators of high-intensity sexual harassment.

DISCUSSION

In this chapter, we add the concept of preventive management to the literature on sexual harassment by using a framework that has been successfully used with other chronic psychosocial problems (e.g., suicide). Though considerable research and, recently, the Supreme Court, has suggested that organizations should actively work to prevent sexual harassment, this chapter is the first to clearly and specifically provide measures of prevention that are linked to a well-supported approach for prevention of other chronic problems. That the prevention model has been successful in other arenas may be particularly helpful, given the reluctance of organizations to allow empirical research of the existence of sexual harassment.

A possible criticism of this model is that in many cases of chronic illness, the person suffering from the illness is the one whose behavior or lifestyle must change. For example, a person suffering from heart disease would need to stop smoking and begin exercising to avoid further deterioration of health. In contrast, if one accepts a medical model for sexual harassment, the target or victim is "suffering" from harassment, but it is the behavior of the harasser, rather than the behavior of the victim, that must change. Alternatively, if one looks at the unit of analysis, the chronic medical problems are of an individual nature, while chronic organizational problems are of a collective or communal nature. Therefore, while the individual with heart disease must change his or her individual behavior, the organization with sexual harassment disorders must change its collective behavior, to include changing the behavior of the perpetrator(s). Further, organizational and situational components, such as skewed sex ratios and policies, also may need to be changed. Once the precursors are identified, the sexual harassment can be arrested and further deterioration prevented, regardless of whose behavior or what attributes must be changed. Given that sexual harassment has negative consequences for both individuals and organizations, it is reasonable that multiple preventive measures would be necessary.

Implications for Practice

In an ideal preventive situation, a newly formed organization would apply primary preventive steps to avoid any harassment. Management would work to ensure that skewed gender ratios and other forms of discrimination were avoided and that power between men and women was balanced. The organization would formulate and communicate its harassment policy, educate and train managers and employees, conduct regular attitude surveys, and maintain a professional environment. These preventive steps should greatly reduce the likelihood of the occurrence of sexual harassment. In this ideal situation, a strategy of affirmative defense should rarely be necessary, as the environment should remain harassment free.

Existing organizations may find precursors, low-to-medium harassment, or high-intensity harassment in existence at the time at which they decide to engage in preventive management. Unfortunately, this may be after a charge or complaint of sexual harassment has been made or a lawsuit has been filed. Preventive management would still be useful for such organizations, though not for affirmative defense for the charge at hand. In applying this model to an existing organization, the preventive strategy appropriate for each stage should be utilized. If there is no harassment policy in existence, a written harassment policy should be developed, communicated, and followed. Multiple complaint procedures, investigation and discipline, and the other secondary prevention methods should be included. If high-intensity harassment is present, the tertiary prevention and treatment strategies should also be applied. In this case, the organization would need to develop in its employees a sense that sexual harassment will no longer be tolerated. To do so, changes must be clearly visible, zero tolerance should be applied, and upper management must be committed to change.

Implications for Research

As noted previously, organizations may be reluctant to allow empirical research on sexual harassment because of the risk of litigation. Nonetheless, several important aspects of this model may be tested with little risk to specific organizations. Of particular interest and importance are attention to organizations that exemplify the best- and worst-case scenarios. For example, organizations with strong prevention measures may indeed be free of harassment. What may be learned from such organizations that may be applicable to preventive management? What cultural aspects exist in these organizations (Hulin, Fitzgerald, & Drasgow, 1996)?

On the other hand, organizations replete with sexual harassment, noteworthy from media accounts and damage awards (e.g., Asta, Mitsubishi, Ford Motor Company), may also provide information useful to the study of harassment. What about these organizations made sexual harassment so pervasive? Were there any safe havens within them, in which women were free of harassment? What characteristics were evident in such safe havens?

Another area of importance is what may drive the perpetrators of hard core, high-intensity harassment. In the Bank One case discussed previously, it appears that, in firing the perpetrator, Bank One did what it should have done to stop the harassment. Yet, the target and her family were ultimately killed by the harasser. What can be learned from such instances, though rare, to prevent them in the future? Would a background check or personality test have identified this employee as a potential harasser? What, if any, selection mechanisms can be employed prior to selection to avoid hiring hard core harassers or opportunists?

CONCLUSION

Sexual harassment is an important problem for workers and their organizations. It affects morale, job satisfaction, turnover and other withdrawal behaviors, and is associated with negative physical and psychological outcomes. The opportunity to mount an affirmative defense provides organizations with financial impetus to work actively to prevent sexual harassment. More importantly, applying the preventive management approach may not only help ensure success in defending lawsuits, but also in preventing sexual harassment from occurring. Given that the legal liability and potential costs of sexual harassment are minor when compared with other costs (e.g., turnover, productivity, and absenteeism) the preventive management approach has the potential to provide organizations with cultural and structural benefits that far exceed potential legal liabilities.

REFERENCES

Airforce suicide rates show significant decline. (1999, November 26) *Wall Street Journal*, p. A12.

Biaggio, M., Watts, D., & Brownell, A. (1990). Addressing sexual harassment: Strategies for prevention and change. In M. Paludi (Ed.), *Ivory power: Sexual harassment on campus* (pp. 213–230). Albany, NY: SUNY Press.

Bresler, S. J., & Thacker, R. (1993). Four-point plan helps solve harassment problems. *HR Magazine, 38,* 117–124.

Buhler, P. M. (1999). The manager's role in preventing sexual harassment. *Supervision, 60,* 16–18.

Burleigh, N., & Goldberg, S. (1989). Breaking the silence: Sexual harassment in law firms. *ABA Journal, 75,* 46–52.

Burlington Industries v. Ellerth, 524 U.S. 775, 118 S. Ct. 2275 (1998).

Cadwallader, B. (1996, August 30). Hessler had plot, gun and motive to kill, jury told. *The Columbus Dispatch,* p. A1.

Charney, D. A., & Russell, R. C. (1994). An overview of sexual harassment. *American Journal of Psychiatry, 151,* 10–17.

Clark, R., Anderson, N. B., Clark, V. R., & Williams, D. R. (1999). Racism as a stressor for African Americans. *American Psychologist, 54,* 805–816.

Crull, P. (1982). Stress effects of sexual harassment on the job: Implications for counseling. *American Journal of Orthopsychiatry, 52,* 539–544.

Dandeker, N. (1990). Contrasting consequences: Bringing charges of harassment compared with other cases of whistle-blowing. *Journal of Business Ethics, 9,* 151–158.

Deadrick, D. L., McAfee, R. B., & Champagne, P. J. (1996). Preventing workplace harassment: An organizational change perspective. *Journal of Organizational Change Management, 92,* 66–75.

Decision 1517-94-OH Au v. Lyndhurst Hospital. (1997). *Ontario Labour Relations Board Reports,* 616–636.

Dekker, I., & Barling, J. (1998). Personal and organizational predictors of workplace sexual harassment of women by men. *Journal of Occupational Health Psychology, 31,* 7–18.

DuBois, C. L. Z., Faley, R. H., Kustis, G. A., & Knapp, D. E. (1999). Perceptions of organizational responses to formal sexual harassment complaints. *Journal of Managerial Issues, 112,* 198–212.

Equal Employment Opportunity Commission (1980). Guidelines on discrimination because of sex. *Federal Register, 45,* 74676–74677.

Equal Employment Opportunity Commission (1995). *Guidelines on Discrimination Because of Sex, 29,* C.F.R. Sex. 1604.11.

Faragher v. City of Boca Raton, 524 U.S. 742, 188 S. Ct. 2257 (1998).

Fine, L. M., Shepard, C. D., & Josephs, S. L. (1999). Insights into sexual harassment of salespeople by customers. The role of gender and customer power. *Journal of Personal Selling and Sales Management, 19,* 19–34.

Fitzgerald, L. F. (1993). Sexual harassment: Violence against women in the workplace. *American Psychologist, 48,* 1070–1076.

Fitzgerald, L. F., Drasgow, R., Hulin, C. L., Gelfand, M. J., & Magley, V. J. (1997). Antecedents and consequences of sexual harassment in organizations: A test of an integrated model. *Journal of Applied Psychology, 82,* 578–589.

Fitzgerald, L. F., & Omerod, A. J. (1991). Perceptions of sexual harassment: The influence of gender and context. *Psychology of Women Quarterly, 15,* 281–294.

Fitzgerald, L. F., & Shullman, S. L. (1993). Sexual harassment: A research analysis and agenda for the 1990s. *Journal of Vocational Behavior, 42,* 5–27.

Fitzgerald, L. F., Swan, S., & Fischer, K. (1995). Why didn't she just report him? The psychological and legal implications of women's responses to sexual harassment. *Journal of Social Issues, 51,* 117–138.

Gelfand, M. J., Fitzgerald, L. F., & Drasgow, F. (1995). The structure of sexual harassment: A confirmatory analysis across cultures and settings. *Journal of Vocational Behavior, 47,* 164–177.

Griffin, R. W., O'Leary-Kelly, A., & Collins, J. (Eds.), (1998). *Dysfunctional behavior in organizations* (Vols. 1–2). Greenwich, CT: JAI Press.

Gruber, J. E. (1990). Methodological problems and policy implications in sexual harassment research. *Population Research and Policy Review, 9,* 235–254.

Gruber, J. E. (1997). An epidemiology of sexual harassment: Evidence from North America and Europe. In W. O'Donohue (Ed.), *Sexual harassment: Theory, research, and treatment* (pp. 84–98). Boston: Allyn & Bacon.

Gruber, J. E., & Bjorn, L. (1982). Blue-collar blues: The sexual harassment of women autoworkers. *Work and Occupations, 93,* 271–298.

Gruber, J. E., & Smith, M. E. (1995). Women's responses to sexual harassment: A multivariate analysis. *Basic and Applied Social Psychology, 17,* 543–562.

Grundmann, E. O., O'Donohue, W., & Peterson, S. H. (1997). The prevention of sexual harassment. In W. O'Donohue (Ed.), *Sexual harassment: Theory, research, and treatment* (pp. 175–184). Boston: Allyn & Bacon.

Gutek, B. A. (1985). *Sex and the workplace.* San Francisco: Jossey-Bass.

Gutek, B. A. (1997). Sexual harassment policy initiatives. In W. O'Donohue (Ed.), *Sexual harassment: Theory, research, and treatment* (pp. 185–199). Boston: Allyn & Bacon.

Gutek, B. A., Cohen, A. G., & Konrad, A. M. (1990). Predicting social–sexual behavior at work: A contact hypothesis. *Academy of Management Journal, 33,* 560–577.

Gutek, B. A., & Koss, M. P. (1993). Changed women and changed organizations: Consequences of and coping with sexual harassment. *Journal of Vocational Behavior, 42,* 28–48.

Hulin, C. L, Fitzgerald, L., & Drasgow, F. (1996). Organizational influences on sexual harassment. In M. S. Stockdale (Ed.), *Sexual harassment in the workplace* (pp. 127–150). Thousand Oaks, CA: Sage.

Jones v. USA Petroleum, 20 F. Supp. 2d 1379, 1384 (S.D. Ga. 1998).

Knapp, D. E., Faley, R. H., Ekeberg, S. E., & DuBois, C. L. Z. (1997). Determinants of target responses to sexual harassment: A conceptual framework. *Academy of Management Review, 223,* 687–729.

Kulik, C. T., Perry, E. L., & Schmidtke, J. M. (1997). Responses to sexual harassment: The effect of perspective. *Journal of Managerial Issues, 91,* 37–53.

Last, J. M. (1988). *A dictionary of epidemiology* (2nd ed.). New York: International Epidemiological Association.

Last, J. M., & Wallace, R. B. (Eds.), (1992). *Public health & preventive medicine* (13th ed.). Norwalk, CT: Appleton & Lange.

Lengnick-Hall, M. L. (1995). Sexual harassment research: A methodological critique. *Personnel Psychology, 484,* 841–864.

Littler-Bishop, S., Seidler-Feller, D., & Opaluch, R. E. (1982). Sexual harassment in the workplace as a function of initiator's status: The case of airline personnel. *Journal of Social Issues, 38,* 137–148.

Mansfield, P. K., Koch, P. B., Henderson, J., Vicary, J. R., Cohn, M., & Young, E. W. (1991). The job climate for women in traditionally male blue-collar occupations. *Sex Roles, 25,* 63–79.

Meritor Savings Bank v. Vinson, 477 U.S. 57 (1986).

Morrow, P. C., McElroy, J. C., & Phillips, C. M. (1994). Sexual harassment behaviors and work related perceptions and attitudes. *Journal of Vocational Behavior, 45*, 295–309.

Munson, L. J., Hulin, C., & Drasgow, F. (2000). Longitudinal analysis of dispositional influences and sexual harassment: Effects on job and psychological outcomes. *Personnel Psychology, 53*, 21–57.

O'Farrell, B., & Harlan, S. L. (1982). Craftworkers and clerks: The effects of male coworker hostility on women's satisfaction with nontraditional jobs. *Social Problems, 29*, 252–264.

O'Hare, E. A., & O'Donohue, W. (1998). *Archives of Sexual Behavior, 376*, 563–580.

O'Leary-Kelly, A. M., Paetzold, R. L., & Griffin, R. W. (2000). Sexual harassment as aggressive behavior: An actor based perspective. *Academy of Management Review, 25*, 372–388.

Piotrkowski, C. S. (1997). Sexual harassment. In J. M. Stellman (Ed.), *ILO Encyclopaedia of Occupational Health and Safety*, (pp. 34.28–34.29). Geneva, Switzerland: International Labour Office, & Chicago: Rand McNally.

Piotrkowski, C. S. (1998). Gender harassment, job satisfaction, and distress among employed white and minority women. *Journal of Occupational Health Psychology, 3*, 33–43.

Pryor, J. B., & Day, J. D. (1988). Interpretations of sexual harassment: An attributional analysis. *Sex Roles, 18*, 405–417.

Pryor, J. B., Giedd, J. L., & Williams, K. B. (1995). A social psychological model for predicting sexual harassment. *Journal of Social Issues, 51*, 69–84.

Quick, J. D., Quick, J. C., & Nelson, D. L. (1998). The theory of preventive stress management in organizations. In C. L. Cooper (Ed.), *Theories of organizational stress* (pp. 246–268). Oxford, England: Oxford University Press.

Quick, J. C., Quick, J. D., Nelson, D. L., & Hurrell, J. J., Jr. (1997). *Preventive stress management in organizations*. Washington, DC: American Psychological Association.

Ragins, B. R., & Scandura, T. A. (1995). Antecedents and work-related correlates of reported sexual harassment: An empirical investigation of competing hypotheses. *Sex Roles, 32*, 429–455.

Richman, J. A., Rospenda, K. M., Nawyn, S. J., Flaherty, J. A., Fendrich, M., Drum, M. L., et al. (1999). Sexual harassment and generalized workplace abuse among university employees: Prevalence and mental health correlates. *American Journal of Public Health, 893*, 358–363.

Riger, S. (1991). Gender dilemmas in sexual harassment policies and procedures. *American Psychologist, 46*, 497–505.

Rowe, M. P. (1996). Dealing with harassment: A systems approach. In M. S. Stockdale (Ed.), *Sexual harassment in the workplace* (pp. 241–272). Thousand Oaks, CA: Sage.

Sbraga, T. P., & O'Donohue, W. (2000). Sexual harassment. *Annual Review of Sex Research, 11*, 258–286.

Schneider, K. T., Swan, S., & Fitzgerald, L. F. (1997). Job-related and psychological effects of sexual harassment in the workplace: Empirical evidence from two organizations. *Journal of Applied Psychology, 82,* 401–415.

Shaffer, M. A., Joplin, J. R. W., Bell, M. P., Lau, T., & Oguz, C. (2000). Gender discrimination and job-related outcomes: A cross-cultural comparison of working women in the United States and China. *Journal of Vocational Behavior, 57,* 395–427.

U.S. Equal Employment Opportunity Commission (EEOC) (1980). Discrimination because of sex under Title VII of the 1964 Civil Rights Act as amended: Adoption of interim guidelines—sexual harassment. *Federal Register, 45,* 25024–25025.

U.S. Merit Systems Protection Board (1981). *Sexual harassment in the Federal workplace: Is it a problem?* Washington, DC: U.S. Government Printing Office.

U.S. Merit Systems Protection Board (1988). *Sexual harassment in the Federal workplace: An update.* Washington, DC: U.S. Government Printing Office.

Winett, R. A. (1995). A framework for health promotion and disease prevention and programs. *American Psychologist, 50,* 341–350.

Yoder, J. D., & Aniakudo, P. (1996). When pranks become harassment: The case of African American women firefighters. *Sex Roles, 35,* 253–270.

13

DO FAMILY-FRIENDLY POLICIES FULFILL THEIR PROMISE? AN INVESTIGATION OF THEIR IMPACT ON WORK–FAMILY CONFLICT AND WORK AND PERSONAL OUTCOMES

HAZEL M. ROSIN AND KAREN KORABIK

The expression "family-friendly" has, during the past decade or so, appeared with increasing frequency in scholarly and popular writing on topics relevant to human resource management in organizations. According to Scheibl and Dex (1998), although the term lacks a concise definition, it may be understood as a shorthand for describing the growing variety of policies and programs that organizations are introducing with the aim of facilitating the ability of employees to fulfill their family-based responsibilities.

In recent years, there has been a substantial expansion in the number of employers providing family-friendly options, a development that was almost unthinkable less than two decades ago (Kossek, Dass, & DeMarr, 1994; Osterman, 1995). The motivations underlying this transformation have been attributed primarily to the profound changes that have swept the workplace over the past quarter century (see chapter 1). Because of these changes, employed individuals, particularly women, find it extremely difficult to reconcile the competing responsibilities inherent in their work/professional and family roles, and consequently suffer from stress and chronic fatigue (Gonyea, 1993; Hughes & Galinsky, 1988).

There is evidence that individuals with family responsibilities increasingly seek employment with companies that demonstrate a sincere commitment to helping employees balance their work and family lives, and also are more likely to stay with such organizations (Allen, Herst, Bruck, & Sutton, 2000). For example, 59% of parents in a recent study reported that one of the reasons they chose their present job was because of the presence of family-friendly policies (Galinsky, Bond, & Friedman, 1996). With respect to retention, family-friendly initiatives have been linked to reduced turnover (Lobel, 1999).

The provision of family-friendly programs to employees, therefore, is predicated on the calculation that they will produce a variety of beneficial effects—reduced absenteeism and stress, and increased satisfaction, commitment, and productivity—by reducing the work–family conflict that researchers and pollsters have found afflict contemporary families. However, while there is substantial literature examining the outcomes associated with either work–family conflict or family-friendly policies, a recent meta-analysis noted that there were "only a handful of studies that measured the relation between work–family conflict, policies, and job and personal outcomes" (Kossek & Ozeki, 1998, p. 140).

We will not review the literature on work–family conflict here because it has been covered in chapters 6–8. Instead, we will focus on the research that has examined the impact of family-friendly policies as well as those few studies that have examined policies, work–family conflict, and outcomes in combination. Subsequent to this, we will describe the results of a three-wave study we conducted that systematically examined the impact of family-friendly policies on work–family conflict and on organizational and personal outcomes.

FAMILY-FRIENDLY POLICIES

Assessments of the impact of family-friendly initiatives present a contradictory picture. Evaluations are often anecdotal and consist of glowing "testimonials"—claims by company spokespersons that though they may be accurate, are not based on empirical research (Lobel, 1999). Some empirical studies indicate that family-friendly initiatives have a positive impact on organizations and employees by reducing absenteeism and turnover, and improving work attitudes (Lobel, 1999). However, as will be apparent from the following review, the results of others are more equivocal (see also Gonyea & Googins, 1992).

Work-Related Outcomes

Stress. Research on the effects of family-friendly benefits, such as flexible work arrangements (FWAs), on reducing stress-related outcomes does not seem to provide a strong endorsement of their efficacy. One study found that a reduction in feelings of stress was reported by a majority of the (mostly female) users of an FWA program implemented in a large Canadian bank (Tombari & Spinks, 1999). Similarly, another study found that the number of family-friendly benefits used by working mothers with at least one preschool child in daycare was related to reduced role strain (Warren & Johnson, 1995). In contrast, other research indicates that, despite employees' beliefs that greater flexibility would ease their burdens, formal FWAs had little effect on perceived stress among working parents (Shinn, Wong, Simko, & Ortiz-Torres, 1989).

Frequently, research shows that the greatest benefits are derived by those least in need of the programs. For example, Bohen and Viveros-Long (1981) found that although flextime decreased role strain and family stress in general, it made little difference to working parents, with most of the benefits experienced by single and childless workers. Similarly, the use of family-friendly benefits has been found to be related to decreased role strain for single women, but increased role strain for married women (Greenberger, Goldberg, Hamill, O'Neil, & Payne, 1989).

Satisfaction and Commitment. Several theories suggest that family-friendly policies should contribute to enhanced job satisfaction and organizational commitment. For instance, Hackman and Oldham's job characteristics theory suggests that the increased autonomy and control permitted by flexible working hours should result in increased job satisfaction (Baltes, Briggs, Huff, Wright, & Neuman, 1999). Similarly, according to the work adjustment model, "high correspondence between an employee's needs and the reinforcement system of the work environment should lead to more positive job attitudes" (Baltes et al., 1999, p. 498). Also relevant is the notion of the psychological contract (Rousseau, 1995). According to Scandura and Lankau (1997), family-friendly policies should strengthen this contract by enhancing employees' perceptions that the organization cares about their needs, thus contributing to greater job satisfaction and organizational commitment.

In support of the theories, Kossek and Ozeki's meta-analysis reported that "there is a consistent relationship between access to or use of work–family policies (particularly those perceived as supporting flexibility in role integration) and job satisfaction" (1998, p. 146). Another meta-analysis (Baltes et al., 1999) found that both flextime and compressed work week schedules were significantly related to enhanced job satisfaction. However, the positive effects dissipated over time and were greater for programs with less flexibility. Moreover, the effect was significant only for general employees and not for those in managerial positions or professional occupations. Baltes et al. attribute this result to the fact that managers and professionals already have jobs that afford them greater autonomy, making them less reliant on flexible policies.

The results of other studies, however, are less consistent. Whereas several have found that job satisfaction is enhanced by the presence of family-friendly policies (Burud, Aschbacher, & McCroskey, 1984, as cited in Gonyea, 1993; National Council of Jewish Women, 1987; Youngblood & Chambers-Cook, 1984), in others, job satisfaction has been found to be unrelated to them. For example, job satisfaction has been found to be unrelated to the degree of formal flexibility (Shinn et al., 1989), to satisfaction with flexibility of job schedules (Rothausen, 1994), or to use of an employer-sponsored daycare center (Marquart, 1988, as cited in Gonyea, 1993). In addition, although Judge, Boudreau, and Bretz's (1994) study of male executives found that job satisfaction was positively correlated with the extensiveness of work–family policies, Greenberger et al. (1989) found that the number of family-friendly benefits used was positively related to job satisfaction for single women, but not married women or men.

The impact of family-friendly initiatives on organizational commitment is also inconclusive. Some studies have found increased commitment as a result of family-friendly policies in general, or as a result of specific initiatives such as schedule flexibility or daycare centers (Aryee, Luk, & Stone, 1998; Grover & Crooker, 1995; Kropf, 1999; Tombari & Spinks, 1999; Youngblood & Chambers-Cook, 1984). On the other hand, Marquart (1988, as cited in Gonyea, 1993) found no differences in commitment between users and nonusers of an employer-sponsored daycare center.

One explanation for these inconsistencies may be that family-friendly options have a differential impact on men and women. Because family demands are still primarily women's preoccupation and responsibility, the availability of family-friendly policies may be more likely to increase their commitment than it would that of men. This is consistent with Scandura and Lankau's (1997) contention that the nature of the psychological contract may be different for women versus men and for parents versus those with no children. In support of this argument, Greenberger et al. (1989) found that the number of family-friendly benefits used was related to organizational commitment among married and single women, but not among men. Likewise, Scandura and Lankau (1997) found that the perception that flexible working hours were available was related to increased commitment and satisfaction among women and those with family responsibilities, but not men or those without families. By contrast, two other studies have found no sex differences in organizational commitment as a function of family-friendly policies. This could be due to the fact that the men and women in their samples had equally high levels of family involvement (Aryee et al., 1998; Marsden, Kalleberg, & Cook, 1993). In sum, the relationship between commitment and family-friendly policies is complex and not yet well understood.

Turnover and Turnover Intentions. A number of studies suggest that family-friendly benefits result in lower turnover or turnover intentions (see reviews by Gonyea, 1993; Lobel, 1999). For example, access to family-friendly policies (Grover & Crooker, 1995) and satisfaction with schedule flexibility (Aryee et al., 1998) are correlated with lower turnover intentions. Moreover, satisfaction with flexibility of job scheduling is negatively related to turnover for parents (Rothausen, 1994). Several employer policies, most importantly length of maternity leave and the ability to avoid mandatory overtime, were found by Glass and Riley (1998) to reduce mothers' attrition in the first year following childbirth. Similarly, Glass and Estes (1996, as cited in Scheibl & Dex, 1998) found higher productivity and retention among mothers who were allowed to work at home after childbirth. Additionally, a number of studies have demonstrated that employer-sponsored daycare is related to lower turnover and an increased ability to attract and retain employees (Burud et al., 1984; Dawson, Mikel, Lorenz, & King, 1984; Perry, 1978, all as cited in Gonyea, 1993; Youngblood & Chambers-Cook, 1984).

Personal Outcomes. In addition to potential improvements in employee work attitudes and retention, researchers also have been interested in whether family-friendly initiatives have a positive impact on family and life satisfaction. In this regard, schedule flexibility has been associated with increased satisfaction with family life (Parasuraman, Purohit, Godshalk, & Beutell, 1996). In addition, Judge et al. (1994) found a significant positive relationship between the extensiveness of work–family policies and life satisfaction among male executives. However, other research has shown that the degree of flexibility in scheduling was not significantly related to family satisfaction or life satisfaction among working parents (Shinn et al., 1989).

Although there is some inconsistency in the outcomes of the research, family-friendly initiatives appear to have a variety of positive outcomes overall. Still, little is known about the mechanisms through which these policies bring about favorable outcomes, or the extent to which they affect men and women differently.

FAMILY-FRIENDLY POLICIES, WORK–FAMILY CONFLICT, AND OUTCOMES

As noted earlier, very little research has examined the assumption that family-friendly policies produce their beneficial effects by reducing work–family conflict. Of the few studies that have examined this issue, only one has found clear evidence that work–family policies ameliorate work–family conflict. Gooler's (1996) study showed that organizational provision of support (e.g., flextime, family leave, telecommuting) had direct effects in reducing work–family conflict both in terms of work interference with family (WIF) and family interference with work (FIW), absenteeism, and turnover intentions, and in increasing job satisfaction. Thomas and Ganster (1995), however, found that flexible schedules had only an indirect effect in reducing work–family conflict and enhancing job satisfaction. Moreover, in a study of working parents with children under the age of five, Goff, Mount, and Jamison (1990) concluded that there were no significant differences in work–family conflict between users and nonusers of an on-site daycare center. Rather, it was supportive supervisors and satisfaction with childcare (regardless of its location) that were the significant predictors. Furthermore, Galinsky et al.'s research (1996) indicated that although employed parents reported experiencing higher levels of work–family conflict and stress than nonparents, access to family-friendly policies was not associated with lower levels of work–family conflict and only slightly predictive of lower stress among both groups. These discouraging findings seem to contradict the generally favorable effects that have been shown to be associated with the implementation of family-friendly policies and the reduction of work–family conflict, as we discussed previously. Further investigation is warranted in order to understand these perplexing results.

LIMITATIONS OF PAST RESEARCH

Some of the inconsistencies in the results of past studies may be attributable to methodological limitations. For example, almost all studies have been cross-sectional (e.g., Galinsky et al., 1996; Grover & Crooker, 1995; Rothausen, 1994; Shinn et al., 1989), making them susceptible to common method bias. Moreover, research has often been company specific (e.g., Kossek & Nichol, 1992; Rothausen, 1994; Youngblood & Chambers-Cook, 1984) and findings, therefore, might be biased by peculiarities of the company setting (Grover & Crooker, 1995). In addition, some studies have only sampled parents (Goldberg, Greenberger, Koch-Jones, O'Neil, & Hamill, 1989; National Council of Jewish Women, 1987), whereas others (e.g., Grover & Crooker, 1995) have used demographically diverse, national random samples.

Relatively few studies have specifically set out to examine gender differences, despite the fact that men and women may be differentially affected. Men and women may have distinct experiences of work–family conflict (Duxbury & Higgins, 1991), and men's utilization of family-friendly policies is also unlike women's (Pleck, 1993).

Most studies on the outcomes associated with either family-friendly policies or work–family conflict consider only one or two dependent variables. In addition, some research has not distinguished WIF from FIW. Kossek and Ozeki (1998) conclude on the basis of their meta-analysis that measures that separate the two dimensions perform better than global measures that do not. This may be important if, as Frone and Yardley (1996) suggest, FIW is more likely to be related to the utilization and importance ratings of family-friendly policies than is WIF.

Studies are also inconsistent in what aspects of family-friendly policies they examine (i.e., access to, utilization of, satisfaction with, or importance of). "Researchers usually have focused on the availability of particular benefits or the number of benefits available, without consideration of whether these benefits satisfy the need of the employee" (Greenberger et al., 1989, p. 760). This may explain why mere access to or utilization of family-friendly policies does not appear to have direct effects on work and family outcomes (Goldberg et al., 1989). Instead, employees' perceptions of the importance of workplace policies or their satisfaction with them seem to be more critical.

THE STUDY

The study we now describe examines the extent to which perceptions of, satisfaction with, and importance of family-friendly policies impact work–family conflict (both WIF and FIW) and a variety of outcome variables within the work and family domains. This exploratory research was part of a larger investigation of the career patterns and attitudes of men and women professionals. The participants were drawn from four occupations: bankers, accountants, managers, and engineers. Data were collected at three points in time over a 20 month period via three separate mail surveys. From an initial mailing of 2,707 questionnaires, those who responded to all three totaled 1,102 (a 41% response rate). Only the 533 men (11% bankers, 14% certified accountants, 22% managers, and 10% engineers) and 412 women (10% bankers, 14% certified accountants, 13% managers, and 6% engineers) who were organizationally employed are included in this study. Their average age was 41 and they had an average of 16.5 years of work experience.

In the first survey, single item questions were used to assess a variety of demographic characteristics (i.e., age, education, income, marital status, and number of children), as well as hours worked per week.

The second survey included a number of measures of stress including role ambiguity and role conflict (Rizzo, House, & Lirtzman, 1970), role overload (Beehr, Walsh, & Taber, 1976), job-induced tension (House & Rizzo, 1972), and perceived stress (Cohen, Kamarch, & Mermelstein, 1983). WIF and FIW (Gutek, Searle, & Klepa, 1991) were also assessed.

In addition, respondents rated each of seven family-friendly policies (parental leave, paid days off for family concerns, job sharing, policies dealing with family responsibilities, daycare, flextime, and telecommuting) as to how important each of these policies was to them, and how satisfied they were with each policy.

The third survey assessed a variety of work- and family-related outcomes. The work-related outcomes were job involvement (Kanungo, 1982), job satisfaction (Quinn & Staines, 1979), and organizational commitment (Mowday, Steers, & Porter, 1979). Intention to leave was assessed using a scale composed of seven items drawn from three sources (Camman, Fichman, Jenkins, & Klesh, 1979; Mitchell, 1981; Rosin & Korabik, 1991). The family-related outcomes were family involvement (Frone & Rice, 1987), family satisfaction (Kopelman, Greenhaus, & Connolly, 1983), and life satisfaction (Quinn & Staines, 1979). All scales had acceptable levels of internal consistency and reliability.

Following the method specified by Kerlinger and Pedhauzer (1973), a series of separate path analyses was conducted via ordinary least squares regression. These were used to examine the importance of and satisfaction with family-friendly policies as predictors of work–family conflict (WIF and FIW) and several outcome variables in the work and family domains. Separate path models were estimated for each outcome variable for men and for women. At each stage of the path analysis, the variable considered to be the dependent variable was regressed on all of the variables on which it was assumed to depend. Thus, during the first stage of the analysis, the paths between importance of and satisfaction with family-friendly policies and a set of control variables (age, education, income, hours worked per week, marital status, and number of children) were estimated. Subsequently, the paths between importance of and satisfaction with family-friendly policies and the work–family conflict variables were estimated, followed by the paths between WIF and FIW and the outcome variable of interest (see Figure 1a).

Figures 13.1 and 13.2 provide the standardized regression coefficients (i.e., beta weights) that were obtained when WIF and FIW were predicted from policy satisfaction and importance during Step 2 of the analysis. For both men and women, ratings of policy importance were not significantly associated with either WIF or FIW. In contrast, higher satisfaction with family-friendly policies was significantly associated with both lower WIF and lower FIW (see Figures 13.1 and 13.2).

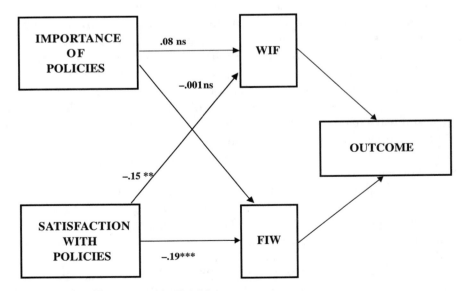

Figure 13.1. Diagram of path model for men.

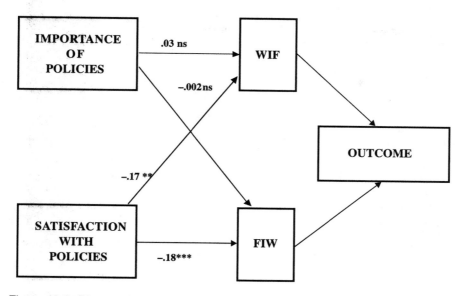

Figure 13.2. Diagram of path model for women.

The results for Step 3 of the path analysis are presented separately for men and women in Table 13.1. Table 13.2 provides the standardized regression coefficients (i.e., beta weights) that were obtained for each of the dependent variables in Step 3 of the analysis.

For men, lower WIF predicted significantly lower role conflict, role overload, job-induced tension, perceived stress, and job involvement, and

TABLE 13.1
Path Analysis Results for Women and Men

Dependent Variables	Women			Men		
	R^2	F (10, 254)	p	R^2	F (10, 254)	p
Role ambiguity	.07	1.9	.05	.22	9.14	0
Role conflict	.15	4.52	0	.16	5.88	0
Role overload	.28	10.2	0	.33	15.71	0
Job induced tension	.32	12.49	0	.35	17.07	0
Perceived stress	.32	12.09	0	.35	16.92	0
Job involvement	.08	1.9	.05	.1	2.29	.02
Job satisfaction	.19	5.93	0	.18	6.45	0
Organization commitment	.1	2.57	0	.16	3.34	0
Quit intentions	.12	3.01	0	.1	2.8	0
Family involvement	.19	5.18	0	.15	4.47	0
Family satisfaction	.16	4.98	0	.19	7.35	0
Life satisfaction	.11	2.82	0	.2	6.41	0

TABLE 13.2
Standardized Regression Coefficients for Men and Women

Dependent variables	Work interference with family		Family interference with work	
	Men	Women	Men	Women
Role ambiguity	−.17**	−.16*	−.19***	−.16*
Role conflict	.27***	.31***	.17**	.11
Role overload	.52***	.45***	.06	.02
Job induced tension	.53***	.57***	.14**	−.06
Perceived stress	.50***	.46***	.22***	.25***
Job involvement	.23**	.17*	−.02	−.02
Job satisfaction	−.20***	−.37***	−.08	.06
Org. commitment	−.11	−.12	−.14*	.04
Quit intentions	.12	.23**	−.12	−.02
Family involvement	−.17**	−.07	−.07	−.05
Family satisfaction	−.23***	−.15*	−.13*	−.20**
Life satisfaction	−.41***	−.30***	−.05	−.01

Note. $* p < .05; ** p < .01; *** p < .001.$

significantly higher role ambiguity, job satisfaction, family involvement, family satisfaction, and life satisfaction. Lower FIW predicted significantly lower role conflict, job-induced tension, and perceived stress and significantly higher role ambiguity, organizational commitment, and family satisfaction (see Table 13.2).

For women, lower WIF predicted significantly lower role conflict, role overload, job-induced tension, perceived stress, job involvement, and turnover intentions, and significantly higher role ambiguity, job satisfaction, family satisfaction, and life satisfaction. Lower FIW predicted only significantly lower perceived stress and significantly higher role ambiguity and family satisfaction (see Table 13.2).

In order to examine whether there were any differences between the sexes, t-tests were computed comparing the unstandardized regression coefficients for men and women on each of the dependent variables. There were no significant differences ($p < .05$).

Discussion. This study has a number of strengths that distinguish it from most previous research. Firstly, whereas previous research often has not made gender comparisons, or has relied on samples from a single organization, this study used a large sample composed of men and women from four different occupations and from a wide variety of organizations. Secondly, past research has not always used reliable measures (Allen et al., 2000); FIW and WIF often have not been measured separately, a wide range of dependent variables usually has not been examined, and analyses have not controlled for potential confounds. By contrast, this study incorporated a number of control variables and used psychometrically sound measures of both WIF and FIW, as well as of a large number of outcome variables in the work and personal domains. Thirdly, whereas almost all previous research has been cross-sectional (Allen et al., 2000), this study employed a three-wave design. This allowed us to eliminate common method bias as an alternative explanation for our results.

Although the data were collected at different points in time, one limitation of the study was that the measures of work–family conflict, satisfaction with and importance of family-friendly policies, and some of the outcome variables (i.e., the stress-related measures) were all collected at the time of Survey 2. This meant that mediating effects could not be ascertained and limited the degree to which causal interpretations could be made. Another potential limitation of our study is that all participants were professionals. Recent research has suggested that family-friendly initiatives are more available to professionals than nonprofessionals and that organizations derive greater productivity benefits when providing work–life programs to professionals (Konrad & Mangel, 2000). Therefore, care should be exercised when generalizing from the results of our study, and the findings should be replicated on nonprofessional samples.

Through use of a more rigorous methodology, however, we were able to establish that satisfaction with family-friendly policies is associated with the amelioration of work–family conflict and, in turn, is related to favorable outcomes in both the work and family domains. These included reduced stress, increased satisfaction and commitment, and lower turnover intentions. This is consistent with Gooler's (1996) study that, like ours, distinguished between WIF and FIW. By contrast, those studies in which family-friendly policies were not found to reduce work–family conflict used global measures of conflict (i.e., Galinsky et al., 1996; Goff et al., 1990; Thomas & Ganster, 1995).

Our results indicated that, once the control variables had been partialed out, there were no gender differences. For both men and women, higher satisfaction with family-friendly policies was associated with significant reductions in both WIF and FIW. In terms of work-related outcomes for both sexes, reduced levels of WIF were associated with significantly decreased role conflict, role overload, job-induced tension, perceived stress, and job involvement, and with significantly increased role ambiguity and job satisfaction. In the family domain, lower WIF predicted significantly higher family and life satisfaction. For both sexes, reduced levels of FIW were related to significantly lower perceived stress and significantly higher role ambiguity in the work domain, and to significantly higher family satisfaction in the family domain. For both men and women, a reduction in WIF had more significant effects, particularly in the work domain, than a reduction of FIW. This is not surprising, given that in professional occupations, it is more likely for work to interfere with family than vice versa (Frone, Russell, & Cooper, 1992).

While the reductions in the stress-related variables and increases in satisfaction are what might be hoped for, the reduction in job involvement associated with lower WIF, as well as the increase in role ambiguity associated with both WIF and FIW, appeared puzzling initially. With respect to role ambiguity, it may be that the use of family-friendly programs contributes to a reduction in role rigidity by making the boundaries between family and work more fluid. If this is so, increased role ambiguity could be seen as a positive consequence of family-friendly initiatives.

The lower scores on job involvement that were associated with reduced WIF may at first appear to be negative from the point of view of corporations. We should recall, however, that the job involvement measure (Kanungo, 1982) contains statements such as "the most important things that happen to me involve my present job." Thus, lower scores may actually be indicative of the fact that employees are more closely achieving the desired balance between their work and family lives which is, after all, the stated purpose of family-friendly policies. It is important for corporations to recognize that having more balanced employees is not detrimental. A linkage between job involvement scores and employee effectiveness has not been established, and the amount of time spent at work is not related to the quality and quantity of the work produced (Bank of Montreal, 1991).

Our results provide clear evidence that for both men and women it is satisfaction with family-friendly policies (rather than their perceived importance, availability and use) that predicts a reduction of work–family conflict and positive personal and work outcomes. This is consistent with the findings of other studies (Galinsky et al., 1996; Thomas & Ganster, 1995). Our results raise the question, "what makes family-friendly policies satisfying to their recipients?" It has been suggested that policies are perceived as satisfying when they meet workers' needs (Greenberger et al., 1989). Research has shown that giving workers increased control over the management of their personal and professional obligations, and ensuring supervisor or organizational support reduces work–family conflict (Gooler, 1996; Thomas & Ganster, 1995). Thus, it is likely that when individuals are satisfied with family-friendly policies, it is because these policies not only are suited to the employees' requirements, but also allow them to increase their control and are implemented in the context of a supportive environment.

CONCLUSION

This study lends empirical support to the assumption made by a growing number of companies that the provision of family-friendly initiatives to employees has positive effects on work–family conflict reduction. This, in turn, produces a variety of positive outcomes including decreased stress, increased work and family satisfaction, organizational commitment, and decreased turnover intentions. It is important to note that these may be only a few of the potential beneficial consequences associated with the provision of family-friendly policies. Others that were not included in our study, and have generally been neglected thus far in the literature, include higher productivity and job performance, and lower absenteeism and actual turnover (Allen et al., 2000). Future research should address the moderating effects of family-friendly policies on the relationship between work–family conflict and these outcomes. Furthermore, research is needed that explicates the mechanisms through which family-friendly policies bring about their desirable results.

With respect to our research, it is critical to recognize that the positive outcomes that emerged were a function of employee satisfaction with family-friendly initiatives, not with their simple presence. In other words, if companies are to benefit from the institution of such initiatives, they need to ensure—via consultation with their employees—that the programs provided meet employee needs, and that the programs are implemented in a supportive environment that encourages employees to use them without fear of being penalized in terms of salary, promotions, or career development. This suggests that an organization's culture and management must support and recognize the value of these initiatives. If organizations take these caveats seriously, they will avoid wasteful and unnecessary expenditures on programs that are underutilized or fail to achieve their purpose. Instead, careful implementation of the desired initiatives should produce substantial benefits for employees and organizations.

REFERENCES

Allen, T. D., Herst, D. E. L., Bruck, C. S., & Sutton, M. (2000). Consequences associated with work-to-family conflict: A review and agenda for future research. *Journal of Occupational Health Psychology, 5,* 278–308.

Aryee, S., Luk, V., & Stone, R. (1998). Family-responsive variables and retention-relevant outcomes among employed parents. *Human Relations, 51,* 73–87.

Baltes, B. B., Briggs, T. E., Huff, J. W., Wright, J. A., & Neuman, G. A. (1999). Flexible and compressed workweek schedules: A meta analysis of their effects on work-related criteria. *Journal of Applied Psychology, 84,* 496–513.

Bank of Montreal Report to Employees. (1991, November). *The task force on the advancement of women in the bank.* Montreal: Author.

Beehr, T. A., Walsh, J. T., & Taber, T. D. (1976). Relationship of stress to individually and organizationally valued states: Higher order needs as a moderator. *Journal of Applied Psychology, 61,* 41–47.

Bohen, H. H., & Viveros-Long, A. (1981). *Balancing jobs and family life.* Philadelphia, PA: Temple University Press.

Camman, C., Fichman, M., Jenkins, D., & Klesh, J. (1979). *The Michigan Organizational Assessment Questionnaire.* Unpublished manuscript, University of Michigan, Ann Arbor.

Cohen, S., Kamarch, T., & Mermelstein, R. (1983). A global measure of perceived stress. *Journal of Health and Social Behavior, 24,* 385–396.

Duxbury, L. E., & Higgins, C. A. (1991). Gender differences in work-family conflict. *Journal of Applied Psychology, 76,* 60–74.

Frone, M. R., & Rice, R. W. (1987). Work-family conflict: The effect of job and family involvement. *Journal of Occupational Behavior, 8,* 45–53.

Frone, M. R., Russell, M., & Cooper, M. L. (1992). Prevalence of work-family conflict: Are work and family boundaries asymmetrically permeable? *Journal of Organizational Behavior, 13,* 723–729.

Frone, M. R., & Yardley, J. K. (1996). Workplace family-supportive programmes: Predictors of employed parents' importance ratings. *Journal of Occupational and Organizational Psychology, 69,* 351–366.

Galinsky, E., Bond, J. T., & Friedman, D. E. (1996). The role of employers in addressing the needs of employed parents. *Journal of Social Issues, 52,* 111–136.

Glass, J. L., & Riley, L. (1998). Family responsive policies and employee retention following childbirth. *Social Forces, 76,* 1401–1435.

Goff, S. J., Mount, M. K., & Jamison, R. L. (1990). Employer supported child care, work/family conflict, and absenteeism: A field study. *Personnel Psychology, 43,* 793–809.

Goldberg, W. A., Greenberger, E., Koch-Jones, J., O'Neil, R., & Hamill, S. (1989). Attractiveness of childcare and related employer-supported benefits and policies to married and single parents. *Child and Youth Care Quarterly, 18,* 23–37.

Gonyea, J. G. (1993). Family responsibilities and family-oriented policies: Assessing their impacts on the work place. *Employee Assistance Quarterly, 9,* 1–28.

Gonyea, J. G., & Googins, B. K. (1992). Linking the worlds of work and family: Beyond the productivity trap. *Human Resources Management, 31,* 209–226.

Gooler, L. (1996, August). *Coping with work-family conflict: The role of organizational support.* Paper presented at the annual meeting of the Academy of Management, Cincinnati, OH.

Greenberger, E., Goldberg, W., Hamill, S., O'Neil, R., & Payne, C. (1989). Contributions of a supportive work environment to parents' well-being and orientation to work. *American Journal of Community Psychology, 17,* 755–783.

Grover, S. L., & Crooker, K. J. (1995). Who appreciates family-responsive human resource policies: The impact of family-friendly policies on the organizational attachment of parents and non-parents. *Personnel Psychology, 48,* 271–288.

Gutek, B. A., Searle, S., & Klepa, L. (1991). Rational versus gender role explanations for work-family conflict. *Journal of Applied Psychology, 76,* 560–568.

House, R. J., & Rizzo, J. R. (1972). Role conflict and ambiguity as critical variables in a model of organizational behavior. *Organizational Behavior and Human Performance, 7,* 467–505.

Hughes, D., & Galinsky, E. (1988). Balancing work and family life: Research and corporate application. In A. E. Gottfried, & A. W. Gottfried (Eds.), *Maternal employment and children's development: Longitudinal research.* New York: Plenum Press.

Judge, T. A., Boudreau, J. W., & Bretz, R. D. (1994). Job and life attitudes of male executives. *Journal of Applied Psychology, 79*, 767–782.

Kanungo, R. (1982). Measurement of job and work involvement. *Journal of Applied Psychology, 67*, 341–349.

Kerlinger, F. N., & Pedhauzer, E. J. (1973). *Multiple regression in behavioral research.* New York: Holt, Rinehart, & Winston, Inc.

Konrad, A. M., & Mangel, R. (2000). The impact of work-life programs on firm productivity. *Strategic Management Journal, 21*, 1225–1237.

Kopelman, R., Greenhaus, J., & Connolly, T. (1983). A model of work, family, and inter-role conflict: A construct validation study. *Organizational Behavior and Human Performance, 32*, 198–215.

Kossek, E. E., Dass, P., & DeMarr, B. (1994). The dominant logic of employer-sponsored work and family initiatives: Human resource managers' institutional role. *Human Relations, 47*, 1121–1149.

Kossek, E. E., & Nichol, V. (1992). The effects of on-site child care on employee attitudes and performance. *Personnel Psychology, 45*, 485–509.

Kossek, E. E., & Ozeki, C. (1998). Work-family conflict, policies, and the job-life satisfaction relationship: A review and directions for organizational behavior–human resources research. *Journal of Applied Psychology, 83*, 139–149.

Kropf, M. B. (1999). Flexibility initiatives: Current approaches and effective strategies. *Women in Management Review, 14* 177–185.

Lobel, S. A. (1999). Impacts of diversity and work-life initiatives in organizations. In G. N. Powell (Ed.), *Handbook of gender and work* (pp. 453–474). Thousand Oaks, CA: Sage.

Marsden, P. V., Kalleberg, A. L., & Cook, C. R. (1993). Gender differences in organizational commitment: Influences of work positions and family roles. *Work and Occupations, 20*, 368–390.

Mitchell, J. O. (1981). Effect of intentions, tenure, personal and organizational variables on managerial turnover. *Academy of Management Journal, 24*, 742–751.

Mowday, R. T., Steers, R. M., & Porter, L. W. (1979). The measurement of organizational commitment. *Journal of Vocational Behavior, 14*, 224–247.

National Council of Jewish Women (1987, November). *Accommodating pregnancy in the workplace.* NCJW Center for the Child report. New York: Author.

Osterman, P. (1995). Work/family programs and the employment relationship. *Administrative Sciences Quarterly, 40*, 681–700.

Parasuraman, S., Purohit, Y. S., Godshalk, V. M., & Beutell, N. J. (1996). Work and family variables, entrepreneurial career success, and psychological well-being. *Journal of Vocational Behavior, 48*, 275–300.

Pleck, J. H. (1993). Are family supportive employer policies relevant to men? In J. C. Hood (Ed.), *Men, work and family* (pp. 217–237). Newbury Park, CA: Sage.

Quinn, R. P., & Staines, G. L. (1979). *The 1977 Quality of Employment Survey.* Institute for Social Research, University of Michigan, Ann Arbor.

Rizzo, J. R., House, R. J., & Lirtzman, S. I. (1970). Role conflict and ambiguity in complex organizations. *Administrative Sciences Quarterly, 15*, 150–163.

Rosin, H. M., & Korabik, K. (1991). Workplace variables, affective responses, and intention to leave among women managers. *Journal of Occupational Psychology, 64*, 317–330.

Rothausen, T. J. (1994). Job satisfaction and the parent worker: The role of flexibility and rewards. *Journal of Vocational Behavior, 34*, 317–336.

Rousseau, D. M. (1995). *Psychological contracts in organizations: Understanding written and unwritten agreements,* Thousand Oaks, CA: Sage.

Scandura, T. A., & Lankau, M. J. (1997). Relationships of gender, family responsibility and flexible work hours to organizational commitment and job satisfaction. *Journal of Organizational Behavior, 18*, 377–391.

Scheibl, F., & Dex, S. (1998). Should we have more family-friendly policies? *European Management Journal, 16*, 585–599.

Shinn, M., Wong, N. W., Simko, P. A., & Ortiz-Torres, B. (1989). Promoting the well-being of working parents: Coping, social support, and flexible job schedules. *American Journal of Community Psychology, 17*, 31–55.

Thomas, L. T., & Ganster, D. C. (1995). Impact of family-supportive work variables on work/family conflict and strain: A control perspective. *Journal of Applied Psychology, 80*, 6–15.

Tombari, N., & Spinks, N. (1999). The work/family interface at Royal Bank Financial Group: Successful solutions—A retrospective look at lessons learned. *Women in Management Review, 14*, 186–193.

Warren, J. A., & Johnson, P. J. (1995). The impact of workplace support on work–family role strain. *Family Relations, 44*, 163–169.

Youngblood, S. A., & Chambers-Cook, K. (1984, February). Child care assistance can improve employee attitudes and behavior. *Personnel Administrator,* 93–95.

IV

CONCLUSION

14

NEW DIRECTIONS FOR STUDYING GENDER, WORK STRESS, AND HEALTH

DEBRA L. NELSON, RONALD J. BURKE, AND SUSAN MICHIE

As this collection bears out, the research on gender, work stress, and health is eclectic both in terms of subject matter and study methods. As a body of knowledge, it has contributed to our understanding of the different stressors faced by men and women, the varied ways they cope, the challenge of managing the work–home interface, and the interventions that organizations can use to assist individuals. To move forward in this understanding, we believe that researchers must concern themselves with some additional questions of a provocative, contemporary, and holistic nature.

Although many unanswered questions remain, we propose six that we believe should occupy research efforts in the new millennium.

1. In what ways have the new economy and a new psychological contract affected men and women's work stress and health, and how has the contemporary work environment influenced (changed) gender role expectations?
2. Are there particular occupational and demographic or family structure groups that need greater research attention?
3. Are the differences we think of as gender based really biological in nature?
4. Is a more positive approach possible, focusing on health rather than distress?
5. Is a focus on gender, stress, and health at odds with higher education programs and the demands of corporate life?
6. How can employers be encouraged to take an active role in supporting women and men's health?

CHANGING WORK, CHANGING ROLES

In the 1990s, organizations were facing a new reality characterized by turbulence and increasingly rapid change, increased economic and competitive pressures, the internationalization and globalization of business, the introduction of new technology, and a changing workforce (Gowing, Kraft, & Quick, 1998a; Martin & Freeman, 1998). Organizations throughout the industrialized world responded to these changes in a number of ways (Burke & Nelson, 1998). These included restructuring and downsizing, plant closings, mergers and acquisitions, and increased use of outsourcing as a way to contain costs. These initiatives resulted in increased levels of workplace stress and diminished quality of worklife among the women and men who survived these changes (Burke & Nelson, 1998; Worrall, Cooper, & Campbell, 2000). Individuals who lost their jobs, the victims of these changes, also suffered increasing levels of hardship and distress (*New York Times*, 1996).

There is accumulating evidence that organizational downsizing is associated with health risks of survivors (Kivimaki, Vahtera, Griffiths, Cox, & Thomson, 2000; Vahtera, Kivimaki, & Pentti, 1997). There is also a suggestion that women may experience unique demands during restructuring and downsizing (Karambayya, 1998).

One work stressor that has been shown to be on the increase is job insecurity (Burke & Nelson, 1998; Worrall et al., 2000). Job insecurity typically is found to be associated with negative health symptoms. Few studies have examined gender and job insecurity, however (Westman, 2000). Men may report greater job insecurity than women since men have typically fulfilled the provider roles within families. There is some evidence that financial concerns play a bigger role in job security for men than for women. In addition, job insecurity affected more work attitudes among women than among men (see Westman, 2000, for a review of these studies).

Westman raises some intriguing hypotheses on the impact of job insecurity on gender roles. The erosion of job security among men may challenge the male provider role and increase the female's role in economically providing for the family. Increasingly, long-term job insecurity may require families to reconsider gender identities and roles in relation to work and family. In addition, as women increasingly work longer hours (job insecurity among women being related to working harder to keep their jobs), women may experience even greater work–home conflicts. Finally, the stresses associated with restructuring and downsizing (job insecurity being one important example) are likely to be transmitted to other family members. Women have traditionally shouldered the burden of these nonwork concerns (Hochschild, 1997).

These organizational changes also have brought about a shift in the nature of the employment relationship—the psychological contract—between employer and employees (Noer, 1993; Rousseau, 1995; Sparrow,

2000). These changes have direct implications for organizational forms, the future of work, and societies as a whole. One reads phrases such as "job security is dead," "employers do not owe employees a career," and "loyalty is dead" in the popular press. What is clear is that the nature of the employer–employee relationship has changed (McCarthy & Hall, 2000; Rousseau, 1995). What was primarily a relational contract (open-ended with ambiguous performance requirements attached to continued membership) has increasingly become a transactional contract (limited duration with well-specified performance requirements).

These changes in the employment relationships place increasing demands on employees in the form of ambiguity and uncertainty as these changes unfold; the need for additional employee skills and competencies (career self-management, resiliency, lifelong learning); and negotiating a relationship with one's employer that provides opportunities for contribution, learning, and development. The new psychological contract, with its greater uncertainty and demands, will prove difficult for some and beneficial but challenging to others. Women may have greater difficulty than men under these conditions, since the development of a managerial self-identity has typically been more difficult for women. To the extent that women are still responsible for a disproportionate share of second-shift work, they may experience greater work and life demands and greater health risk.

UNDERRESEARCHED CONSTITUENCIES

One of the limitations of the recent literature on gender and work is its tendency to treat women and men as homogenous groups. It is often assumed that gender, because it creates naturally occurring groups, means women and men are more similar to members of their own gender than they may be to members of the other. This may not be the case, given that there are many groupings besides gender for determining similarity in terms of stress and health issues related to work. Intragroup differences in the study of gender and work may be as important as intergroup differences, and they are often overlooked (Matuszek, Nelson, & Quick, 1995). The questions of interest focus on identifying individuals and/or groups at particular risk for distress and the attendant health risks.

If we move to a consideration of at-risk individuals and groups, it becomes evident that particular occupational and demographic or family structure groups must receive greater research attention. Many studies of working women have focused on professional and managerial jobs rather than blue-collar jobs. Women in blue-collar jobs may be particularly vulnerable to distress, yet they are an understudied group. Women's presence in traditionally male blue-collar jobs is quite small; while 45% of men are in such jobs, only 10% of women hold blue-collar jobs (Williams, 1999). The most desirable blue-collar jobs, those in precision, craft, and production occupations, are predominately held by white males.

The mechanisms for excluding women from these prized jobs differ from those faced by managerial women. In the blue-collar world, the equipment used and the industrial processes employed were designed around men's bodies. The job ladder often starts with shop floor jobs that require heavy physical work, excluding women who cannot lift such heavy burdens. The net result is that they cannot climb the ladder because they cannot get the shop floor jobs that comprise the lower rungs. Blue-collar men are more apt to feel their provider status threatened by the intrusion of women into their jobs than are white-collar men. Manual labor, with its requisite physical endurance and tolerance of discomfort, is indelibly tied to the masculine image, and men may see women who can do these jobs as threats to their egos. Blue-collar women are especially at risk for sociosexual behaviors and harassment (Williams, 1999).

We also need to broaden our concept of family structure, and to ensure that family structure is included as an important variable in studies of gender, work stress, and health. Schneer and Reitman (1993) proposed three dimensions of family structure (marital status, parental status, and spousal employment) as being important for both men and women. One particular group that we need to learn more about is single parents. Because childcare is seen mainly as a female responsibility, single-parent women face extreme risks of work–home conflicts. For single women who have children, there is no division of labor. They have no partners they can rely on to "pick up the slack" when childcare demands clash with work demands. They may also experience social isolation and exclusion from social networks that involve mostly married couples. Discrimination may also play a role when employers operate on the assumption that single women are incapable of fully managing both careers and children.

Single fathers may face similar stressors in terms of childcare and work–home conflicts, but they may also encounter role stressors because they are taking on what some may see as a traditionally female role. These men are a relative minority in our society, and consequently their peer group is small and scattered. Employers may be less likely to recognize the plight of single fathers and less likely to extend them the flexibility they need to manage their work and family lives.

We also know little about the stress and health consequences of work for gays and lesbians. Undoubtedly they share common stressors experienced by their heterosexual colleagues, but there must be unique stressors as well. A review by Croteau (1996) cited both subtle and overt discrimination and indecision about whether to be open about one's orientation at work as issues for gays and lesbians. Harassment and exclusion from social networks may also be stressors for these individuals. Further, gay men and lesbians may be more different than they are similar in their work–life experiences. A study of gay and lesbian graduates of Harvard Business School indicated that gay men have advantages in terms of well-developed networks, but lesbians fare better by coming out at work in terms of encountering positive reactions (Friskopp & Silverstein, 1995).

Disabled individuals' experiences of work stress merits further study. We know, for example, that the unemployment rate for disabled individuals (those employable) approaches 60%; therefore, simply finding work is a challenge. Do women with disabilities experience different stressors than men with disabilities? Does work have different health consequences for men and women with disabilities? Many unanswered questions remain concerning disabled individuals and other underresearched groups.

NATURE OR NURTURE?

We need a better understanding of the relationship between evolved biobehavioral responses and adopted social roles that are gender specific. Due to concerns about stereotyping and discrimination, biological explanations of gender differences in human behavior have fallen out of favor in recent years. Still, it may be unwise, or even impossible, to ignore biological factors in studies concerning gender differences in social behavior. Rather than viewing social roles and biological factors as distinct dichotomies (nurture versus nature), we need to learn more about how these two bases of behavior interact to account for obvious differences between sexes.

One of the most well-documented gender differences in adult human behavior is a strong tendency for women to affiliate with others when coping with stress. Women maintain more same-sex close relationships and mobilize more social support during stressful events than do men. Men, on the other hand, engage less in purely social networking and rely more heavily on their spouses for social support.

Recently, Taylor et al. (2000) developed a new theory of stress response for women that complements the traditional fight-or-flight response. They propose a "tend-and-befriend" behavioral response pattern that attempts to link neuroendocrine responses to female preferences for affiliation during stress. This pattern involves "tending" for offspring under stressful circumstances and "befriending" social groups to reduce vulnerability and to facilitate the exchange of resources and responsibilities. Aspects of these response patterns may be linked to female attachment—caregiving processes and related neuroendocrine underpinnings. For females, stress-induced responses appear to be downregulated by estrogen-enhanced oxytocin, a hormone that is associated with calming effects during fearful responses to stress. Oxytocin coupled with other sex-linked hormones and mechanisms may induce maternal and affiliative behaviors in stressful situations. For example, on days when women reported higher levels of stress at work, their children reported that their mothers were more loving and nurturing (Repetti, 1997, 2000)

In contrast, fathers are more likely to withdraw from their families following a stressful day at work or to engage in familial conflict after they experience interpersonal conflict at work (Repetti, 1989). This behavior is more consistent with the traditional view of a fight-or-flight response to stress. Early research on stress indicates that fight-or-flight may be linked to an androgenic organization of an aggressive response to threat that is activated by testosterone. Although female aggression is well documented, it is not organized by testosterone or androgens. The typically low levels of these predominantly male hormones in females indicate that they are unlikely to evoke the same response in women that they do in men.

We need more studies that attempt to link physiological responses to behavioral outcomes. Do women who display competitive behavior in challenging situations have physiological responses that are more similar to men than to women who tend to avoid rivalry? When men experience depression, are there physiological underpinnings that are different than those experienced by women? How do physiological responses differ when men and women work together as opposed to working solely among members of their own gender?

Although hormonal influences on human behavior are scientifically appealing, it may be impossible to determine whether any behavioral response is purely biological or sociological. According to Taylor et al. (2000), biology is a central tendency that interacts with social, cultural, cognitive, and emotional factors. Thus, physiological explanations for gender differences are likely to be influenced or reinforced by social and cultural roles as well.

Gender differences in the content and quality of social roles usually are not advantageous to women and may have adverse affects on their health. Turner & Turner (1999) found that interpersonal dependence represents a significant risk factor for depression that is gender specific. In general, women tend to experience higher levels of emotional reliance and depression than do men. Gender socialization processes that begin in early childhood may initially encourage women's dependence on interpersonal relationships; however, adult status differences involving variations in power, respect, and opportunity are also likely to be involved. According to Turner & Turner (1999), higher education and occupational prestige are more likely to reduce emotional reliance in women than in men. Marriage increases emotional reliance for both men and women; however, emotional reliance for men is offset by an increase in spousal social support and is less likely to lead to depression. Emotional reliance appears to have a positive influence on interpersonal relationships and mental health among men in comparison to women.

Today more than ever, women are adopting roles that have tradition-ally been occupied by men—entrepreneur, administrator, politician, head of household, and major breadwinner. Men are beginning to engage more in household and caregiving roles that were traditionally the domain of women. Will the adoption of new role behaviors that cross traditional boundaries influence biological tendencies in the next generation?

A MORE POSITIVE APPROACH

Like much of the literature on work stress and health, the studies related to gender differences view health as the absence of disease rather than as a state of well-being. Stress is viewed predominately as distress, with its attendant negative consequences. Gender differences, similarly, are stud-ied in terms of which gender experiences more symptoms of which type (e.g., women report more depression while men report more heart disease). Prevention efforts, then, focus on preventing distress. We believe the field would benefit from a more positive approach, that is, examining gender dif-ferences as they relate to generating eustress and enhancing health.

Eustress is the healthy, constructive, positive side of stress, and is asso-ciated with desirable health consequences and high performance (Quick, Quick, Nelson, & Hurrell, 1997). Rather than being the absence of nega-tive psychological states, it is more properly viewed as involving the pres-ence of positive psychological states. Simmons (2000) defined eustress as "a psychological state that represents a degree of positive response to any given demand." He further examined several indicators of eustress, including meaningfulness of work, manageability, hope, and positive affect. From a study of hospital nurses, he concluded that *meaningfulness*—a state in which work makes sense emotionally, is worth investing energy in, and represents active engagement—was a particularly strong indicator of eustress. Follow-ing this line of research, it makes sense to study those conditions at work that are associated with active engagement, meaningfulness, and hope.

Other potential indicators of eustress are worth investigating, includ-ing optimism. This positive psychological characteristic has been associated with positive mood, perseverance, high achievement, and enhanced physi-cal health (Peterson, 2000). Positive emotional states such as positive affect are associated with healthy perceptions and physical well-being (Salovey, Rothman, Detweiler, & Steward, 2000). It makes sense, therefore, to explore gender differences in optimism and positive emotional states.

There are probably gender differences involved in eustress, both in terms of the stressors that produce a eustressful response, the conditions at work that promote eustress, and the personality factors that affect the indi-vidual's propensity to experience eustress. In fact, it might be argued that the construct of eustress at work may differ by gender. If, as the work of Taylor and her colleagues indicates, the distress response differs by gender, perhaps the eustress response differs as well. Studying gender differences in eustress will allow researchers to gain insight into facilitating this positive response at work. In essence, it means moving from a model of distress prevention toward a model of eustress generation.

MBA PROGRAMS, CORPORATE LIFE: AT ODDS WITH HEALTH?

Is a focus on gender, stress, and health at odds with higher education programs and the demands of corporate life? Probably. But that doesn't mean that this emphasis is not warranted.

There is little empirical evidence on the experiences of women and men in their training programs in preparation for corporate life (e.g., MBA programs, law school, engineering, and computer science). The information that is available suggests, not surprisingly, that women students may experience greater stress in their academic programs than do men (Catalyst, 2000a, 2000b). A recent study undertaken by Catalyst of women and men MBA graduates from 12 leading universities sheds some light on these issues. In the 1990s, the percentage of women MBA students rose from single digits to about 30%. There was an expectation that women might reach the 50% mark. Women's interest in pursuing graduate education in business has fallen slowly in the past five years. There are several possible explanations for this, including the MBA experience itself. There are few women faculty members. Relatively few business cases involve female decision makers. Much of the emphasis still remains on the quantitative content (finance, accounting operations), though women typically can handle this material as well as men. Women also believed they were perceived as less qualified than men.

More information is available on women's experiences in corporate life and how these experiences are reflected in stress and health concerns (Burke, 1996; Nelson & Burke, 2000a, 2000b). This body of writing will not be discussed in detail here. Suffice it to say that while women and men share some common stress and health factors, women also report unique stressors that are gender-related.

There are several reasons why organizations should be interested in gender, stress, and health issues. First, organizations are currently involved in a war for talent. There is a shortage of highly skilled, motivated, and productive employees. Employers of choice will be those that care about the well-being of their employees (Gowing, Kraft, & Quick, 1998b). Second, organizations are likely to require even greater creativity, learning, development, and contribution from all employees if they are to remain competitive. Firms are more likely to obtain these responses from staff members that are invigorated, responsive, and healthy. Third, as more women move into increasingly more responsible jobs, it makes sense to consider the intersection of gender stress and health since both genders have vital roles to play in corporate success. Finally, the interplay of gender, stress, and health has an impact on family functioning. Women and men who work are often parents. Society at large has a stake in the experiences and development of its children. It has been shown that children can sense when their parents are facing work stress concerns, and many children wish that their parents were less stressed. This reality conveys important messages to our next generation of leaders.

Gowing, Kraft, & Quick (1998b) link the health of the workforce and the health of the organization in ways that are relevant here. They observe that the good health of employees is a necessary condition for productivity. In addition, investing in employees as long-term assets (Leana & Van Buren, 2000) will offer firms a competitive advantage. Organizations, in turn, need to transform and change in ways that responsibly maintain and restore employee health, human capital, and partnership. As Gowing et al. conclude, firms that manage the health and development of all employees— women and men—and the health of the organization during these chaotic times will be successful on all measures (Kaplan & Norton, 1996).

ENERGIZING AND INVOLVING EMPLOYERS

Employers must take an active role in supporting the health and well-being of all workers, regardless of their gender. In order to do so, they must realize that employee health is greatly affected by the interaction of work and personal life for both sexes, that mental and physical stress or strain may have differential effects on men and women, and that coping mechanisms may also differ according to gender. However, awareness of gender differences in response to work stress should not lead to labeling health issues as "male" or "female" or to creating work roles that are gender specific. Employers can avoid such pitfalls by addressing individual concerns through enhanced social support and cooperative relationship learning.

Perhaps the most consistent finding in the literature on stress in the workplace is the positive effects of employer social support (Dorman & Zapf, 1999; Seers, McGee, Serey, & Graen, 1983). Whereas the intrinsic benefits of social support to workers and organizations are well-documented, social support may have extrinsic benefits for the organization as well. In a recent study involving both blue- and white-collar workers in two different organizations, Manning, Jackson, & Fusilier (1996) found that the amount and quality of social support an employee received was negatively related to health care costs. This relationship was more prominent for those experiencing higher levels of stress or strain. Furthermore, high strain accompanied by high social support was associated with a lower level of costs than was apparent under the low-strain condition. According to Manning et al. (1996), some stress, if coupled with social support, may result in a healthy level of arousal. When the effects of stress are positive, medical attention may not be sought. The individual's perception of these strains as eustress rather than distress may be closely connected to the quality and amount of social support received.

There is substantial evidence that men and women may be affected differentially by work stressors; for example, women who work consistently report they are in poorer mental health relative to employed men. In contrast, men report fewer symptoms of mental distress on the job, but they tend to suffer from chronic physical conditions or illnesses more so than women. However, in a study of more than 900 working men and women in various occupations, Roxburgh (1996) reported that job characteristics known to positively affect men's well-being (i.e., full-time, nonroutine, moderate perceived demands) also had a positive affect on women's well-being, and that differences in the impact of job conditions account for only a modest portion of the variance in gender differences in well-being. Roxburgh suggested that exposure to work-place stressors, such as structural and normative constraints on advancement opportunities, and gender differences in coping with work stressors, may contribute to higher levels of mental distress for women as opposed to men.

For example, global companies often require overseas assignments to prepare managers for promotion to more challenging levels of management. Catalyst (2000c) interviewed and surveyed 450 women and men who were current and former expatriates, as well as their employers. Almost half of all executives said developing global talent is a growing priority in their organizations and 80% agreed that the trend will continue over the next 5 years. Although expatriates are usually selected from middle management ranks where women comprise half of the talent pool, only 13% of expatriates in U.S. corporations are women.

Survey responses from executives of *Fortune 500* firms report that women are not considered as globally mobile as men. Yet women frequent flyers were more likely than their male counterparts to say they would relocate in the future. Of expatriates who have relocated, 80% of women had never turned down a relocation, compared to 71% of men (Catalyst, 2000c). Many executives believe that women encounter more work–life conflict working on a global schedule. In reality, men were just as likely as women to report they find work–life balance difficult.

Women in international assignments often find themselves more isolated than their male counterparts, without the naturally occurring networks and mentors available to men. Women say they want, but often fail to get, the formal support they need to stay connected to their companies.

A silver lining in the new world of rapidly changing technology, accelerated learning, and global corporate growth is the opportunity to recreate work roles that are sexually integrated. Such roles attempt to create challenging work for all employees, capitalizing on the positive effects of eustress and downplaying the negative effects of work and relational activities that lead to distress. Successful organizations will be those that encourage employees to help each other learn new skills and competencies needed to promote these integrated work roles. Although formal training programs can accomplish some of this learning, most real training comes from peer-assisted, self-directed learning through integrated project teams, enhanced electronic communication, access to social and work-related networks, support groups, and cooperative working relationships between customers, employees, and managers (Hall & Moss, 1998). Employers who encourage cooperative relationship learning may increase the level of social support throughout their organizations.

By promoting the give and take of social support that meets the individual needs of both genders, and encouraging cooperative relationship learning across genders, employers can develop organizational cultures that emphasize the health and well-being of all employees. Through redesigning work roles to make them equally challenging and rewarding for both men and women, employers may capitalize on the positive effects of eustress on employee health.

In conclusion, this collection of work is testament to the fact that our knowledge of gender, work, and health has been significantly expanded in the recent past; yet many fascinating questions remain. The questions we have raised in this chapter, along with others that undoubtedly will arise, can occupy researchers for years to come.

REFERENCES

Burke, R. J. (1996). Work experiences, stress and health among managerial and professional women. In M. J. Schabracq, J. A. M. Winnubst, & C. L. Cooper (Eds.), *Handbook of work and health psychology* (pp. 205–230). New York: John Wiley.

Burke, R. J., & Nelson, D. L. (1998). Mergers and acquisitions, downsizing and privatization: A North American perspective. In M. K. Gowing, J. D. Kraft, & J. C. Quick (Eds.), *The new organizational reality* (pp. 21–54). Washington, DC: American Psychological Association.

Catalyst (2000a). *Study of women and men MBA graduates.* New York: Author.

Catalyst (2000b). *Women and the MBA: Gateway to opportunity.* New York: Author.

Catalyst (2000c). *Passport to opportunity: U.S. women in global business*. New York: Author.

Croteau, J. M. (1996). Research on the work experiences of lesbian, gay and bisexual people: An integrative review of methodology and findings. *Journal of Vocational Behavior, 48*, 195–209.

Dormann, C., & Zapf, D. (1999). Social support, social stressors at work, and depressive symptoms: Testing for main and moderating effects with structural equations in a three-wave longitudinal study. *Journal of Applied Psychology, 84*, 874–884.

Friskopp, A., & Silverstein, S. (1995). *Straight jobs, gay lives: Gay and lesbian professionals, the Harvard Business School, and the American workplace*. New York: Scribner.

Gowing, M. K., Kraft, J. D., & Quick, J. C. (1998a). *The new organizational reality*. Washington, DC: American Psychological Association.

Gowing, M. K., Kraft, J. D., & Quick, J. C. (1998b). A conceptual framework for coping with the new organizational reality. In M. K. Gowing, J. D. Kraft, & J. C. Quick (Eds.), *The new organizational reality* (pp. 259–268). Washington, DC: American Psychological Association.

Hall, D. T., & Moss, J. E. (1998). The new protean career contract: Helping organizations and employees adapt. *Organizational Dynamics* (Winter), 22–37.

Hochschild, A. R. (1997). *The Time Bind*. New York: Metropolitan Books.

Kaplan, R. S., & Norton, D. P. (1996). *The balanced score card*. Boston: Harvard Business School Press.

Karambayya, R. (1998). Caught in the crossfire: Women and corporate restructuring. *Canadian Journal of Administrative Sciences, 15*, 333–338.

Kivimaki, M., Vahtera, J., Griffiths, A., Cox, T., & Thomson, C. (2000). Sickness absence and organizational downsizing. In R. J. Burke, & C. L. Cooper (Eds.), *The organization in crisis* (pp. 78–94). London: Blackwell.

Leana, C. R., & Van Buren, H. I. (2000). Eroding organizational social capital among U.S. firms: The price of job instability. In R. J. Burke, & C. L. Cooper (Eds.), *The organization in crisis* (pp. 220–232). London: Blackwell.

Manning, M. R., Jackson, C. N., & Fusilier, M. R. (1996). Occupational stress, social support, and the costs of health care. *Academy of Management Journal, 39*, 738–750.

Martin, R. E., & Freeman, S. J. (1998). The economic context of the new organizational reality. In M. K. Going, J. D. Kraft, & J. C. Quick (Eds.), *The new organizational reality* (pp. 5–20). Washington, DC: American Psychological Association.

Matuszek, P. A. C., Nelson, D. L., & Quick, J. C. (1995). Gender differences in distress: Are we asking all the right questions? *Journal of Social Behavior and Personality, 10*, 99–120.

McCarthy, J. F., & Hall, D. T. (2000). Organizational crisis and change: The new career contract at work. In R. J. Burke, & C. L. Cooper (Eds.), *The organization in crisis* (pp. 202–219). London: Blackwell.

Nelson, D. L., & Burke, R. J. (2000a). Women executives: Health, stress and success. *Academy of Management Executive, 14,* 107–121.

Nelson, D. L., & Burke, R. J. (2000b). Women, work stress and health. In M. J. Davidson, & R. J. Burke (Eds.), *Women in management: Current research issues* (pp. 177–191). London: Sage.

New York Times (1996). *The downsizing of America.* New York: Time Books.

Noer, D. M. (1993). *Healing the wounds.* San Francisco, CA: Jossey-Bass.

Peterson, C. (2000). The future of optimism. *American Psychologist, 55,* 44–55.

Quick, J. C., Quick, J. D., Nelson, D. L., & Hurrell, J. J., Jr. (1997). *Preventive stress management in organizations.* Washington, DC: American Psychological Association.

Repetti, R. L. (1989). Effects of daily workload on subsequent behavior during marital interactions: The role of social withdrawal and spouse support. *Journal of Personality and Social Psychology, 57,* 651–659.

Repetti, R. L. (1997, April). *The effects of daily job stress on parent behavior with preadolescents.* Paper presented at the biennial meeting of the Society for Research in Child Development, Washington, DC.

Repetti, R. L. (2000). *The differential impact of chronic job stress on mothers' and fathers' behavior with children.* Manuscript in preparation.

Rousseau, D. M. (1995). *Psychological contracts in organizations.* Thousand Oaks, CA: Sage.

Roxburgh, S. (1996). Gender differences in work and well-being: Effects of exposure and vulnerability. *Journal of Health and Social Behavior, 37,* 265–277.

Salovey, P., Rothman, A. J., Detweiler, J. B., & Steward, W. T. (2000). Emotional states and physical health. *American Psychologist, 55,* 110–121.

Schneer, J. A., & Reitman, F. (1993). Effects of alternate family structures on managerial career paths. *Academy of Management Journal, 36,* 830–843.

Seers, A., McGee, G. W., Serey, T. T., & Graen, G. B. (1983). The interaction of job stress and social support: A strong inference investigation. *Academy of Management Journal, 26,* 273–284.

Simmons, B. L. (2000). Eustress at work: Accentuating the positive. Unpublished doctoral dissertation, Oklahoma State University.

Sparrow, P. (2000). The new employment contract. In R. J. Burke, & C. L. Cooper (Eds.), *The organization in crisis* (pp. 167–187). London: Blackwell.

Taylor, S. E., Klein, L. C., Lewis, B. P., Gruenewald, T. L., Gurung, R. A., & Updegraff, J. A. (2000). Biobehavioral responses to stress in females: Tend-and-befriend, not fight-or-flight. *Psychological Review, 107,* 411–429.

Turner, H. A., & Turner, R. J. (1999). Gender, social status, and emotional reliance. *Journal of Health and Social Behavior, 40,* 360–373.

Vahtera, J., Kivimaki, M., & Pentti, J. (1997). Effect of organizational downsizing on health of employees. *Lancet, 350,* 1124–1128.

Westman, M. (2000). Gender and job insecurity. In R. J. Burke, & C. L. Cooper (Eds.), *The organization in crisis* (pp. 119–131). London: Blackwell.

Williams, J. (1999). *Unbending gender: Why family and work conflict and what to do about it*. New York: Oxford University Press.

Worrall, L., Cooper, C. L., & Campbell, F. (2000). The impact of organizational change on UK managers' perceptions of their working lives. In R. J. Burke, & C. L. Cooper (Eds.), *The organization in crisis* (pp. 20–43). London: Blackwell.

AUTHOR INDEX

Numbers in italics refer to listings in reference sections.

Ackerman, P. L., 75, 84
Adams, G., 104, *112*
Adler, N. J., 22, *30*
Aguinis, H., 80, *82*
Allen, E., 117, *127*, 142, *147*
Allen, S. J., 24, 25, *32*
Allen, T. D., 211, 220, 221, 223, *223*
Alliger, M., 86, 96, 105, *114*
Almeida, D. M., 9, *13*
Altmaier, E., 102, *114*
Alvesson, M., 6, *12*
Amabile, T. A., 55, *66*
Ambrose, D., 58, *66*
Anderson, C. R., 26, *30*
Anderson, N. B., 197, *206*
Aniakudo, P., 197, *210*
Apter, T., 23, *30*
Armenakis, A. A., 56, *67*
Armstrong-Stassen, M., 57, *66*
Arnetz, B. B., 29, *30*
Arroba, T., 23, *30*
Aryee, S., 103, 104, *112*, 116, 117, 124,
    126, 214, *223*
Au v. Lyndhurst Hospital, 192, *207*
Azar, B., 8, *12*

Bacharach, S. B., 86, *93*
Baglioni, A. J., 27, *31*, 137, *147*
Bailyn, L., 161, *167*
Bala, M., 24, 25, *30*
Baldini, V., 21, 28, *30*
Ball, G. A., 8, *12*
Baltes, B. B., 213, *223*
Bamberger, P., 86, *93*
Bandura, A., 25, *30*, 136, *146*
Bank of Montreal report to employees
    (1991), 222, *223*
Banyard, V. L., 88, *93*
Bardwick, J., 42, *50*
Barker, V. L., 55, *68*
Barling, J., 10, *12*, 193, *207*
Barnes, G. M., 9, *13*
Barnett, R. C., 5, 7, *12*, 21, 22, *30*, 67,
    139, 142, *146*, 169, 170, 186,
    187, *188*
Baruch, G. K., 7, *12*, 56, 57, 67, 139, *146*

Beatty, C. A., 7, 9, *12*
Becker, J., 27, *33*
Bedeian, A. G., 56, 67, 116, *127*
Beehr, T. A., 72, 82, 103, 104, 111, *112*,
    113, 130, 137, *146*, *147*, 217, *223*
Beilin, L. J., 7, *13*
Beiner, L., 7, *12*, 56, 57, *67*
Belk, S. S., 41, *53*
Bell, E., 63, *67*
Bell, E. L., 22, *30*
Bell, M. P., 192, *210*
Bell, N. E., 72, *84*
Belle, D., 56, 67, 88, *93*
Bennett, R. C., 56, *57*
Ben-Porath, Y., 88, 90, 94, 137, *147*
Bernstein, I. H., 80, *83*
Beutell, N. J., 102, 104, *113*, *114*, 117, 119,
    120, 124, *127*, 128, 215, *225*
Biaggio, M., 202, *206*
Bianchi, S. M., 86, *96*
Biener, L., 139, *146*
Billing, A. D., 6, *12*
Billings, A. G., 87, *93*
Bjorn, L., 191, 197, *208*
Blalock, J. A., 88, *93*
Bliese, P. D., 71, *83*
Blossfeld, Hans-Peter, 169, *188*
Bohen, H. H., 213, *223*
Boles, J., 87, *95*
Boles, J. S., 117, *128*
Bolger, N., 68, 74, 129, *146*
Bond, J. T., 4, *12*, 158, *166*, 211, 216, 221,
    222, *224*
Bond, T., 161, *166*
Booth, A., 140, 141, *146*
Borgen, F. H., 79, *82*
Borrelli, L., 170, 178, *189*
Borysenko, J., 8, *13*
Boudreau, J. W., 116, 119, *127*, 214,
    215, *225*
Bouthillette, F., 57, *68*
Brannon, R., 37, 39, 49, *50*
Brennan, R. T., 21, 22, *30*, 139, 142, *146*
Brenner, S. O., 29, *30*
Bresler, S. J., 203, *206*
Brett, J. M., 80, *83*

Bretz, R. D., 116, 119, *127*, 214, 215, *225*
Brief, A. P., 72, 73, 79, *82*
Briggs, T. E., 213, *223*
Bristor, J. M., 23, *30*
Brockner, J., 56, 57, *67*
Brod, H., 38, 48, *50*
Bronfenbrenner, U., 130, *146*, 171, *188*
Brooks, G. R., 41, *50*
Brousseau, R., 28, *33*, 139, *148*
Brownell, A., 202, *206*
Bruck, C. S., 211, 220, 221, 223, *223*
Buck, M. L., 115, *126*, 170, 178, *188*, *189*
Buffardi, L. C., 104, *112*
Buhler, P. M., 191, 200, *206*
Bunting, A. B., 39, *50*
Bureau of Labor Statistics (2001), 155,
    166
Burke, M. J., 72, 73, 79, *82*
Burke, P. J., 117, 124, *126*
Burke, R., 140, *148*
Burke, R. J., 3, 5, 6, 8, *13*, *14*, 19, 21, 23,
    28, 29, *30*, *31*, *33*, 43–45, 49,
    50, 57, *67*, 68, 88, 90, 94, 95,
    140, 141, 143, *146*, 230, 236,
    239, 241
Burleigh, N., 191, *206*
Burleson, B. R., 144, *147*
Burlington Industries v. Ellerth, 193, *206*
Butts, D., 38, *50*
Buzzell, S., 71, *83*

Cacioppo, J. T., 103, *114*
Cadwallader, B., 199, *206*
Cameron, K. S., 55, *67*
Camman, C., 107, *112*, *114*, 217, *223*
Campbell, F., 230, *242*
Caplan, R. D., 27, *30*, 120, *126*, 136, *148*,
    171, *188*
Carlson, D. S., 102–104, *112*, 117, *126*
Carver, M. C., 104, *112*
Cascio, W. F., 55, 56, 58, *67*
Casper, W. J., 104, *112*
Catalano, R., 136, *148*
Catalyst, 155–159, 161–166, *166*, 170,
    188, 236, 238, 239, *240*
Celentano, E., 37, *52*
Chambers-Cook, K., 213–216, *226*
Champagne, P. J., 202, *207*
Charney, D. A., 191, 198, 203, *206*
Chen, P. Y., 73, 79, *82*, *84*
Cherrington, D. J., 26, *31*
Chesney, M., 43, *50*

Chin, J., 7, *13*, 38, *50*, *51*
Chrisler, J. C., 23, *33*
Claes, M. E., 89, *93*
Clark, L. A., 8, *14*, 72, 73, 80, *84*
Clark, R., 197, *206*
Clark, V. R., 197, *206*
Clark, V. S., 170, *189*
Clausen, J. A., 72, *84*
Cobb, S., 120, *126*
Cohen, A. G., 197, *208*
Cohen, J., 72, 80, *82*
Cohen, P., 80, *82*
Cohen, S., 88, 93, 103, *112*, 217, *224*
Cohen, T. F., 35, *50*
Cohn, M., 197, *208*
Collins, J., 193–194, *207*
Conley, S., 86, *93*
Connolly, T., 218, *225*
Constable, J. F., 102, *112*
Contant, F., 26, *33*
Conti, R., 55, *66*
Cook, C. R., 214, *225*
Cook, J. H., 76, *83*
Cooper, C. L., 20–24, 27, 28, *31*, *33*, 34,
    137, *147*, 170, 171, *189*, 230, *242*
Cooper, C. R., 20, *31*
Cooper, M., 86, *93*
Cooper, M. L., 22, *31*, 107, *113*, 117, *127*,
    217, *224*
Corcoran-Nates, Y., 23, *31*
Courtenay, W. H., 38, *50*
Cox, C., 22, *34*
Cox, R. S., 86, *95*
Cox, T., 230, *240*
Cox, T. H., 86, *93*
Coyne, J. C., 137, *146*
Cozza, T., 37, *52*
Cronkite, R. C., 27, *33*
Crooker, K. J., 214, *224*
Croteau, J. M., 232, *240*
Crull, P., 192, *206*
Cummings, L. L., 24, *33*
Cunningham, D. A., 43, *52*
Cvetanovski, J., 24, 25, *32*

Daly, P. S., 74, *84*
Dandeker, N., 201, *207*
Danon, E., 142, 143, *149*
Dass, P., 211, *225*
Davidson, M. J., 19–24, 27, 28, *31*, 66, *66*
Davis, F., 40, *50*
Dawkins, M. C., 26, *32*

Day, J. D., 200, *209*
Deadrick, D. L., 202, *207*
Deaux, K., 76, *82*
Decker, P. J., 79, *82*
Deddens, J., 5, *13*
Dekker, I., 193, *207*
Dell, D. M., 40, *51*
DeLongis, A., 90, *93*, 129, *146*
DeMarr, B., 211, *225*
Deszca, E., 43, *50*
Detweiler, J. B., 235, *241*
Devlin, A., 23, *33*
Dex, S., 211, 215, *226*
DiClemente, C. C., 91, *95*
Diener, E., 75, 77, 78, *82, 83*
DiSalvo, V., 139, *146*
Dodge, K., 89, *95*
Dodge, K. L., 137, *148*
Dooley, D., 136, *148*
Dormann, C., 237, *240*
Downey, G., 137, *146*
Drasgow, F., 192, 196, 205, *207–209*
Drum, M. L., 191, *209*
Dubin, R., 129, *146*
DuBois, C. L. Z., 191, 193, 197, 201, 202, *207, 208*
Dunahoo, C. L., 57, *67*, 88, 90, 137, *147*
Dunham, R. B., 24, *33*
Dunseath, J., 104, *112*
Dupre, K. E., 10, *12*
Dutton, J. E., 55, 59, *69*
Duwors, R. E., 43, *50*, 143, *146*
Duxbury, L. E., 105, *112*, 216, *224*
Dwyer, D. J., 72, *83, 84*, 118, *126*
Dytell, R. S., 9, *14*

Eaker, E. D., 140, *147*
Eaker, L. H., 20, *30*
Eastburg, M. C., 102, *112*
Eckenrode, J., 136, 137, *146, 148*
Eckerman, L., 28, *31*
Edwards, J., 101, *112*
Edwards, J. R., 27, *31*, 115, *126*, 137, *147*
Ehrenreich, B., 36, *51*
Eisler, R. M., 40, 44, *51, 52*, 88, *93*
Ekeberg, S. E., 193, 197, *208*
Elkin, A., 21, *31*
Elliott, S. J., 29, *31*
Ely, R. J., 59, *67*
Eneroth, P., 29, *30*
Engler, L., 169, 170, *189*
Epstein, C. F., 159, *166*, 170, *189*

Equal Opportunities Commission, 21, *31*, 191, 196, *207, 210*
Erdwins, C., 104, *112*
Erdwins, P., 26, *33*
Etzion, D., 9, *14*, 91, *93*, 106, *113*, 130, 142, 143, *149*
Eyles, J., 105, *114*

Fagan, C., 169, *189*
Faley, R. H., 191, 193, 197, 201, 202, *207, 208*
Faludi, S., 35, *51*
Faragher v. City of Boca Raton, 193, 200, *207*
Farrell, D., 65, *67*
Fassel, D., 44, *51, 53*
Feinleib, M., 140, *147*
Feldman, D. C., 57, *68*
Fendrich, M., 191, *209*
Fenlason, K. J., 103, *113*
Ficarrotto, T., 7, *13*, 38, *51*
Fichman, M., 107, *112*, 217, *223*
Fielden, S., 66, *67*
Fielden, S. L., 20, 27, *31*
Fiksenbaum, L., 88–90, 92, *93, 94*
Fine, L. M., 192, *207*
Finn, J., 40, *51*
Fischer, K., 200, *207*
Fitzgerald, L., 205, *208*
Fitzgerald, L. F., 191, 192, 196, 199–201, *207, 210*
Flaherty, J. A., 191, *209*
Fletcher, B., 130, 137, 142, 143, *147*
Fletcher, J. K., 61, *67*
Flynn, P. M., 159, 164, *166*, 170, *189*
Folger, R., 56, *67*
Folkman, A., 118, *127*
Folkman, S., 87, 88, *93, 94*
Fortunato, V. J., 80, *82*
Fox, M. L., 72, 73, *83*, 118, *126*
Frankenhaeuser, M., 4, 5, 9, *13*, 21, *32*
Freeman, S. J., 55, *67*, 230, *240*
Freeston, M., 26, *33*
French, J. R. P., 120, *126*
French, S., 105, *114*
Friedman, D. E., 211, 216, 221, 222, *224*
Friedman, M., 42–44, 46, 49, *51*
Friedman, S. D., 118, 125, *126*, 158–160, *166*
Fromm, E., 42, *51*
Frone, M., 86, *93*
Frone, M. R., 9, *13*, 22, *31*, 103, 104, 107, *113*, 117, 119, 124, *127*, 216, 217, *224*

Frosh, S., 28, *32*
Frost, P., 56, 61, *67*
Frydenberg, E., 91, *93*
Fudge, D. A., 140, 141, *148*
Fujita, F., 75, *83*
Fusilier, M. R., 237, 238, *240*

Galambos, N. L., 9, *13*, 143, *147*
Galinsky, E., 4, *12*, 158, 161, *166*, 211, 216, 221, 222, *224*
Ganster, D., 101, 104, 110, *114*
Ganster, D. C., 72, 73, *83*, 118, *126*, 215, 221, 222, *226*
Gardner, D. G., 24, *33*
Gareis, K. C., 169, 170, 186, *188*
Garnsey, E., 23, *30*
Gelfand, M. J., 192, 196, *207*
Geller, P. A., 57, *67*
Gencoz, F., 76, *83*
George, J. M., 72, 73, 79, *82*
Giedd, J. L., 197, *209*
Glass, J. L., 215, *224*
Godshalk, V. M., 104, *114*, 117, 119, 124, *128*, 215, *225*
Goff, S. J., 215, 221, *224*
Goffee, R., 60, *67*
Goldberg, H., 40, *51*
Goldberg, S., 191, *206*
Goldberg, W. A., 213, 214, 216, 217, 222, *224*
Goldenhar, L. M., 5, *13*
Gonyea, J. G., 211–215, *224*
Good, G. E., 40, *51*
Googins, B. K., 212, *224*
Gooler, L., 215, 221, 222, *224*
Gordon, D. M., 55, 58, *68*
Gore, S., 136, *146*
Gorsuch, R., 102, *112*
Gottlieb, B. H., 171, *189*
Gould, R. E., 36, *51*
Gowing, M. K., 230, 236, 237, *240*
Graen, G. B., 237, *241*
Graham-Bermann, S. A., 88, *93*
Granrose, C. S., 103–105, *114*, 120, 121, *127*, *128*, 139, 142, *148*
Grayson, C., 76, *83*
Greenberger, E., 104, *113*, 118, *127*, 213, 214, 216, 217, 222, *224*
Greenglass, E., 88, 92, *93*, 95
Greenglass, E. R., 23, 27, *32*, 57, *67*, 86–91, *94*
Greenhaus, J., 218, *225*

Greenhaus, J. H., 10, *13*, 22, *32*, *51*, 101–105, 111, *113*, *114*, 115, 116, 118–121, 125, *126–128*, 139, 140, 142, *147*, *148*, 159, 160, *166*
Griffin, R. W., 194, *209*
Griffin, R. W., 193, 194, *207*
Griffiths, A., 230, *240*
Grigsby, T. D., 117, *127*, 142, *147*
Grisanti, C., 39, *54*
Grover, S. L., 214, 216, *224*
Gruber, J. E., 191, 193, 197, 199–201, *207*, *208*
Gruenewald, T., 8, *14*
Gruenewald, T. L., 144, *148*, 233, 234, *241*
Grundmann, E. O., 193, 200, 202, *208*
Gurung, R. A., 8, *14*, 144, *148*, 233, 234, *241*
Gutek, B., 106, 107, *113*
Gutek, B. A., 116, *127*, 191, 197, 201, 202, *208*, 217, *224*

Hakim, C., 169, *188*
Hall, D. T., 231, 239, *240*
Hamill, S., 213, 214, 216, 217, 222, *224*
Hammarstrom, A., 29, *32*
Hammer, L. B., 117, *127*, 142, *147*
Harlan, S. L., 192, 197, *209*
Harquail, C. V., 86, *93*
Harrison, J. C., 7, 38, 41, *51*
Harrison, R. V., 120, *126*
Havlovic, S. J., 57, *68*
Hawkins, R. C., 41, *53*
Hawthorne, F., 42, *51*
Haynes, S. G., 140, *147*
Hearn, J., 35, *51*
Hegelson, V. S., 41, *52*
Heinisch, D. A., 77–80, *82*, *83*
Helmreich, R. L., 41, *53*
Henderson, J., 197, *207*
Hepburn, C. G., 10, *12*
Heppner, P. P., 40, *53*
Herst, D. E. L., 211, 220, 221, 223, *223*
Hertz, R., 63, *68*
Higgins, C. A., 105, *112*, 216, *224*
Hildreth, K., 116, *128*
Hill, D. R., 89, *96*
Hill, S., 37, *52*
Hirsch, L., 37, *52*
Hirschman, A., 64, *68*
Hite, L. M., 22, *32*
Hitt, M. A., 5, 7, *14*, *33*
Hobfoll, S. E., 57, 64, *67*, *68*, 88, 90, 91, *94*, 136–138, 140, *147*

Hochschild, A. R., 42, *52*, 57, 68, 230, *240*
Hochwarter, W. A., 26, *32*, 101, *114*
Holahan, C. K., 41, *53*
House, J., 137, *147*
House, J. S., 103, *113*
House, R. J., 217, *224*, *225*
Howard, J. M., 43, *52*
Huard, J., 26, *33*
Huberman, A. M., 173, *189*
Huff, A., 61, 68
Huff, J. W., 213, *223*
Hughes, D., 211, *224*
Hulin, C., 192, *209*
Hulin, C. L., 192, 205, *207*, *208*
Hunt, R. G., 106, *113*
Hurrell, J. J., 5, *13*
Hurrell, J. J., Jr., 7, 10, *14*, 194, *209*, 235, *241*

Ilgen, D. R., 116, *128*
Institute for Women's Policy Research, 86, *94*
Institute of Management and Remuneration Economics, 19, *32*
Iwanicki, E. F., 88, *96*

Jackson, C. N., 237, 238, *240*
Jackson, S. E., 88, *95*, 102, *113*, 137, *147*
Jacobs, J. A., 89, *96*
Jakubiec, D., 89, *94*
James, K., 22, 23, 30, *32*
James, L. R., 80, 88
Jamieson, L., 21, 23, *32*
Jamison, R. L., 215, 221, *224*
Janlert, U., 29, *32*
Jenkins, D., 107, *112*, 217, *223*
Jenkins, R., 6, *13*
Jex, S. M., 24, 25, *32*, 71–73, 77–80, 82–84, 130, *147*
Jick, T., 8, *13*
Jick, T. D., 75–77, 79, 83, 139, *147*
Johnson, L. B., 137, *146*
Johnson, P. J., 213, *226*
Johnson, S., 41, *54*
Joiner, T. E., 76, 83
Jones, F., 130, 137, 142, 143, *147*
Jones, W. H., 104, *112*
Jones v. USA Petroleum, 200, *208*
Joplin, J. R. W., 192, *210*
Josephs, S. L., 192, *207*
Jourard, S. M., 38, 39, *52*

Judge, T. A., 116, 119, *127*, 214, 215, *225*
Juni, S., 39, *50*

Kahn, R., 102, *113*
Kahn, R. L., 116, *127*, 130, 144, *147*
Kalleberg, A. L., 214, *225*
Kamarch, T., 217, *224*
Kangas, R., 29, *32*
Kanter, R. M., 5, *13*, 59, 68
Kanungo, R., 217, 222, *225*
Kapalka, G. M., 26, *32*
Kaplan, R. S., 237, *240*
Karambayya, R., 58–60, 62, 63, 65, 68, 230, *240*
Karasek, R. A., 170, 177, *189*
Katz, D., 102, *113*
Kaufman, H. G., 24, *32*
Kaufman, M., 37, 38, 47–49, *50*, *52*
Keita, G. P., 86, *95*
Keizer, W. A. J., 25, *33*
Kejner, M., 120, *127*
Kellogg, D. M., 159, 164, *166*, 170, *189*
Kelloway, E. K., 171, *189*
Kerlinger, F. N., 218, *225*
Kessler, R., 129, *146*
Kessler, R. C., 86, *95*, 140, 144, *147*
Kiecolt-Glaser, K. G., 103, *114*
Kiewitz, C., 101, *114*
Kimmel, M. S., 35, 49, *52*
King, D. W., 104, 111, *112*
King, L. A., 104, 111, *112*
Kinicki, A. J., 26, *32*
Kinnunen, U., 9, *13*, 86, *94*, 101, *113*
Kivimaki, M., 230, *240*, *241*
Klein, L., 8, *14*
Klein, L. C., 144 *148*, 233, 234, *241*
Klepa, L., 106, 107, *113*, 116, *127*, 217, *224*
Klesh, J., 107, *112*, 217, *223*
Knapp, D. E., 191, 193, 197, 201, 202, *207*, *208*
Knuiman, M. W., 7, *13*
Koch, P. B., 197, *208*
Koch-Jones, J., 216, 217, *224*
Kofodimos, J., 41, 45–47, *52*
Kolaric, G. C., 9, *13*
Konrad, A. M., 197, *208*, 221, *225*
Kopelman, R., 218, *225*
Korabik, K., 36, *52*, 87, *95*, 217, *226*
Korman, A., 42, 43, 45–47, *52*
Korman, R., 42, 43, 45–47, *52*
Koss, M. P., 201, *208*
Kossek, E., 87, *94*, 101, *113*
Kossek, E. E., 211–213, 216, *225*

Kraft, J. D., 230, 236, 237, *240*
Kropf, M. B., 214, *225*
Ku, L. C., 39, *53*
Kulik, C. T., 199, 200, *208*
Kunkel, A. W., 144, *147*
Kustis, G. A., 191, 201, 202, *207*

Labour Market Trends, 19, *32*
Lachenmeyer, J. R., 26, *32*
Lahelma, E., 29, *32*
Lakshmi, M., 24, 25, *30*
Lambert, S. J., 140, *147*
Landers, S., 41, *52*
Lankau, M. J., 213, 214, *226*
Larsen, R. J., 75, 77, 78, *82*
Larson, S., 76, *83*
Lash, S. J., 40, *52*
Last, J. M., 194, 196, *208*
Latack, J. C., 26, *32*
Lau, T., 192, *210*
Lawler, E. E., 107, *114*
Lazarus, R. S., 87, 88, 93, 94, 118, *127*
Leana, C. R., 57, 68, 237, *240*
Leavy, R. L., 105, *113*
Lee, M. D., 60, 63, 68, 115, *126*, 159, 160,
      164, *166*, 169, 170, 178, 188, *189*
Lefcourt, H. M., 26, *32*
Lemieux, B., 26, *33*
Lengnick-Hall, M. L., 193, 194, 198, 201,
      208
Lenton, R., 105, *114*
Lerew, D. R., 76, *83*
Leung, A., 104, *112*, 117, *126*
Levant, R. F., 35–37, 39, 41, *52*
Levi, L., 29, *30*
Levy, E. S., 159, 164, *166*, 170, *189*
Lewis, B., 8, *14*
Lewis, B. P., 144, *148*, 233, 234, *241*
Lewis, J., 139, *146*
Lewis, R., 91, *93*
Lewis, S., 23, *31*
Lim, V. K., 104, *113*
Lindquist, T. L., 7, *13*
Linnehan, F., 115, *128*
Lirtzman, S. I., 217, *225*
Littler-Bishop, S., 191, *208*
Lo, S., 104, *112*, 117, *126*
Lobel, S. A., 116–118, 124, *127*, 212,
      214, *225*
Locke, E., 102, *113*
Lodahl, T. M., 120, *127*
London, J., 136, 138, *147*

Long, B., 21, *32*
Long, B. C., 86, 87, *95*
Long, N. R., 130, *147*
Lubbers, C., 139, *146*
Luckow, A. E., 89, *95*
Luk, V., 103, 104, *112*, 117, *126*, 214, *223*
Lundberg, U., 5, 9, *13*, 21, *32*
Lyness, K. S., 75, *83*

MacDermid, S. M., 115, *126*, 159, 160,
      164, *166*, 170, 178, 188, *189*
MacEachern, M., 37, *52*
Maddock, S., 59, *68*
Maddux, J., 25, *32*
Magley, V. J., 192, *207*
Maier, M., 11, *13*, 41, *52*
Maile, S., 59, *68*
Maiuro, R. D., 27, *33*
Manderbacka, K., 29, *32*
Mangel, R., 221, *225*
Manning, M. R., 237, 238, *240*
Mansfield, P. K., 197, *208*
Mardberg, B., 9, *13*
Markel, K. S., 103, 104, 117, 119, 124,
      127
Marsden, P. V., 214, *225*
Marshall, J., 22, 23, *32*, 60, 63, *68*
Marshall, N. L., 142, *146*
Martin, R. E., 230, *240*
Martocchio, J. J., 139, *148*
Maslach, C., 88, *95*, 137, *147*
Matsui, T., 117, *127*
Matuszek, P. A., 139, *148*
Matuszek, P. A. C., 6, 8, *14*, 231, *240*
Mauno, S., 9, *13*, 86, *94*, 101, *113*
Mayr, J., 105, *114*
McAfee, R. B., 202, *207*
McCarthy, J. F., 231, *240*
McDonald, L. M., 87, *95*
McElroy, J. C., 192, *209*
McGee, G. W., 237, *241*
McGrath, E., 86, *95*
McIntosh, D. N., 89, *95*
McKinley, W., 55, *68*
McLeod, J. D., 56, 69, 86, *95*, 140, 144,
      147, *149*
McMurrian, R., 87, *95*, 117, *128*
Meiksins, P., 170, *189*
Melhuish, A., 28, *31*
Mellinger, S., 26, *33*
Meritor Savings Bank v. Vinson, 199, *208*
Mermelstein, R., 217, *224*

Messner, M. A., 35, *52*
Mettlin, C., 43, *52*
Miles, A., 28, *33*
Miles, M. B., 173, *189*
Miller, D. I., 25, *34*
Mintz, L. B., 40, *51*
Mirowski, J., 139, *148*
Mirvis, P., 107, *114*
Mitchell, J. O., 217, *225*
Mitchell, R. E., 27, *33*
Mitz, L., 8, *13*
Mitz, L. F., 75–77, 79, 83, 139, *147*
Mone, M. A., 55, 68
Monnier, J., 88, 90, 137, *147*
Mooney, T. F., 41, *53*
Moos, R. H., 27, *33*, 87, *93*
Morris, M. G., 75, *84*
Morrison, E. W., 61, 68
Morrow, P. C., 192, *209*
Mosher, D. L., 40, 41, *53*
Moss, J. E., 239, *240*
Mossholder, K. W., 116, *127*
Mount, M. K., 215, 221, *224*
Mowday, R. T., 217, *225*
Moyle, P., 73, 77, 79, *83*
Munson, L. J., 192, *209*
Murray, M. A., 72, *82*
Mustard, C., 28, 29, *33*

National Council of Jewish Women, 213, 216, *225*
Nawyn, S. J., 191, *209*
Neale, J. M., 87, 96
Near, J. P., 106, *113*
Negrey, C., 169, *189*
Nelson, D. L., 3, 5–8, 10, *13*, *14*, 23, 28, 29, *33*, 57, 68, 139, 140, *148*, 194, 195, *209*, 230, 231, 235, 236, *239–241*
Netemeyer, R., 87, *95*
Netemeyer, R. G., 117, *128*
Neuman, G. A., 213, *223*
New York Times, 230, *241*
Newbold, B., 105, *114*
Nichol, V., 216, *225*
Nicholson, N., 60, 67
Nieva, R., 137, *146*
Noer, D. M., 55, 56, 69, 230, *241*
Nolen-Hoeksema, S., 75, 76, *83*
Norcross, J. C., 91, *95*
Norton, D. P., 237, *240*
Nunnally, J. C., 80, *83*

Oakley, A., 89, *95*
O'Brian, A., 104, *112*
O'Brien, T., 90, *93*
O'Connell, B. J., 73, *84*
O'Donohue, W., 191, 193, 199, 200, 202, 208, 209
O'Driscoll, M. P., 21, *33*, 116, *128*
O'Farrell, B., 192, 197, *209*
Oglensky, B., 159, *166*, 170, *189*
Ogus, E. D., 88, *95*
Oguz, C., 192, *210*
O'Hare, E. A., 199, 200, 202, *209*
Ohsawa, T., 117, *127*
O'Keefe, S. J., 141, *148*
O'Leary, A. M., 139, *148*
O'Leary-Kelly, A., 193, 194, *207*
O'Leary-Kelly, A. M., 194, *209*
Omerod, A. J., 200, *207*
O'Neil, R., 104, *113*, 118, *127*, 213, 214, 216, 217, 222, *224*
O'Neill, C. P., 87, *95*
Onglotco, M., 117, *127*
Opaluch, R. E., 191, *208*
O'Reilly, J., 169, *189*
Ortiz-Torres, B., 213–216, *226*
Orton, R. S., 49, *53*
Osterman, P., 211, *225*
Ozeki, C., 87, 94, 101, *113*, 212, 213, 216, *225*

Paetzold, R. L., 194, *209*
Paley, V. G., 41, *53*
Parasuraman, S., 10, *13*, 22, *32*, *51*, 101–105, 111, *113*, *114*, 115, 117, 119–121, 124, 125, *127*, *128*, 139, 140, 142, *147*, *148*, 215, *225*
Parkes, K. R., 73, 74, 77, 79, *83*
Parkin, D., 59, 68
Payne, C., 213, 214, 217, 222, *224*
Pedhauzer, E. J., 218, *225*
Pentti, J., 230, *241*
Perlow, L. A., 158, *167*
Perrewé, P. L., 26, *32*, 101–104, *112*, *114*
Perry, E. L., 199, 200, *208*
Peterson, C., 235, *241*
Peterson, S. H., 193, 200, 202, *208*
Petrini, B., 29, *30*
Phillips, C. M., 192, *209*
Piechowski, L. D., 88, *95*
Pierce, J. L., 24, *33*

Pines, A., 91, 93
Pinneau, S. R., 120, *126*
Piotrkowski, C., 129, *148*
Piotrkowski, C. S., 192, 199, *209*
Pleck, J. H., 6, *14*, 36, 37, 39, 41, *53, 54,*
    88, *95*, 104, 107, *114*, 142, *146,*
    216, *225*
Pollack, W. S., 40, 41, 44, *52, 53*
Porter, G., 44, *53*
Porter, L. W., 217, *225*
Pottic, K. G., 140, 141, *148*
Powell, G. N., 35, *53*, 86, 96, 116, *127*
Price, R. H., 136, *148*
Price, V. A., 44, *53*
Primeau, J., 71, *83*
Prochaska, J. O., 91, *95*
Prussia, G. E., 26, *32*
Pryor, J. B., 197, 200, *209*
Ptacek, J., 89, *95*
Ptacek, J. T., 89, 96, 137, *148*
Purohit, Y. S., 104, *114*, 117, 119, 124,
    128, 215, *225*

Quick, J. C., 5–8, 10, *14*, 33, 139, *148,*
    194, 195, *209*, 230, 231,
    235–237, 240, *241*
Quick, J. D., 7, 10, *14*, 194, 195, *209*, 235,
    241
Quinn, R. P., 116, *127*, 130, 144, *147,*
    217, 218, *225*

Raabe, P., 170, *189*
Rabinowitz, S., 120, *127*
Ragins, B. R., 201, *209*
Rapoport, R., 161, *167*
Rashbaum, B., 47, *53*
Raudenbush, S. W., 142, *146*
Rechnitzer, P. A., 43, *52*
Rees, D., 27, *33*
Reeves, J. B., 39, *50*
Reheiser, E. C., 139, *148*
Reifman, A., 89, *95*
Reilly, A. H., 42, *54*
Reise, S. P., 80, *84*
Reitman, F., 159, *167*, 232, *241*
Reitzes, D. C., 117, 124, *126*
Repetti, R. L., 234, *241*
Rice, R. W., 106, *113*, 217, *224*
Richman, J. A., 191, *209*
Ridley, C., 102, *112*
Riger, S., 201, 202, *209*
Riley, D., 137, *148*

Riley, L., 215, *224*
Rizzo, J. R., 217, *224, 225*
Robbins, A. S., 8, *14*
Roberts, K., 23, *31*
Roberts, R., 141, *148*
Robinson, B. E., 44, 49, *53*
Robinson, B. S., 72, 73, 79, *82*
Robinson, S., 56, 61, *67*
Robinson, S. L., 61, 65, 68, *69*
Rogers, R., 25, *32*
Rook, S. K., 136, *148*
Rosch, P., 21, *31*
Rosenfield, S., 140, 141, *148*
Rosenman, R., 42–44, 46, *51*
Rosenman, R. H., 43, *50*
Rosenthal, R. A., 116, *127*, 130, *147*
Rosin, H. M., 217, *226*
Rospenda, K. M., 191, *209*
Ross, C. E., 139, *148*
Ross, J., 72, *84*
Rossi, A. M., 139, *146*
Rothausen, T. J., 214, 216, *226*
Rothbard, N., 101, *112*
Rothbard, N. P., 115, *126*
Rothblum, E. D., 90, *96*
Rothman, A. J., 235, *241*
Rothstein, M. G., 23, *30*
Rotter, J. B., 25, *33*
Rousseau, D. M., 61, 62, 69, 213, *226,*
    230, 231, *241*
Rowe, M. P., 199, 201–203, *209*
Roxburgh, S., 238, *241*
Ruder, A., 5, *13*
Russell, D. W., 102, *112, 114*
Russell, M., 9, *13*, 22, *31*, 86, 93, 107,
    113, 117, *127*, 217, *224*
Russell, R. C., 191, 198, 203, *206*
Russo, J., 27, *33*
Russo, N. F., 86, *95*

Sachs, R., 23, *33*
Salovey, P., 235, *241*
Sanchez, C. M., 55, *68*
Sandelands, L. E., 55, 59, *69*
Sandvik, E., 75, 77, 78, 82, *83*
Saute, R., 159, 166, 170, *189*
Sbraga, T. P., 191, *209*
Scandura, T. A., 201, *209*, 213, 214, *226*
Schabracq, M., 170, 171, *189*
Schaef, A. W., 44, *53*
Schaubroeck, J., 73, *83*
Scheibl, F., 211, 215, *226*

Schein, V. E., 19, 23, 25, 28, *33*
Schick, A. G., 55, 68
Schilling, E. A., 74, *82*
Schmidt, N. B., 76, *83*
Schmidtke, J. M., 199, 200, *208*
Schneer, J. A., 159, *167*, 232, *241*
Schneider, K. T., 192, *210*
Schor, J., 44, *53*
Schreiber, C., 170, 178, *189*
Schuler, R. S., 102, *113*
Schulman, R. S., 40, *52*
Schwab, R. L., 88, 96, 102, *113*
Schwartzberg, N. S., 9, *14*
Schwarzer, R., 89, *94*
Searle, S., 106, 107, *113*, 116, *127*, 217, *224*
Sears, H. A., 9, *13*
Seashore, S. E., 107, *114*
Seers, A., 237, *241*
Segev, K., 142, *149*
Seidler-Feller, D., 191, *208*
Seligman, M. E., 76, *84*
Serey, T. T., 237, *241*
Seron, C., 159, *166*, 170, *189*
Serpe, R. T., 117, 124, *128*
Shaffer, M. A., 192, *210*
Sharpe, M. J., 40, *53*
Shen, Y. C., 5, *12*
Shepard, C. D., 192, *207*
Sherer, M., 25, *32*
Shinn, M., 213–216, *226*
Shirom, A., 137, 140, *147*, *149*
Shullman, S. L., 201, *207*
Shumaker, S. A., 89, *96*
Silverstein, O., 47, *53*
Silverstein, S., 233, *240*
Simko, P. A., 213–216, *226*
Simmons, B. L., 235, *241*
Sims, H. P., Jr., 8, *12*
Sirkin, M., 40, 41, *53*
Skarlicki, D. P., 56, *67*
Skidmore, J. R., 40, *51*
Sloan, S. J., 20, *31*
Smith, L. L., 80, *83*
Smith, M. E., 193, 200, *208*
Smith, R., 89, *95*
Smith, R. E., 137, *148*
Smith, S., 115, *126*, 170, 178, *188*
Snell, W. E., 41, *53*
Snoek, J. D., 116, *127*, 130, 144, *147*
Society for Human Resource Management, 159, *167*

Solomon, L. J., 90, *96*
Sonenstein, F. L., 39, *53*
Spain, D., 86, *96*
Sparrow, P., 230, 231, *241*
Spector, P. E., 72, 73, 79, *82–84*
Spence, J. T., 8, *14*, 41, *53*
Spielberger, C. D., 139, *148*
Spinks, N., 212, 214, *226*
St. Clair, L., 118, *127*
St. Yves, A., 26, *33*
Stacy, B. A., 72, *82*
Staines, G. L., 107, *114*, 129, 140, 141, *148*, 217, 218, *225*
Staw, B. M., 55, 59, 69, 72, *84*
Steers, R. M., 217, *225*
Steward, W. T., 235, *241*
Stone, A. A., 87, *96*
Stone, R., 214, *223*
Stone-Romero, E. F., 80, *82*
Strickland, B. R., 86, *95*
Stroh, L. H., 42, *54*
Stryker, S., 117, 124, *128*
Sutton, M., 211, 220, 221, 223, *223*
Swan, S., 192, 200, *207*, *210*
Swanberg, J. E., 4, *12*, 158, *166*
Swanson, N. G., 5, *13*
Syme, S. L., 88, *93*

Taber, T. D., 217, *223*
Taubert, S., 89, *94*
Taylor, S., 8, *14*
Taylor, S. E., 144, *148*, 233, 234, *241*
Tellegen, A., 81, *84*
Thacker, R., 203, *206*
Theorell, T., 170, 177, *189*
Thoits, P. A., 117, *128*
Thomas, L., 101, 104, 110, *114*
Thomas, L. T., 215, 221, 222, *226*
Thompson, D. E., 75, *83*
Thompson, E. H., 36, 37, 39, *54*
Thomson, C., 230, *240*
Tombari, N., 212, 214, *226*
Topping, J. S., 25, *34*
Tremblay, L., 28, *33*, 139, *148*
Trevino, L. K., 8, *12*
Tuosignant, M., 28, *33*, 139, *148*
Turner, H. A., 234, *241*
Turner, R. J., 234, *241*

U.S. Census Bureau, Special Populations Branch, Population Division, 86, *96*

U.S. Merit Systems Protection Board, 191, 199, *210*
Uchino, B. N., 103, *114*
Ulmer, D., 46, 49, *51*
Unger, R., 88, *96*
Updegraff, J., 8, *14*
Updegraff, J. A., 8, 144, *148*, 233, 234, *241*

Vahtera, J., 230, *240*, *241*
Van Buren, H. I., 237, *240*
Van der Wal, R., 57, *68*
Van Heck, G. L., 26, 27, *33*
Van Velzen, D., 102, *114*
Venkatesh, V., 75, *84*
Verbrugge, L. M., 28, *33*
Vermeulen, M., 28, 29, *33*
Vianen, A. E. M., 25, *33*
Vicary, J. R., 197, *208*
Vingerhoets, A. J. M., 26, 27, *33*
Vinokur, A., 131, 136, 142, *148*, *149*
Vitaliano, P. P., 27, *33*
Viveros-Long, A., 213, *223*
Voges, K. E., 130, *147*
Vroman, W., 169, *189*

Wahl, A., 22, *34*
Waldron, I., 41, *54*, 89, *96*
Wallace, R. B., 194, *208*
Wall Street Journal, 194, *206*
Walsh, J. T., 217, *223*
Walsh, W. B., 40, *50*
Walters, B. J., 143, *147*
Walters, V., 28, *34*, 105, *114*
Ward, C. H., 40, *51*
Warren, J. A., 213, *226*
Wasserman, J., 29, *30*
Watson, D., 8, *14*, 72, 73, 80, *84*
Watts, D., 202, *206*
Webster, J., 72, 73, 79, *82*
Weir, T., 43, *50*, 140, 141, 143, *146*
Weiss, R. S., 38, *54*
Weiten, W., 26, *34*

Wells-Parker, E., 25, *34*
Welsh, M. S., 23, *34*
Wenger, J., 169, *189*
West, C., 36, *54*
Westman, M., 9, *14*, 130, 131, 136, 137, 142, 143, *149*, 230, 241
Wethington, E., 56, 69, 129, 144, *146*, *149*
Whalley, P., 170, *189*
White, B., 22, *34*
Whitty, M., 38, *50*
Williams, D. R., 197, *206*
Williams, J., 5, 8, 9, *14*, 86, *96*, 105, *114*, 231, 232, *242*
Williams, K. B., 197, *209*
Williams, M., 170, 178, *189*
Williams, M. L., 170, 178, *189*
Williams, R., 47, *54*
Williams, S., 20, *31*
Williams, V., 47, *54*
Williamson, M., 102, *112*
Wills, T. A., 103, *112*
Winett, R. A., 196, *210*
Winnubst, J. A. M., 170, 171, *189*
Wofford, J. C., 74, *84*
Wolfe, D. M., 116, *127*, 130, 144, *147*
Wong, N. W., 213–216, *226*
Working Mother Magazine, 160, *166*
Wormley, W. M., 22, *32*
Worrall, L., 230, *242*
Wright, J. A., 213, *223*
Wright, L., 169, 170, *189*

Yardley, J. K., 103, 104, *113*, 117, 119, *124*, *127*, 216, *224*
Yoder, J. D., 197, *210*
Young, E. W., 197, *208*
Youngblood, S. A., 213–216, *226*

Zapf, D., 237, *240*
Zedeck, S., 129, *149*
Zeichner, A., 87, *95*
Zimmerman, D. H., 36, *54*

SUBJECT INDEX

Affect intensity, 75
  gender-based differences in, 77–79

Behavioral responses, 233–234
Business networking, 23–24

Career models, 60
Career success and personal failure syn-
      drome, 45–46
Children, effects of parental stress on, 9–10
Coping, 7, 26–27
  in crossover, 137, 143–144
  depersonalization in, 88
  emotion-focused, 27, 57
  gender differences in, 87–88
  and individual behavior, 88
  in organizational restructuring, 62–65
  proactive, 89–90
  problem-focused, 26–27, 57
  ruminative, 76
  and social support, 88–90, 90–92. See
      also Social support
  Type A behavior in, 8, 27
Corporate restructuring. See Organiza-
      tional restructuring
Crossover, 9
  bidirectional, 142
  coping strategies in, 137
  direct empathetic, 131, 136
  gender differences in, 140–141
    coping, 143–144
    direction of process, 141–143
    social support, 144
  gender role in, 129, 131, 145–146
    summary of findings, 132–135
  indirect, 136–137
  job–stress model in, 130–131
  mediators, and moderators in,
      130–131, 138
  personal attributes in, 138
  process of, 131, 136
    five dimensions of, 130, 131
  social support in, 137–138
  stressors in, 129–130, 136
    role, 131
  systems theory in, 130–131
  unidirectional, 142–143

Demand–control model, job, 170, 177,
      182–184, 185–186
Depersonalization, 88
Disabled individuals, in workplace, 233
Downsizing
  definition of, 55
  See also Organizational restructuring

Family
  broadening concept of, 232
  gender and roles in, 9–10. See also
      Work–family domains
  social support from, 104
    gender and, 105–106
  work and. See also Time allocation;
      Work arrangements;
      Work–family domains
Family identity salience, 118
Fight-or-flight response, 7–8, 144, 234

Gender
  in affect intensity, differences, 77–79
  concepts of, 3–4, 233–235. See also
      Gender roles
  considerations of, in stress research,
      138–140
  and coping, differences, 87–88. See also
      Coping
  and crossover, 140–141. See also
      Crossover
  in family dynamics, 9–10. See also
      Work–family domains
  harassment and, 196
  in health outcomes, stressors, and differ-
      ences, 4–7, 28–29. See also
      Health outcomes
  and individual characteristics, 7–10. See
      also Individual characteristics
  and negative affectivity, differences,
      75–77. See also Negative affec-
      tivity
  and occupational stress, 56–57. See also
      Occupational stress
  role strain, 6
    and concept of masculinity, 39
  and social support, differences, 88–90.
      See also Social support

and socially constructed roles, 3–4. *See also* Gender roles; Men; Women managers; Work–family domains

Stereotyping, 22

and stress in managerial positions, 19–30. *See also* Managerial stress; Men

and stress management, 10–12

and work–home conflict, 9–10. *See also* Time allocation; Work arrangements; Work–family domains

Gender roles, 6

ambiguity in, 221–222

and concept of masculinity, 39

conflicting, 86–87, 125

in crossover, 129, 131, 145–146

summary of findings, 132–135

in negative affectivity and occupational stress, 74–75

overload in, 5

socially constructed, 3–4. *See also* Men; Women managers; Work–family domains

Gendered cultures, 59–60

Glass ceiling, 5, 57

Health outcomes, 85–87, 92–93

behavioral symptoms, 7

chronic conditions, 7, 194

gender, stressors and, 3–12, 28–29

heart disease, 7, 29, 194

infectious disease, 29

life expectancy, 7

in men, 38–39, 40–41

physical vs. mental manifestations, 28, 139

and preventive stress management, 10

psychopathology, development of, 91

psychophysiologic symptoms, 6

Health preservation/stress prevention, 235–236

employer support of, 236–237

Homosexuals, in workplace, 232–233

Human ecology model, 170, 186–188

Individual characteristics, 7–10

affect intensity and, 75

gender-based differences in, 77–79

coping and, 88. *See also* Coping

as moderators in crossover, 138

personal control, 25–26

self-efficacy, 25

self-esteem, 24–25

See also Negative affectivity

Integrity of functioning, 171, 184–185

Job demand–job control model, 170, 177, 182–186

Job insecurity, 230

Labor market

changing, 230–231

growth of part-time work in, 169–172. *See also* Work arrangements, reduced load

labor force participation, women aged 25 and older, 159

women entering, 19–20, 86, 140, 145–146. *See also* Work–family domains

Managerial stress, gender differences and, 19–20

coping styles, 26–27

occupational stress, 20–21

outcomes, 28–29

response to stressors, individual, 24–26

stressors, 21–26

business networking, 23–24

gender stereotyping, 22

glass ceiling, 5

marital support, 22–23

maternal wall, 5

minority ethnicity, 22

organizational culture, 23

role overload, 5

tokenism, 5–6

workload, 4–5

Marital support, 22–23

Masculinity, concept of, 36–37

consequences of, 37–38

corporate, 11, 41–42

gender role strain and, 39

implications in men's health, 38–41

reconstructing, 48–49

Maslach Burnout Inventory (MBI), 88

Maternal wall, 5

MBI. *See* Maslach Burnout Inventory

Men, stressors in,

career success and personal failure syndrome, and, 45–46

educational and counseling initiatives for, 46–48

health and, 35–36

health management and, 40–41
masculinity concept and, 36–37
consequences of, 37–38
corporate, 41–42
gender role strain and, 39
implications in men's health, 38–41
reconstructing, 48–49
organizational change and, 46–48
single fatherhood, 232
Type A behavior and, 42–44
workaholism and, 44–45
Minority ethnicity, 22

Negative affectivity, 8
as component of cognitive–affective
stress propensity, 74
definition of, 71
gender-based differences in, 75–77
impact of, substantive, 73
mediational models of, 73
as moderator variable, 74
and occupational stress
gender's role in, 74–75
incorporating gender in research on,
79–82
overview of research, 72–74

Occupational stress, 20–21, 56–57
costs of, 21
managerial stress, gender differences,
19–20
coping styles, 26–27
outcomes, 28–29
stressors, 21–26
response to stressors, individual, 24–26
and negative affectivity, 71–72
gender-based differences in, 74–77
impact of, substantive, 73
incorporating gender in, research on,
79–82
as moderator variable, 74
overview of research, 72–74
organizational restructuring, 55–56,
65–66
coping strategies in, 62–65
research on stress in, 57–62
100 Best Companies for Working Mothers,
167
Organizational culture, 23
Organizational restructuring, 55–56,
65–66, 230–231
coping strategies in, 62

exit, voice, loyalty, or neglect, 64–65
reevaluation of work, in life's context, 63
separation of work from rest of life,
63–64
social support, 64
research on stress in, 57–58
gendered culture issues, 59–60
psychological contract issues, 61–62
relational practice issues, 61
structural and functional issues,
58–59
Outcome expectancy, 25

Part-time work. *See also* Work arrange-
ments, reduced load
PCI. *See* Proactive coping inventory
Perceived breach, definition of, 61–62
Personal attributes. *See also* Individual
characteristics
Personal control, 25–26, 87
Preventive stress management, 10
Proactive Coping Inventory (PCI), 89–90
Psychological contract, 61–62
in changing labor market, 230–231
definition of, 61

Rational view, 115–116
Relational practice, 61
Research, future directions, 229
gender differences/gender roles,
233–235
health preservation/stress prevention,
235–236
employer support of, 236–237
labor market/employment changes,
230–231
social support from employer, 237–239
underresearched constituencies,
231–233
Restructuring. *See also* Organizational
restructuring
Role ambiguity, 221–222
Role overload, 5
Ruminative coping, 76

Self-efficacy, 25
Self-efficacy expectancy, 25
Self-esteem, 24–25
Sexual harassment, 5–6, 191–192
court rulings cited
Au v. Lyndhurst Hospital, 192, 207

Burlington Industries v. Ellerth, 193
Faragher v. City of Boca Raton,
     193, 200
Jones v. USA Petroleum, 200
Meritor v. Vinson, 199
as dysfunctional organizational
     behavior, 194
indicators of, 195–198
  discrimination, 197
  high intensity, 198–199
  low/medium intensity, 198
  perpetrator characteristics, 198
  power differentials, 197
  precursor, 197–198
  skewed sex ratios, 197
outcomes of, 192
perpetrators of, characteristics, 198
preventive management of, 199, 204
  employer motivation, 193
  example of, 194
  framework for, 195–196
  harassment reporting, 193
  implementation of, 204–205
  primary, 195–196, 199–202
  research on, 205–206
  secondary, 196, 202–203
  strong policy against harassment,
       193–194
  tertiary, 196, 203
Social identity, 117–118, 124
Social psychological view, 115–116
Social support, 64, 85–86, 92–93
  and coping, 90–92
  in crossover, 137–138, 144
  definition of, 103
  emotional, 103
  from employer, 103–104, 237–239
  in family, 104
  gender differences in, 88–90
  instrumental, 103
  interaction with gender, in work–family
       domains, 104–105
  and satisfaction in work–family
       domains, 103–104
Spillover stress, 129
Stress
  coping with, 7, 26–27. *See also* Coping
  definition of, 20
  gender differences in, 3–10, 28–29. *See
       also* Gender
  in men, 28–29. *See also* Masculinity;
       Men

occupational, 20–21, 56–57
  costs of, 21
  managerial stress, gender differences,
       20–29. *See also* Managerial stress
  and negative affectivity, 71–82. *See
       also* Negative affectivity
  organizational restructuring and,
       55–66. *See also* Organizational
       restructuring
  sexual harassment in, 5–6, 191–203.
       See also Sexual harassment
  programs for, gender-specific, 11–12
  social support in, 64, 85–86, 92–93. *See
       also* Social support
  spillover, 129
  in women, 28–29. *See also* Managerial
       stress
  and work–family conflict, 9, 101–102.
       See also Crossover; work–family
       domains
  responses to, 115–116, 155, 164–166.
       See also Time allocation; Work
       arrangements, reduced load
  See also Stressor(s)
Stress hormones, 5
Stressor(s)
  and expression of dissatisfaction, 64–65
  and gender, health outcomes, 3–12,
       28–29
  managerial stress, gender differences,
       21–26
  in men, 35–49. *See also* Masculinity,
       concept of
  career success and personal failure syn-
       drome, 45–46
    educational and counseling initia-
         tives, 46–48
    gender role strain, 39
    health implications, 35–36, 38–41
    health management, 40–41
    masculinity concept, 36–38
      corporate, 41–42
    organizational change, 46–49
    Type A behavior, 42–44
    workaholism, 44–45
  and time allocation, 116–117. *See also*
       Time allocation
  in women, 19–30, 85–87. *See also* Man-
       agerial stress; Work–family
       domains
    business networking, 23–24
    gender stereotyping, 22

glass ceiling, 5
marital support, 22–23
maternal wall, 5
minority ethnicity, 22
multiple roles, and role conflict,
    86–87
organizational culture, 23
role overload, 5
sexual harassment, 5–6
tokenism, 5–6
workload, 4–5
Survivor's syndrome, 56

Tend-and-befriend response, 8, 144,
    233–234
Time allocation, 115–116
    gender differences in, 118
    identity salience and, 117–118, 125
    involvement vs. role conflict, 125
    social identity and, 124
    spousal involvement and, 124–125
    and stress, 116–117, 118–119
    study of
        conclusions, 124–126
        findings, regression analyses, 121–123
        future directions, 125–126
        hypotheses, 117–119
        measures used, 120–121
        samples, 119–120
    work overload and, 124
Tokenism, 5–6, 20
Trauma strain, 6
Type A behavior, 8
    in coping styles, 27
    and stressors in men, 42–44

Underresearched constituencies, 231–233

Women managers, 19–20
    coping styles, 26–27
    occupational stress, 20–21
    outcomes, 28–29
    stressors, 4–7, 21–26
        response to, individual, 24–26
    See also Work–family domains
Women workers, blue-collar employment,
    231–232
Work, 9
    See also Coping
    See also Crossover; Work–family domains
    See also Work arrangements, reduced
        load

reevaluation of, 63
separation of, from rest of life, 63–64
social support from, 103–104. See also
    Social support
    gender and, 105
stress at, and gender differences. See also
    Managerial stress; Masculinity;
    Occupational stress
See also Labor market
Work arrangements, reduced load, 155,
    164–166, 169–172, 211–212
    acceptance of, 160
    availability of, 159–160
    implementation of, 162
        at individual level, 162
        at organizational level, 161
        at supervisory level, 161
    labor force participation, women aged
        25 and older, 159
    models of, 170–172
    motivation for, 175–178
    motivation vs. outcome in, 170
    need for, 157–159
    outcomes of, 163, 172–186
    preferred, 158
    studies of, 172
        analyses of data, success rating and,
            173–174
        catalyst, 155–156
            findings, 157–164
            research methodologies, 156–157
        control findings, 170, 175, 177,
            182–186, 188
        data sources and methodologies, 172
        human ecology findings, 170,
            186–188
        integrity of functioning findings, 171,
            184–185
        participants, interviews and, 172–173
    success of, 160, 179–181, 211–212,
        220–223
        limitations of past research, 216–217
        satisfaction and commitment,
            213–214
        stress reduction, 212–213
        study of
            analyses, 218–220
            data collection/participants, 217
            findings, 221–223
            strengths and limitations of,
                220–221
            survey questions, 217–218

turnover, 214–215
    work–family conflict, 215–216
  success strategies for, 163
    evolvement of arrangement, 164
    formalizing/evaluating arrangement, 164
    trusting relationships, 164
    understanding of work options, 163–164
Work–family domains, 101–102
  allocation of time in, 115–128. *See also* Time allocation
  compensation relationship between, 129
  conflict between, 9–10, 64, 85–87, 92–93, 102. *See also* Work arrangements
  crossover stress in, 129–130. *See also* Crossover

culture and, 9
gender and social support in, studies of, 106
  analyses, 107
  conclusions, 110–111
  measures, 106–107
  regression analyses, 108–109
  results, 107–109
satisfaction in, 102–103
  social support and, 103–104
    gender and, 104–106
segmentation of, 129
spillover stress in, 129
Work identity salience, 118
Work overload, 4–5, 116–117, 124
  increase in, in restructuring, 58–59
Workaholism, 8
  and concept of masculinity, 44–45